ESCHATOLOGY AND HOPE

THEOLOGY IN GLOBAL PERSPECTIVE SERIES

Peter C. Phan, General Editor
Ignacio Ellacuría Professor of Catholic Social Thought,
Georgetown University

At the beginning of a new millennium, the *Theology in Global Perspective* series responds to the challenge to reexamine the foundational and doctrinal themes of Christianity in light of the new global reality. While traditional Catholic theology has assumed an essentially European or Western point of view, *Theology in Global Perspective* takes account of insights and experiences of churches in Africa, Asia, Latin America, Oceania, as well as from Europe and North America. Noting the pervasiveness of changes brought about by science and technologies, and growing concerns about the sustainability of Earth, it seeks to embody insights from studies in these areas as well.

Though rooted in the Catholic tradition, volumes in the series are written with an eye to the ecumenical implications of Protestant, Orthodox, and Pentecostal theologies for Catholicism, and vice versa. In addition, authors will explore insights from other religious traditions with the potential to enrich Christian theology and self-understanding.

Books in this series will provide reliable introductions to the major theological topics, tracing their roots in Scripture and their development in later tradition, exploring when possible the implications of new thinking on gender and sociocultural identities. And they will relate these themes to the challenges confronting the peoples of the world in the wake of globalization, particularly the implications of Christian faith for justice, peace, and the integrity of creation.

Other Books Published in the Series

Orders and Ministries: Leadership in a Global Church, Kenan Osborne, O.F.M.
Trinity: Nexus of the Mysteries of Christian Faith, Anne Hunt
Spirituality and Mysticism: A Global View, James A. Wiseman, O.S.B.

THEOLOGY IN GLOBAL PERSPECTIVE
Peter C. Phan, General Editor

ESCHATOLOGY AND HOPE

ANTHONY KELLY, C.Ss.R.

ORBIS BOOKS
Maryknoll, New York 10545

Founded in 1970, Orbis Books endeavors to publish works that enlighten the mind, nourish the spirit, and challenge the conscience. The publishing arm of the Maryknoll Fathers and Brothers, Orbis seeks to explore the global dimensions of the Christian faith and mission, to invite dialogue with diverse cultures and religious traditions, and to serve the cause of reconciliation and peace. The books published reflect the opinions of their authors and are not meant to represent the official position of the Maryknoll Society. To obtain more information about Maryknoll and Orbis Books, please visit our website at www.maryknoll.org.

Library of Congress Cataloging-in-Publication Data

Kelly, Anthony, 1938-
  Eschatology and hope / Anthony Kelly.
      p. cm. — (Theology in global perspective)
  Includes bibliographical references and index.
  ISBN-13: 978-1-57075-651-1 (pbk.)
  1. Eschatology. 2. Hope—Religious aspects—Christianity. I. Title.
  II. Series.

  BT821.3.K44 2006
  236—dc22
                              2005031825

Contents

Foreword

by Peter C. Phan

Eschatology—the theological discourse about the end of the human person and of history — was given a tremendous boost at the beginning of the third Christian millennium. As the New Year revelries in 2000 receded with no cosmic catastrophes, however, public interest in "raptures," Armageddon, and the second coming of Christ fizzled like wet firecrackers and stale champagne. Perhaps all to the good, since, as Anthony Kelly makes abundantly clear, Christian eschatology is not about these alleged apocalyptic events but essentially about human hope.

This hope is the red thread unifying Kelly's wide-ranging and rich reflections on Christian eschatology. Hope, Kelly points out, is a trustful movement forward; it is also a defiant posture toward the present situation of incompletion—or what the Buddha calls *dukkha* (existential unsatisfactoriness)—since it holds out the promise of a better future. Hope is more than optimism or mere wishing. Its world is that of meanings and values, and its scope is personal and cosmic fulfillment.

For Christians, this hope is not guaranteed by an ideology but is focused on and guaranteed by, in Kelly's memorable phrase, "the parable of hope," that is, the life, death, and resurrection of Jesus. This parable in turn is rooted in God's trinitarian love—love as origin (the Father), love as self-giving (the Son), and love as communicative (the Spirit). Eternal life, then, is this love consummated for the individual person, human society, and the cosmos.

Eschatology is the "intelligence of hope," and Kelly offers us challenging and fresh perspectives on the traditional themes of eschatology—death, purgatory, hell, and heaven. In line with the thrust of our Theology in Global Perspective series, he elaborates these themes in dialogue with themes from contemporary science and insights from other religious traditions. Rather than "interfaith," Kelly prefers to speak of "inter-hope" dialogue, emphasizing its more open-ended and interpersonal dimensions. Finally, he draws attention to the sacramental and spiritual aspects of eschatology, showing how the Eucharist is the foretaste of eternal life and how Christian spirituality is living in hope.

It is theologically significant that Kelly dedicates his book to the hundreds of thousands of victims of the 2005 tsunami in the northeastern regions of the Indian Ocean, with the prayerful hope that they might be "gathered into the Light." That this hope of salvation is prayed for these victims, most of whom were not Christians, bears eloquent witness to Kelly's largeness of heart and the all-embracing inclusiveness of his theological vision. May his book, which he says is not a "hope pill" or a "hope book," inspire in readers the same Christian hope and vision.

Preface

It is some fifteen years since I last turned to eschatological themes. The book that resulted is long out of print, and its Melbourne publisher subsumed into some higher form of existence. I was pleased, then, when Orbis invited me to return to this theme and contribute to a new theological series, keeping in mind the ever-broadening context of Christian theology.

The dialogue between theology and science continues to be very productive as scientists and theologians have their different ways of envisaging the end. The works of Ian G. Barbour, John Polkinghorne, George F. R. Ellis, David Toolan, William R. Stoeger, Denis Edwards and many more provide excellent resources for eschatology today. Of course, some eminent scientists, indeed Nobel Prize laureates such as Jacques Monod and Steven Weinberg, become rather dismal when they consider the chanciness and—to them—the essential pointlessness of the cosmic process, and the eventual heat-death of the physical universe. Most forms of religious hope, however, are not essentially troubled by the inevitable death of the individual or the physical universe itself, billions of years hence. On the other hand, the scale of the cosmos and wondrous fertility inscribed into its emergence are a backdrop, at the very least, to cosmic dimensions of Christian hope. Discussing, say, the resurrection of the body—or the resurrection of Jesus himself—cannot but profit from current explorations into the nature of matter/energy and the meaning of time. Our common emergence within this immense cosmic process leaves us all humbled, not only as brought back to earth but as reimmersed in the great cosmic cauldron that brewed the constituent elements of carbon-based life on our little planet. The universe is full of surprises. Hope in its highest forms suggests that there are more surprises yet. I do not think this is the time for religious hope to lose its nerve in the dialogical exchanges that are taking place.

Just as we are all the more one in our recognition of our cosmic origins, a good Spirit is at work making the times propitious for dialogue between the great religious traditions and spiritualities that have long nourished our different histories. A little phrase kept occurring to me in the course of writing these pages: it is time for "inter-hope" dialogue. I find that this suggests something more open-ended and interpersonal than the more usual "inter-faith" description. For that can give the impression that all believers are so clear about the realities they believe in that their differences have the last word. Hope implies a waiting for another kind of last word: the inclusion of everyone in its scope and the expectation of a vast communion of life in which we all belong to one another in the end. I write this as a Christian theologian, of course, and obviously influenced by the Catholic tradition. But far from a sense of narrowness or defensiveness, I feel that Christian hope implies a limitless overture to an eschatological companionship from which no one is excluded.

These are hopeful stirrings, but the immediate reality is often despair and depression, to say nothing of the calamities that many of our fellow human beings have suffered. I am writing these words just days after the earthquake-tsunami event that caused so much loss of life in the northeastern regions of the Indian Ocean. Hope is not an academic issue in the face of such devastation. Nor is it when so many, leading otherwise secure lives, see no point to it and look for nothing more. There is no "hope pill" or even "hope book" that solves their problems. Still there is Someone, and this book is about that One on whom alone our hopes ultimately rely—in life, in death, and in all that happens in between. If this particular book does not point the reader beyond itself to the Other who is the source, sustainer, and goal of true life, it will have failed: but that is the challenge for all theology.

I have tried to keep the order and treatment of the various topics reasonably simple. In some sense, a "systematic" theology of hope is a contradiction in terms. For hope comes into its own when the system breaks down, and when the dreadful or fascinating "otherness" of reality breaks in. I have chosen to present these reflections on key eschatological themes in a certain order: the first three chapters deal with the experience of hope, the history of eschatology, and the eschatological style of thinking. These are followed by a reflection on the paschal mystery of Christ's death and resurrection. In that context, we reflect on death, and in the chapters that follow, the topics of purgatory, hell, and heaven. After that, the concluding chapters return to earth, so to speak, to focus on the eucharist and the continual conversion that is called for in living Christian hope. This particular order could be varied in any number of ways, and other themes may well have demanded a chapter-length treatment. Some may prefer to separate the individual and collective dimensions of our human and cosmic destiny more clearly, and so to give less space to the traditional topics of purgatory, hell, and heaven. I realize that my option not to have a separate chapter on judgment may be contested. Still, there is no end to the ways hope can express itself, nor is there any perfect expression of what we hope for. But by focusing on the paschal mystery of Christ and its eucharistic celebration, there is always a point from which to begin and to which to return. It is less a question of discussing hope in the linear form and sequences of a book, and more a matter of letting ourselves be captured by the symphony of hope, in its different movements of lament and joy, conversion and patience, thanksgiving and final assurance.

I would like to dedicate this book to the victims of the tsunami disaster, with the prayer that the thousands who died might be gathered into the Light, and that those who survived might witness to the kind of hope that keeps us all going in the midst of loss and suffering.

I must express my gratitude to Orbis Books and its editorial staff. Special thanks are owed to Peter C. Phan of Georgetown University, who has been so encouraging at every stage in the preparation of this manuscript. I am also very indebted to theological colleagues such as Anne Hunt of Australian Catholic University and Father Tom Norris of St. Patrick's Maynooth for the expertise and discretion with which they alerted me to errors and obfuscations in the later drafts of this book. Hope always needs its allies!

1

The World of Hope

HOPE IN ALL ITS REGISTERS implies a trustful and confident movement toward the future. It is trustful, for it is relying on something or someone for the help that is needed. There is confidence, too: whatever the evils that threaten, hope anticipates an escape or release into a fuller dimension of life. It is always about a movement forward. While it is not always easy to find words for what we are hoping for, at the very least hope is moving from despair to something more positive. It shows a certain defiance: the future has to be more than the present situation of suffering or incompletion. It might even extend to everything and everyone. In that case, it outstrips what can be controlled and planned for, and senses, however implicitly, that, hidden in the present, there is a promise that can and will be kept.

A GENERAL DESCRIPTION OF HOPE

A Dwindling Hope?

But hope seems to be becoming a nonrenewable resource. The fund of trust and confidence that our different cultures once had has dwindled. There is an oppressive dearth of good news. Our staple media diet is largely one of doom-laden reports and the record of death, violence, and catastrophe of one kind or another. Given the dire predictions concerning the world economy, the ecological well-being of the planet, to say nothing of the intractability of peacemaking efforts in many regions, it is clear that there is no easy path to a promising future.

Basic human experiences that once held their own promise are now far more ambiguous. Marriage and family, for instance, were once the sturdy intergenerational basis of a confident world. But now that life is problematic. There is overpopulation in some regions and increasing sterility in others. The fragility of human relationships is evidenced in divorce and family breakdowns in most cultures. In the West, the aging populations go from retirement villages to nursing homes. A naïve "happy families" view of things is no longer sustainable.

Many entered the professions, say, of education, medicine, law, politics, media, or business with youthful enthusiasm. They were motivated by high ideals of serving and protecting society. Not uncommonly, they now feel trapped in enormous networks of influences. Their confidence in doing something worthwhile for society is undermined. They cannot avoid quite radical questions: Who, or what, am I working for? What possible difference can my contribution make?

In the face of cultural and social dislocation, many, too, are searching for a new sense of community. But in the present culture of pluralism, common moral norms are hard to find. The promotion of human rights remains one of the noblest carriers of hope for a community of justice and personal dignity. Yet even this can be imperiled. A consumerist world favors an endless litigious catalogue of "my rights against all others." As a result, those who are most defenseless are forgotten.

Refined planning skills can express a great deal of what needs to be done. They can outline a probable future development by extrapolating from current trends. Planning for probable future outcomes is surely a good resource to have. But planning by itself cannot do much about changing human beings. The greater the vision, the more it is faced with the question of how the human heart can be transformed. Despite the good will and intelligence of the participants, no "peace process," no "Justice and Reconciliation Commission," is assured of a happy conclusion.

At what point, then, do great human hopes turn to despair? Global or regional peace proves elusive. The term "peacekeepers" is euphemistically attributed to military forces of occupation. Security is tied to superior weaponry. Little wonder that the peacemaking children of God (see Mt 5:9) can be discouraged. When do people begin to despair over the possibilities of justice? When do they begin to accept that social divisions built on power, possession, and privilege are an inescapable reality? When, then, does despair become part of the situation, and the heart freeze into autistic loneliness? If the rich get richer and the poor get poorer, why bother about social justice at all? In the meantime, an anxious intelligence is busy about other things. It devises new techniques of damage control and defense—with weapons of mass destruction targeted on the menacing masses of "those others."

When societies have been uprooted from any history, the meaning of faith, hope, and deep culture shrinks in a consumerist—and manipulable—present. In one way or another, governments have to cope with the culturally uprooted and disorientated populations of citizens who share no hopes. Drug addiction, violence, and youth suicide are just some of the faces of hopelessness. A liberal social system might promise success and inspire expectations. But on matters closest to the human heart, it cannot deliver what the society most needs. When the evils are so obvious, the language of hope seems too good to be true. And yet the gods of progress promised so much; but *this* is what they delivered. As a result, the deepest self remains unemployed, lost and wandering in a consumerist world with nowhere to go.

In any number of ways the future has already been shaped by decisions made without any political or moral controls. When the logic of "what can be done, must be done" remains unquestioned, the world of human values limps embarrassingly behind. Its protests are dismissed as recalcitrant conservatism. Moral reflection is caught in a time lag. Pragmatic, short-term decisions make it difficult for those who wish to take time over the whole human good and to build a human moral consensus on the way things ought to be going. Genetic engineering, the production of new and more deadly weapons, the machinations of international business and banking, the unilateral decisions of powerful national states, all these are far from guaranteeing a promising future for the many. Powerful new communications technologies, instead of unifying the world, are used for surveillance and control and a more deadly way of targeting of "the enemy." In other words, the future is already under the control of agencies equipped with enormous impersonal capacities to manipulate and oppress.

Yet some three billion of the world's population are living on two U.S. dollars a day. Serious proposals have been put forward to resolve the international debt of poor countries in order to release funds to meet social needs such as health and education. If the amount of international aid for development could be increased from the current 0.2 percent of GDP to the 0.7 percent (as actually agreed upon at the Monterey Financing for Development Conference in 2002), matters would improve. But unless there is a radical change of heart and a more enlightened organizational intelligence, there can be no betterment of the present desperate situation.

The Stirring of Hope

Still, the times are ripening for a deeper exploration of the meaning of life in its whole mystery. As people of planet earth, we can sense how our hitherto different and often conflicting histories are now being woven together. A sense of one-world history is not the result merely of a sense of common threat—be it ecological, economic, or political. It is powered also by a new aspiration to a new global common good. It dares to suggest the possibility of a new, truly human future in which past enmities can fall away and millions of the forgotten poor can come to share in the still abundant resources of the earth.

Moreover, we can now recognize our existence within the womb of an immense planetary and cosmic history. Fifteen billion years have gone into our making. Within that vast cosmic process, there have been the three and a half billion years of life on this planet. This has led to the emergence of the human race over the last million years or so, from primitive hominids to the *homo sapiens* of today. Each one of us who breathes the air of planet earth can look at the night sky in the realization that there shine in our own galaxy some hundred billion stars the size of our sun—in a physical universe of perhaps a hundred billion galaxies.

We are always part of a larger story.[1] The genetic scripts written into our brains and our bodies, into our land, into our earth—all depend on elements brewed in exploding stars billions of years ago. Unimaginable dimensions of time bring us to this present moment of wonder. The spiritual calling of humanity in the universe expresses itself in thanksgiving and hope on a cosmic scale. Hope is formed in a world of many gifts and many givers, and of some gifts that only the Source of all can give.

If some despairingly have come to accept that the whole emergent reality of life is the result of blind and unfeeling chance, then any hope for something more is pure illusion. On the other hand, if we feel that there is meaning and purpose to life, then the uphill battle begins. We have to keep reclaiming the heights already occupied by the martyrs, saints, mystics, and the great throng of good people who have insisted that there is something worth living and dying for. Despite any number of unfavorable circumstances, a hopeful energy keeps moving us on. For many it can be as matter-of-fact as getting up in the morning and going to work, or addressing the agenda of yet another meeting—and the daily round of leisure and work, study and social interaction.

The eminent Marxist philosopher Ernst Bloch, in his monumental work *The Principle of Hope*, presents hope in creative terms.[2] Hope manifests itself as the dream of the New, the *novum*. It animates all the efforts of freedom to bring a new society into being. As a hunger for the not-yet, it keeps history moving. The restless imagination of hope calls into question the status quo. In doing so, it inspires an awareness of hidden possibilities within the situation. It brings into being what is waiting to be realized. In this manner, hope is an active and realistic anticipation of new forms of a just society. It envisions a "new heaven and new earth" to be realized in human history. Hope is the forward thrust of time. Its energies keep the human journey through history

---

1. See Denis Edwards, *Breath of Life: A Theology of the Creator Spirit* (Maryknoll, N.Y.: Orbis, 2004), 7-15; David Toolan, *At Home in the Cosmos* (Maryknoll, N.Y.: Orbis Books, 2001), 127-55.
2. Ernst Bloch, *The Principle of Hope*, trans. Neville Plaice, Stephen Plaice, and Paul Knight, 3 vols. (Cambridge, Mass.: MIT Press, 1986).

moving through its many exiles toward its true homeland. Yet Bloch remains a Marxist atheist; "God" is the cipher for the as-yet-unrealized possibilities of human freedom, the indeterminate symbol of the good society attracting human history on its forward course.[3] The value and limitations of this view will be treated in the next chapter.

But whether we speak of hope in a non-religious or specifically Christian sense, it is as well to bear in mind the following points.[4]

Features of Hope

First, hope differs from optimism. To the detriment of genuine hope, these two notions are often confused. Optimism is no bad thing in itself. It is a kind of implicit confidence that things are going well in the present situation. Optimism may be simply a feature of temperament expressing itself in a spontaneous logic: we can manage and cope in a world that is reasonably predictable. Optimism is happy enough with the system. In contrast, genuine hope is always "against hope." It begins where optimism reaches the end of its tether. Hope stirs when the secure system shows signs of breaking down. Hope is at home in the world of the unpredictable where no human logic or expectation is in control. It rejects any easy assurances of pretending to manage what in fact intrinsically resists management. It relies on something that comes from outside the system. In this respect, it is never far from humility, for it acknowledges that in birth and in death, in the wonder of life and in the intimations of art, human existence is never a realm of total control. We are not the center of the universe that has brought us forth, and the ultimate reaches of destiny are beyond human planning and control. This humility gives rise to a subversive irony on the hollowness of any cultural pretensions to deliver what in the end can come only as a gift. Genuine hope has no use for idols.

Second, hope operates in a world of meaning and values. It has a conscience and an intelligence that mere optimism lacks. Hope looks beyond self-regarding satisfactions to the transcendent values that alone can nourish life and give it direction. Nor does it repress inconvenient questions. Illusions or lies are no long-term solution to anything. To speak technically, the energies of hope nourish the self-transcending dynamism of our existence. Hope refuses to see the ultimate meaning of life as simply more of the same. It is a

---

3. Ibid., 3:1298.
4. For a good analysis, see James R. Averill, G. Catlin, and K. K. Chon, *Rules of Hope* (New York: Springer-Verlag, 1990).

patient openness to what is and must be "otherwise." Hope refuses to rest in anything less than the truly meaningful and the genuinely good. It increases the scope and momentum of human intelligence in its quest for the fullness of life. Genuine hope radically affects our commitment to the great values of peace, justice, and personal dignity. It breathes the conviction that what is deepest in our aspirations is not ultimately worthless or self-defeating. To this degree, hope is a dimension of the fundamental spirituality of the human person. It allows for the sacred indefinability of who we are. It refuses to be reduced to some form of materialistic determinism.

Third, and more specifically, hope focuses on what is truly important in terms of personal fulfillment. To live in hope is to recognize that we do not live by bread alone. What we most need is not something we can ever simply grasp and possess. It reaches beyond the consumerist imagination. When hope begins, a conversion is happening at the heart of our being. We are not meaningless and worthless phenomena in an absurd universe, but creatures of eternal value. Consequently, hope inspires a personal sense of calling and destiny. It nourishes a feeling of being part of something greater, further, something more human and lasting.

Fourth, hope is not mere *wishing* for something more. It is a conduct of life. It is a mode of living and acting. For this reason it is called a virtue, a *virtus*, a capacity to act well. For hope inspires action. It gives vigor and buoyancy to intelligence. It engenders a deep moral sense and points in the direction of a more passionate self-involvement in the making of the world. Hope's imagination and deepest feelings resist all forms of cultural depression. It enables one to risk even life itself for the greater good of oneself or others. It is capable of taking a stand with the hopeless. Hope anticipates a future fulfillment that is yet to be given. Hoping is therefore not simply wishing. For hope acts in such a way as to bring into the limitations of the present some anticipation of what it ultimately envisions. In acting, it can also pray. To praise the giver of all gifts is an act of hope. It expresses thanksgiving for what is already given. It maintains a receptive openness to what is beyond all imagination and control. Hope for oneself expands to hope for others. The most precious fruit of this is intercession for all who, in life and in death, are our companions in the light and shadow of the history we share.

Deeper Questions

The human "system" is one form of biological life on this planet. Like all other life forms, it unfolds in time and is limited by death. But in contrast to the instinctive life of animals, human beings know time and death as explicit and even dreadful realities. In human memory, there have been times of peace and times of war. Today we are aware of time as threatening ecological destruction and planetary suicide through atomic and bacterial weaponry. Our science knows time as leading eventually to cosmic collapse.[5] History informs human memory with the recollection of empires, oppression, and interminable conflict. While history can recall times of grace, prosperity, social progress, scientific achievement, and religious and artistic inspiration, its memories include a miserable catalogue, personal and social, of grief, guilt, greed, and violence. In the meantime, the aeons roll on. Is this vast fifteen-billion-year cosmic process emptying the present of any personal value? If there is no abiding value in the human person, there can be no resting place, no homecoming. There is only an endless movement onward . . . to what and to where? The force of such radical questionings may make us feel that everything we most treasure is thrown into the lottery of a blind evolutionary advance toward what is both beyond our ken and outside our control. Time appears demonic, an obscure, unfeeling force that in fact has no time for the human or the world as we know it. Death, individual and social, historical and cosmic, is the end.

The question of hope emerges in a new way. Is there any sense in which we can have hope for time itself? What can save time from meaninglessness? Is death its absolute and universal limit? These are deeply disruptive questions when heard in the cultural systems that shape our lives. It must be admitted that there is nothing within the system that can save it. Of itself, religion can offer its obscure consolations by denying the significance of the world of time and by deferring everything to another world, another time, and another place. Meanwhile, we are here, now, in this time and in this place, in the company of these people. Some may opt to work the system for what it is worth. They are the true "survivors." They calculate the odds and look to the main chance. If to survive means sacrificing others, or even our best selves, that is the price to be paid. If death is the end, then life to the full means living now, even if such living may mean a more or less violent exclusion of others as competitors or threats. When victory belongs to the strong, hope appears to be the virtue of the weak. Hope is nothing but a reckless abdication of power and self-assertion. It is built on the illusion that somehow we belong together, and that there is something or someone who has a care for our common destiny.

---

5. For a many-sided treatment of the issues involved, see George F. R. Ellis, ed., *The Far-Future Universe: Eschatology from a Cosmic Perspective* (London: Templeton Foundation, 2002).

Genuine hope will, of course, contest such a crude ideology. Hope is intent not on the "survival of the fittest," but on the fittingness of all finding life's fullness and fulfillment. Nonetheless, to be human is to know the passage of time and the reality of death. And in such realism, hope offers its anticipation of the future and learns to rely on what alone is trustworthy. It inspires a journey through time and history. To be human is always to be "on the way"—as in the title of Gabriel Marcel's book, *Homo Viator*, to which we refer in the next chapter.[6]

DESPAIR AND DEPRESSION

When it lacks any hope for anything beyond itself, a culture manifests the symptoms of depression. This pathological state is characterized by a feeling of isolation. It shows a tendency to "totalize" its failures and indulge in unreal expectations. It manifests a generalized apathy and incapacity to act. Hope begins with a new ability to imagine a larger sense of life and community. Here an outstanding reference is still William F. Lynch's *Images of Hope: Imagination as Healer of the Hopeless*.[7] I will briefly indicate how hope inspires a larger imagination and points the way to recovery, and thereby pose some questions relevant to the cultural situation. The sufferings of the individual suggest an analogy for any larger culture that has lost hope.

Hope begins to stir when the depressed begin to rediscover themselves not as isolated, unreachable and beyond all help but as belonging to a larger community of care. Typically help is represented by the true friend, the counselor, pastor, physician, or spiritual director. These helpers challenge the isolation of the depressed with what amounts to an invitation to rejoin the human race. By allowing themselves to be helped by these "others" who represent the promise of healing, the hitherto depressed begin on the road to recovery. In the presence of the helper, the sufferer begins to imagine things differently. The frozen isolation of depression is melted. Life recovers its momentum. Marcel wisely observes that hope most arises when it comes closest to despair.[8] By defying the temptation to give up, the self ceases to be an isolated, defensive ego. It admits the presence of the other. It finds that existence can be realized only in co-existence with others. For every

6. Gabriel Marcel, *Homo Viator: Introduction to a Metaphysic of Hope*, trans. E. Craufurd (New York: Harper & Row, 1966), 7.
7. William F. Lynch, *Images of Hope: Imagination as Healer of the Hopeless* (Notre Dame, Ind.: University of Notre Dame Press, 1965).
8. Marcel, *Homo Viator*, 30, 32, 36, 41, 45.

human being needs the help of others. Hope thrives on mutual assistance, cooperation, and compassion. It inspires the necessary humility and patience if the promise of life is to be kept.[9]

Both the isolation of despair and its accompanying totalization of evil and failure are destructive illusions. Despair lacks all sense of proportion. It thrives on depression's exaggerated imagination of suffering, guilt, failure, or disgrace. In this depressive state, we might feel that we are nothing but a sum of negativities. But at that bleak point, hope begins when we start to imagine matters in a larger sense of proportion. Life is in fact going on. The feeling of "total" worthlessness begins to meet up with the possibilities of healing, repentance, conversion, forgiveness, and reconciliation. Love and wisdom reveal what had hitherto been hidden. The totalization of personal worthlessness and failure is relativized. Depressed persons begin humbly to rejoin the human race. They find themselves in the company of those who know that the evils we suffer—or inflict—need not be the whole story. It may be that the past has had its say and delivered a crushing judgment on our failures. But agents of hope point to the possibilities of forgiveness, reconciliation, repentance, and the expiation of past evils. The past delivered its verdict, but the future has made no such ultimate and total judgment. The destructive totalization that has been in control yields to a more healthy and gracious sense of proportion.

Without wishing to trivialize the evils that have led to depressive despair, hope introduces a note of humor and irony into the human situation. Given the wonder of existence and the immensity of the mysterious universe, it is possible that we have been taking ourselves too seriously. We have all along been trying to live life without wonder and mercy.

When despair isolates the depressed and exaggerates their problems, it encloses them in the illusion of hopelessly unreal expectations. These have led to a doomed attempt to measure oneself, others, and the larger world against unreachable ideals of perfection. Inevitably, then, despair inhabits a world of endless frustration. The original problems are intensified. Censorious idealism has never learned the saving grace of humility. To the degree that we see ourselves occupying the moral center of the universe, we take on the rather large burden of universal judgment. Depression is born out of conceit and pride. There is no room for patience. If I try to dispense with the long haul, if I reject the need to take time—whatever time it takes—to achieve the goal, then failure is inevitable. To demand some instant outcome is to become locked in unreal time. Energy is first frustrated and then exhausted.

---

9. Ibid., 36.

When patience runs out, despair enters in. And with it comes the depression of living in a world in which everything takes too much time, and everyone, including oneself, is revealed as incapable of delivering what my unreal expectations impatiently demand.

Again, it is easy to see that the dawning of hope is the recovery of a more humble and patient imagination. We are members of a community. We live in a network of dependence. An immense variety of factors and conditions affect our existence. I am not the center of the universe, even though the universe has time and a place for my unique existence. To the degree that we begin to live with humility and the gratitude that comes from it, the way of hope has begun. It grows strong in the recognition that, while there might be instant coffee, or instant communication, or instant meals, there are no instant people. Unless we resist being duped by the consumerist instant, we cannot enter into the multidimensioned "now" in which hope lives.[10] In the patient acceptance of time with all its seasons come both healing and hope.

Yet there is a further aspect of depressive despair. It shows itself in impotence and apathy. The depressed have been deflected from reality. Problems totally determine their world. Isolation is an englobing experience. Life has become a complete disappointment. In such a state, I can stop wanting anything. Desire dies in the heart. Love for anyone or anything presents too big a threat. It will make me vulnerable to further grief and frustration. It is better not to want anything so as to avoid a further letdown. As a result, I cannot permit myself feeling, wanting, desiring anything outside the frozen autism of my depressed state. Sympathy for other sufferers is beyond me. There is another side to this sad state. It can show itself in a blind kind of lashing out at anyone or any group that invites me into a larger world of living and loving. The other is experienced only as invading the privacy of my depressive despair and must be rejected. Life has left me alone and disappointed, and I want nothing of it. A listless inability to act is the result. I can neither do anything about my sorry state, nor do I want to.

Obviously the voice of hope would gently insist on the necessity of learning to desire and to love again, in whatever tentative form. As a beginning, it might suggest the healthy possibilities of tending the garden, looking after a pet, making a phone call or writing a letter to friends or relatives too long ignored. Friends would probably suggest, in one way or another, the need

---

10. On "the sacrament of the present moment," see the eighteenth-century classic by Jean-Pierre de Caussade, *Self-Abandonment to Divine Providence*, trans. Algar Thorold (London: Burns Oates & Washbourne, 1948). In a more current and broadly spiritual idiom, a useful work is Eckhart Tolle, *The Power of Now: A Guide to Spiritual Enlightenment* (Novato, Calif.: New World Library, 1999).

"to get out of yourself." Of these, the more philosophically minded might say that your listless state of self-enclosure has to recover the dynamics of self-transcendence. The hitherto isolated, depressed existence must begin to move again. Wisdom may well suggest the healing possibilities of learning from other sufferers and beginning to think of those "less fortunate than yourself." More sensitive advice might point to the advantages of joining a support group made up of people who have been through something of the same dark night. In an atmosphere of sharing and compassion, the long, but not impossible, journey back into life, step by step, can begin. The inspiring examples here are those who are facing the problems of long-term addiction or dependency. Yet the aim here is not to replace one form of dependency with another. For the goal of such therapy groups is to help their members to regain freedom and, with it, the ability to desire what is truly valuable and meaningful in human life.

In each of these instances, hope is experienced as a gift coming from outside the depressive system altogether.[11] How this hidden grace might be best named will provoke philosophical, psychological, and theological responses. So far, we have merely indicated an experience readily identifiable in most human lives. Hope is the experience of transition. It is expressed in the movement of imagination, taking us beyond feelings of isolation and the totalization of problems. It steps out of the unreality of false expectations and the apathy that desires nothing. What this hopeful movement leads to is a mysterious "other dimension." It is manifest in a new way of imagining our participation in the human community and a deeper, wider appreciation of the promise hidden in our common human experience. The hard, cold, lifeless "heart of stone" is on the way to becoming a "heart of flesh" (Ezek 36:26).

DIMENSIONS OF CHRISTIAN HOPE

The Witness of Christian Hope

A cultural form of depression results from living in a social milieu that tends to negate a hopeful sense of self. But just as a dispirited culture can have an adverse effect on hope, a community alive with the energies of hope affects both the individual and the cultural aspects of our lives. Hope is a social virtue. It enables the individual to join or rejoin the human race with confi-

---

11. On this point, see James Alison, *Raising Abel: The Recovery of Eschatological Imagination* (New York: Crossroad, 1996), 173-77. See also *The Joy of Being Wrong: Original Sin through Easter Eyes* (New York: Crossroad, 1998).

dence and freedom. The hope of each one needs to be sustained by a helping community. If that community is to be a milieu of hope it too must be able to renew itself by drawing on other and deeper resources if it is to bring healing and confidence into any depressed situation. Here we have the beginning of a theology of the church as the community of hope. It has been called into existence by God's grace and mercy. Its life is centered in Christ, the embodiment of divine compassion. As the crucified and risen One, he is in person the divine offer of healing and freedom at the point where human beings most encounter the problem of evil—in themselves, in others, and in the world at large.

The Spirit of hope disturbs the depressed society with other possibilities. Society is more than a loveless collective. The seeds of communion in eternal life have already been planted within it. As the First Letter of John has it,

> . . . this life was revealed, and we have seen it and testify to it, and declare to you the eternal life that was with the Father and was revealed to us—we declare to you what we have seen and heard so that you may have fellowship with us; and truly our fellowship is with the Father and with his Son Jesus Christ. We are writing these things that your joy may be complete. (1 Jn 1:2-4)

This gift of eternal life triumphs over the blind forces of time and death. It redeems time of its lifeless weight and emptiness. The gift that makes all the difference has been given into the hopelessness of the system. For any depressive system freezes our capacity to relate, to desire, and to act. God's gift in Christ means a new way of relating to others. For all are called to the one communion of life. It means, too, a new way of desiring. The Spirit of hope plucks out the heavy, lifeless heart of stone to give the liveliness of a heart of flesh (Ezek 36:26). Desire now awakens to the imperative of loving God with one's whole heart and soul and mind and strength, and of loving one's neighbor as oneself (Mk 12:29-31). Love and hope inspire new capacities to act. Patience, kindness, and the courage to endure what must be patiently suffered become possible. All such activity is sustained by entrusting one's life and destiny to Christ and the workings of his Spirit (cf. 1 Cor 13:4-7).

The life of Christian hope lives by surrendering to the creative and redeeming mystery of love working in time, at every moment in life and death throughout the whole of creation. The divine gift is being given. It precedes all our beginnings. It is more ultimate than any "last thing" that either hope or despair can imagine.[12] The God-given future is finally conditioned not by

---

12. Zachary Hayes, *Visions of a Future: A Study of Christian Eschatology* (Wilmington, Del.: Michael Glazier, 1989), 73.

personal failure and social oppression but by the irrevocable promise of life to the full.[13] Christian hope is always more than the catalogue of particular hopes, for it looks to an incalculable fulfillment in terms of what can never be fully expressed.

The church exists in history to be the space of hope in the world. As that part of the world that has awakened to the plenitude of the divine promise, it expresses not only hope in the world but an unconditional hope for the world. In this regard, the church is the community of those who have a sense of a future so full of promise, so absolute, that nothing and no one is excluded. Christians, as people of God, are the people of hope. They are called to witness to the great transformation now afoot which promises the liberation of all human hopes to their fullest dimensions. Yet it is not as though Christian hope occupies some deathless standpoint, untroubled by the agonies of the world and invulnerable to its sufferings. The life of hope is not a matter of watching in armchair comfort a replay of the highlights once "our team" has won. For in this case the team is everyone, and the game has not yet been played to the end. The followers of Christ are not passive spectators, once or twice removed from the agonizing contest of history. Immersed as they are in the great human and cosmic drama, Christians still have to confront the many faces of despair in themselves and others. Hope must arise and grow in the midst of inexplicable suffering, inevitable death, humiliating failure, meaninglessness, guilt, and fear in all its forms. It is ever up against the sheer power of evil in all its virulent manifestations. Whatever the joy and peace inherent in the gospel of hope, it offers no complacent, passive preview of things. Our hope is called to share in the patience of God. Only in the loving patience of God can the promise latent in the unfolding of human time and the meandering history of human freedom be finally kept and revealed. Because it lacks this final evidence, hope is always being refashioned. Whatever the unpredictable turns of history, whatever the mysteries of the cosmos yet to be discovered, hope is always open to new dimensions of Christ, moving forward with "the assurance of things hoped for, the conviction of things not seen" (Heb 11:1). Despite the unseen goal, and because of the intimate joy and anticipation, Peter urges the early Christian community,

[I]n your hearts, sanctify Christ as Lord. Always be ready to make a defense to anyone who demands from you an accounting of the hope that is within you; yet do it with gentleness and reverence. (1 Pet 3:15-16)

---

13. Gabriel Marcel, *Being and Having: An Existentialist Diary*, trans. K. Farrer (Gloucester, Mass.: Peter Smith, 1976), 74-75.

Somehow words have to be found to give an account of what we hope for. It is a continuing challenge in every age, beginning all over again as the different contexts of Christian life through history unfold. Yet in Christ something radically hopeful has already happened. An ultimate love has appeared in our history. Through the resurrection of the Crucified, the deepest aspirations of our race from below are blessed and fulfilled by God's inexhaustible gift from above. In Christ, history is already moving to a divinely guaranteed future. Through him, a new kind of hoping has entered the world. As the Marxist philosopher Ernst Bloch remarked, "Christianity seems like a final emergence of what religion is—a total hope and an explosive one."[14]

Hope and Time

As Christian hope brings its distinctive vision and energies to the world of hope, it reaches beyond any quick solution to what an infinite love is bringing about. And here it must take time. For hope insists that God has time for the whole of creation and everyone who is part of it. Inevitably, hope is sorely tested when the God-intended future seems to be indefinitely deferred. A more just social order, a more informed ecological responsibility, the achievement of peace and reconciliation, are all long-term projects. Indeed, it is often the case that those who hope and work for such causes will often not see the result of their efforts.

Hope, then, must not only have time for all God's creation, but must have time for time itself. In one perspective, time is simply the measure of waste and slow decay. The passage of time means the erosion of everything we are. It leads eventually to the collapse of the whole physical universe. But hope discerns a blessing hidden in the movement of time. It contains a promise that will be kept. The seed of eternal life will grow and bear fruit. Still, hope must take its time as God has taken time, in patience and waiting.

But there is another angle. Even if we hope for the future, dare we hope for the past? It contains the numberless dead, victims of violence and greed, casualties of progress and conquest, mostly unknown and unacknowledged. They lived, suffered, and died, finally laid to rest in the inescapable finality of the grave. Some were heroic witnesses to another way. Yet all were subject to the same mortality. In this present, they are our past. More dramatically, every history, personal or social, contains a memory of unresolved conflicts,

---

14. As quoted by John Macquarrie on the frontispiece of *Christian Hope* (London: Mowbray, 1978). See also Bloch, *Principle of Hope*, 3:1125-31, 1256-74.

violent conquests, unsleeping hatreds. Can hope look back and not lose itself in the history of such defeat and failure? This cannot but be experienced as a strange question. Still it leads into the deepest dimensions of Christian hope. Whatever the theological explanation, hope must allow for the reconciliation even for those who knew one another in life, or in the longer span of history, only as enemies and aggressors. Can the mercy of the Redeemer of the world outwit, in the end, the human capacity for violence, dissension, and oppression of the weak? As we shall see, hope can positively long for a purgatorial fire that burns only with the love that can change enmity to compassion. Hope can even desire the existence of hell, not to pass any ultimate judgment on anyone, but in the expectation that all the self-vaunting powers of evil will be reduced to nothing and be revealed in their absurdity. Most of all, hope envisages a heaven of ultimate reconciliation in which Christ will join together what human history has set apart (see Eph 2:13-22). In short, hope prays for the last judgment, which, even as it exposes evil and casts the mighty from their thrones, will be a revelation of infinite mercy.

The vision and longing of Christian hope can never exclude such considerations. Hope can never be limited to a particular theology. For it is wholly intent on what only God can do and the manner in which an infinite love can bring it about. But this kind of hopeful thinking does suggest how hope looks forward and looks back to the totality of God's redemptive design.

"INTER-HOPE" DIALOGUE

One of the great signs of hope today is the many levels of interfaith dialogue taking place. All who represent the deeper places of the heart and the higher reaches of the spirit, play a part in the ecology of a global human culture.[15] Such meeting and collaboration cannot but make the world more hospitable to the values of peace and justice, compassion and human dignity. Eminent missiologists recognize the eschatological or hope-oriented aspect of this dialogue.[16] It is focused on the Kingdom of the God and "desires everyone to be saved and to come to the knowledge of the truth" (1 Tim 2:4). Theology predictably oscillates between two polar considerations. There is the universality of God's saving will, as when God so loves *the world* (John 3:16a). But

---

15. Hans Küng, *Eternal Life? Life after Death as a Medical, Philosophical and Theological Problem*, trans. E. Quinn (New York: Doubleday, 1984), 44-70.

16. Standard references here are the comprehensive Stephen B. Bevans and Roger P. Schroeder, *Constants in Context: A Theology of Mission for Today* (Maryknoll, N.Y.: Orbis, 2004), and the much-discussed Jacques Dupuis, *Toward a Christian Theology of Religious Pluralism* (Maryknoll, N.Y.: Orbis Books, 2001).

this is held in tension with the culminating particularity of Christian revelation. God so loves the world "so as to give *his only Son*" (John 3:16b). The universality of God's love and the particularity of the divine self-giving in Christ are necessarily interconnected in any adequate theology. The respective emphases of various theologies of the church's mission to the world give rise to a wide range of missiological approaches. Here I would like to suggest that the language of hope is of special relevance.

In fact, for our present purposes, I would suggest replacing the usual term "interfaith" dialogue with "inter-hope" encounter. There is a certain advantage in looking beyond, say, negotiations regarding civil collaboration and democratic freedom, or beyond theological agreement on a number of themes or doctrines. A new openness or sympathy comes into play when the encounter between different faiths and spiritualities is set within a horizon of hope and its expectation of an ultimate communion in eternal life. Inter-hope dialogue would highlight the unimaginable "otherness" of eschatological fulfillment. It looks beyond what is, to what is to come. While there is continuity between the present apprehensions of all faiths and eternal life, there is also the discontinuity that only humble adoration dimly discerns. What is hidden will, in the end, be made clear. Dialogue between various religious and spiritual traditions reveals, of course, quite complex differences regarding the meanings of the self, God, and the character of eternal life, to say nothing of different understandings of the life of the dead and the place of ancestors, and even the meaning of time.[17]

Yet it remains that the future is what we have in common. At the point where all are united in looking forward to a hoped-for future, Christian hope can be especially creative. For the Christian can turn to each revered partner in dialogue and express an unconditional hope for the gift of eternal life for each and every one. If Christians must never give up hope even for their enemies and persecutors, there is surely a lot that can be said—or left unsaid in the necessary darkness of our present perceptions—regarding the ultimate reconciliation of all in eternal life. There is a breadth and length and height and depth of the mystery (Eph 3:18) that can be disclosed only to hope. The love of Christ "surpasses knowledge" (Eph 3:19). Our trust in this love includes all in whom the Spirit of love and hope is moving. This is not an instance of subtle Christian imperialism. For Christian hope waits on the

---

17. On the relevance of John 4 to this question, see Anthony J. Kelly and Francis J. Moloney, *Experiencing God in the Gospel of John* (New York: Paulist, 2003), 97-114. See also Keith Ward, "Cosmology and Religious Ideas about the End of the World," in *The Far-Future Universe*, ed. Ellis, 235-48. For an early attempt at a more global theology, see N. Smart and S. Konstantine, *Christian Systematic Theology in a World Context* (London: Marshall Pickering, 1991).

unfathomable freedom of the One "who by the power at work within us is able to accomplish abundantly far more than all we can ask or imagine" (Eph 3:20). Interfaith dialogue must continue to work for greater mutual comprehension and collaboration among all peoples of faith as they turn toward one another in reverence. Inter-hope dialogue is more a matter of all looking toward a promised future of communion in eternal life. If such a view is criticized as being too specifically Christian, at least it will be criticized for the right reasons—for having too much hope—in the Other, for all others, rather than too little. The other is essentially welcomed into the communion of ultimate life, and is no longer subject to the distance and fragmentation of our historical differences. Christian hope forbids any imperialistic religiosity. It rather gives us the confidence to take the last place in the service of the world, to act as a force for reconciliation and as a witness to ever-expanding hope for the hopes of the world (Luke 14:1-14).

CONCLUSION

Hope as a Theological Virtue

In formally theological terms, Thomas Aquinas, along with Christian tradition generally, understands hope as a God-given virtue. It is the capacity to act by relying on divine help in order to attain our final end in God. Hope relies on God to achieve what faith reveals and charity most desires.[18] Because of its God-given and God-directed character, hope is classified among the "theological virtues."[19] Hope figures in the three theological virtues of faith, hope, and charity as a middle dimension of three interweaving God-wrought and God-ward activities. Hope without faith would be blind. It would not know who it was trusting or what it was hoping for. Yet faith without hope would be closed in on itself. It would tend to imagine the future looking like a mere repetition or copy of the present. Restricted to the range of images and ideas dealing with the present, the God-determined future would seem to be simply an extension of present, untroubled by any sense of judgment or transformation in the light of the infinite Other. Certainly, faith points the way, but hope drives us forward in an open horizon of trust. Likewise, love without hope would atrophy. It might so settle for union with the beloved in the present as to forget that the other is still to be fully revealed. Yet hope

---

18. Thomas Aquinas, *Summa Theologiae, Pars Prima Secundae*, question 62, article 2 (hereafter *STh* 1-2, q. 62, a. 1).

19. *STh* 1-2, q. 62, a. 1.

without love would be stunted and self-centered. It might veer toward vengeance and retribution in forgetfulness of what the last thing really is.

The adjective "theological," when applied to faith, hope, and charity, is used to point the contrast to what is within the natural scope of human action. Hence, in line with Aquinas's description, theological hope is for *the good*—in fact, the supreme good of God.[20] Yet it is a *future* good, since we are not yet united to God in the face-to-face vision of eternal life. In this regard, hope deals with a *possible* good, since eternal life is exactly what God has promised. Nonetheless, hope is concerned with a *difficult* good. To desire the good that is promised as the supreme goal of our existence is a choice. It involves what is experienced as a risk. It means choosing the greatest good over lesser goods, and this choice is made in the context of a certain tension. An idolatrous bias toward the attractions of power, pleasure, and possessions has radically affected the history of which all are a part. Hence, the theological virtue of hope sustains the courage necessary to rely on God alone for the fulfillment of the divine promise.

A Pauline Description (Romans 5:1-5)

The theological realism of Thomas's account of hope as a virtue for the uphill, long-haul journey of Christian existence resonates with Paul's account. For the Apostle, hope is not a theoretical matter but an energy formed in the core of our being:

> Justified, then, by faith, we have peace with God through our Lord Jesus Christ. Through him we have also obtained access to this grace in which we stand, and we *boast* in our hope of sharing the glory of God. More than that we boast even in our *sufferings*, knowing that suffering produces *endurance*, and endurance produces *character*, and character produces hope, and hope that we have will not let us down, because *God's love* has been poured into our hearts through the Holy Spirit which has been given to us. (Rom 5:1-5)[21]

Paul presumes that the gift of faith gives from the start a kind of ecstatic delight in a new horizon of life. Believers look forward from a position of

---

20. For a concise, culturally relevant, and deeply Thomistic treatment of hope, Joseph Pieper, *Hope and History*, trans. Richard Winston and Clara Winston (London: Burns & Oates, 1969) is outstanding.

21. For commentary, see Brendan Byrne, *Romans*, Sacra Pagina 6 (Collegeville, Minn.: Liturgical Press, 1996).

peace and grace to a sharing in God's own glory. But this first "boasting" leads to the realism of the long haul. Our "sufferings" show that our full liberation is not yet realized. The end is not yet. Our existence is grace under pressure. It awaits the fulfillment that will come only in God's good time. The tension of waiting is paralleled in the petition "lead us not into temptation." This is perhaps best translated as, "do not let us crack under pressure," given the apocalyptic conflict of good and evil in human history.

Yet we can still "boast." There is the assurance of moving in the right direction, even though a radical tension is felt through the whole of creation (see Rom 8:18-21). For the Apostle sees our struggles as forming "endurance" within us. This is the "long-suffering" patience characteristic of Job and the great martyrs of the Old Testament. Interestingly, too, it is a feature of the Book of Revelation. The final book of the New Testament has no word for hope, but speaks constantly of "patient endurance" (e.g., Rev 1:9; 2:2-3, 2:19; 3:10). The pressure bearing down on believers brings a new experience of time. Our temporal existence is one of waiting. It is a matter of exercising faithfulness to the end, whenever it will be. Such endurance means standing strong against all temptations to hurry time. It resists all efforts to escape from the particular place and time given to the believer in this moment of the history of God's saving activity. The sufferings involved produce endurance as the readiness to undergo what has to be borne. It rises to the challenge of embracing what each believer is called to undertake and undergo in the all-inclusive providence of the divine plan.

This kind of endurance produces "character." The meaning of God's saving grace is stamped into our inmost being. The good news of God is crystallized in our minds and hearts. It is embodied in the person that each of us is. Christian identity takes definitive shape. Its character is shaped by surrendering to the grace of God and its future unfolding.

"Character produces hope." From this tried and tested character, hope in its full reality arises. It is unconditional, irreversible, all-enduring in its surrender to what only God can bring about. At this extreme point when everything is risked, hope "will not let us down." It is sustained by an unconditional and inexhaustible gift. Hope draws its deepest energies from the love of God permeating the inmost dimensions of our existence. The Spirit, moving through the whole creation, works within each believer. From the Spirit comes that awareness of love without which hope would be vulnerable to the fragility and scandals inherent in our existence in the world. Yet the Spirit aids us in our weakness. The divine Spirit leads hope to its full range and inspires prayers worthy of what we are called to (Rom 8:26-28). The Spirit "groans" in the "groaning" of our hope, just as our hope participates in the "groaning" of all creation as it awaits its deliverance (Rom 8:22, 23, 26). Paul insists on the resolute character of hope as he writes, "but if we keep hoping for what we do not see, then we wait with endurance" (Rom 8:25). Our waiting lives with the conviction that all things are working for the good of those who have stepped into the universe of God's love (Rom 8:28).

Followers of Christ can boast of the grace, faith, and peace inherent in their calling. But as the church reaches out to the world of hope and hopelessness, it proclaims the gospel to those who have "no hope and are without God in the world" (Eph 2:12). The Christian community learns to boast of inevitable struggles that its mission demands. Such suffering brings about the patient endurance that engagement with the world exacts. It takes shape in the special character formed in a long experience of history and its conflicts. This, in turn, expresses itself in hope. The soul of all hopefulness is the love that "bears all things, believes all things, hopes all things, endures all things" (1 Cor 13:7). At a time when "all things" appear all too much, Christian hope opens to the ever greater dimensions of abundant redemption.[22]

In the next two chapters, we will sketch the particular theological expression of hope that is called "eschatology."

---

22. For a profound historical reflection, see Christopher Dawson, "Christian Culture as a Culture of Hope," in his *The Historic Reality of Christian Culture, A Way to the Renewal of Human Life* (New York: Harper & Row, 1960), 60-68.

2

From Hope to Eschatology

T HE OPENING CHAPTER sketched something of the experience and range of hope. From within that experience, it pointed toward the distinctiveness of Christian hope. We now consider how Christian theology begins to offer "an accounting of the hope that is within you" (1 Pet 3:16). This will mean articulating what we hope in and what we hope for. In other words, hope is expressed as "eschatology." This suggests an exploration of what is termed in Greek *eschaton* ("the final reality") or *eschata*, the plural form, "the last things"—the *De Novissimis* of the Latin, post-Tridentine manuals. It signifies that branch or dimension of theological thinking that deals with a variety of particular issues emerging within the horizon of Christian hope. Typically these include death, particular and universal judgment, purgatory, hell, heaven, the resurrection of the body, and the destiny of the universe itself.

Many aspects of Christian life converge in this account of hope and "the last things" that affect it. The liturgy, the daily pastoral care of the suffering, the dying, and the bereaved, and various forms of spiritual and devotional practice are involved. Eschatology reflects on this multidimensional life of hope in order to enrich and refine it. The theology of the last things must address many questions in this regard. Yet it must keep steadily in mind the most fundamental "last thing" in all the "last things" that come up for consideration. As we shall see, this is the reality of God's saving love, which is the beginning and end of all created existence. Detached from this all-decisive reality, the variety of eschatological themes would remain abstract and ill-focused.[1]

Theological attempts to express "what no eye has seen, nor ear heard, nor the human heart imagined" (1 Cor 2:9) are faced with a special challenge. The language of hope is often poetic and visionary—as in the Book of Revelation and in the sublime poetry of Dante. It is the task of eschatology

---

1. Rowan A. Greer, *Christian Hope and Christian Life: Raids on the Inarticulate* (New York: Crossroad, 2001). Along with New Testament perspectives, Greer considers the approaches of Gregory of Nyssa, Augustine, John Donne, and Jeremy Taylor.

to keep asking what such symbolic and figurative language is really trying to say. This implies, however, no bias against the power, or even the primacy, of poetic and mystical modes of expression. Yet the task is complex, given the extent to which contemporary understanding of the world and its history has changed. For example, how is the risen Lord, the Alpha and Omega of God's creation, to be understood within an evolutionary worldview? How is Christian hope best expressed within the fifteen billion years of the cosmic history of the universe, from the Big Bang to the present? Moreover, how is it best articulated so as to bring its best energies and insights to any given cultural situation in all the variety of economic, political, and interfaith contexts affecting our present experience of history? And, most urgently, how does the gift of eternal life bear on the degradation, oppression, and general powerlessness of so many millions of people today?

It would be presumptuous to think that any eschatology can simply come up with a catalogue of answers to all such questions. The important thing is to contribute, humbly and as intelligently as possible, to the living conversation that makes up the world of hopes. It is a matter of proceeding "with gentleness and reverence" (1 Pet 3:16) in the growing and often daily communication with representatives of other faiths, other hopes, other spiritual traditions. Eschatology, then, aims to provoke a conversation on the practice of hope and its bearing on our individual and collective destiny. The theological tradition of "faith seeking understanding" finds a necessary complement in an eschatology best described as "hope seeking understanding." In this regard, eschatology inspires conversation, dialogue, and hopeful conduct among all people of hope as they ask about the kind of future we share and what might we hope for.

In the light of the immensity of the task and the limits of any one contribution, it is well to remind ourselves that we are not starting from scratch. A rich vocabulary of hope is embedded in the tradition. It continues to call forth fresh efforts to speak of what is to come.[2]

THE RICHNESS OF TRADITION

It goes without saying that the theology of any time is basically a rereading of the Scriptures as primary documents of hope. They contain a fundamental

---

2. I note the rich and balanced development of eschatology occurring in the evangelical tradition, especially as instanced in Stanley J. Grenz, *Theology for the Community of God* (Grand Rapids: Eerdmans, 1994); see especially part 6, pp. 571-660.

witness to the decisive eschatological reality, the risen Christ. Here we can rely on the rich results of recent exegetical scholarship.[3]

Patristic and Medieval Inheritance

Regarding the eschatological vision of the early church, scholars such as Brian Daley supply theology with richly documented studies of the patristic period.[4] Despite the variety of voices and views he brings forward, Daley ends his impressive survey with a brief epilogue entitled, "A Common Hope." He concedes it might be better to speak of "many facets of a rapidly developing, increasingly detailed Christian view of human destiny, of many hopes—and many fears—enveloped within a single, growing, ever more complex tradition of early Christian faith and practice."[5]

Though those formative times do not permit too rigid a schematization, Daley does suggest a number of points. For instance, hope for the future is an essential dimension of Christian faith and practice. It places a positive value on history as leading to eschatological fulfillment. Furthermore, there are clear areas of consensus: history is moving to an end; hope includes the resurrection of body and salvation of the whole person; there will be both a particular and a general judgment; hope inspires a communal sense of relationship with the dead as still involved with the living in a bond of mutual intercession.

Daley also mentions perennially controverted issues. These deal, for example, with the imminence of God's judgment and the time of Christ's return, the materiality of the risen body, the extent of God's saving plan in regard to the sinners and even devils, and the possibilities of spiritual progress and purification of the soul after death.

In a telling conclusion, Daley writes,

From the vantage point of faith in the risen Lord, human time is wrapped in eternal love: the many hopes that rise—gropingly, picturesquely—in the heart of the believer are really only attempts to articulate in words the one abiding "mystery, which is Christ in you, your

---

3. See especially Larry Hurtado, *Lord Jesus Christ: Devotion to Jesus in Earliest Christianity* (Grand Rapids: Eerdmans, 2003); N. T. Wright, *The Resurrection of the Son of God* (Minneapolis: Fortress Press, 2003); and James D. G. Dunn, *Christianity in the Making*, volume 1, *Jesus Remembered* (Grand Rapids: Eerdmans, 2003).

4. Brian E. Daley's research into the patristic period is found in *The Hope of the Early Church: A Handbook of Patristic Eschatology* (Cambridge: Cambridge University Press, 1991).

5. Ibid., 216-24, quotation from p. 216.

hope of glory" (Col 1:27). It is an expression of the mystery of Christ
that all Christian eschatology finds its unity and its meaning.[6]

The fertile influence of this patristic inheritance took many forms in later
centuries, especially in the Middle Ages. It produced polarities that are still
with us. To take one example, an eschatological interpretation of history in
apocalyptic and trinitarian terms was typical of the Calabrian Abbot Joachim
and the Spiritual Franciscans. It was given theological respectability especially through the writings of St. Bonaventure.[7] The history of the church
was understood as a succession of states or eras, culminating in the onset of a
new "spiritual" age of peace, contemplation, and evangelical poverty.

On the other hand, there is the more theoretical but still decidedly eschatological vision of Thomas Aquinas. Inevitably, this was somewhat removed
from any immediate historical interpretations.[8] The polarities between a
"warm" history-oriented, or even overheated apocalypticism, on the one
hand, and a "cooler," more serene systematic account of Christian hope, on
the other, continue as the unfinished business of theology up to the present. In the case of Aquinas, the theological task was unfinished in another
sense, as is clear from the incomplete state of his masterwork, the *Summa
Theologiae*.[9] Aquinas's premature death robbed him of the chance to extend
into a complete eschatological synthesis his profound thinking on the beatific
vision, grace, the trinitarian indwelling, the theological virtues, and the
resurrection of Christ. What is often forgotten, however, is that, from its
first pages, the *Summa* unfolds in an eschatological horizon. The theological
insight proper to *sacra doctrina* (with its combination of faith and theological
reflection) is at every stage a sharing in the divine light of God and the vision
of the blessed (*STh* 1, q. 1, a. 2).

In view of the subsequent influence of Aquinas, the incompleteness of
his *Summa* had its effects. In the later scholastic and manualist tradition,
not only was the deeply eschatological orientation of Thomist theology not

---

6. Ibid., 224. For more detailed considerations of millennialism and so forth, see Charles E.
Hill, *Regnum Caelorum: Patterns of Future Hope in Early Christianity* (Oxford: Clarendon Press,
1992).

7. See Bernard McGinn, *Visions of the End: Apocalyptic Traditions in the Middle Ages* (New York:
Columbia University Press, 1998), a richly documented source.

8. Ibid., 196-200.

9. Because he died before he finished his great systematic presentation of Christian doctrine, a
supplementum was added, cobbled together from his earlier occasional writings. There is something
symbolic in that the compilers of this supplementary material make the treatment of the resurrection of the dead follow on the questions relating to illegitimate children. As a result, various eschatological questions unfold in unhappy isolation from the great parent body of the *Summa*.

appreciated, but the manualist tract *De Novissimis* (concerning the last things) was in a literal sense left to the end of any theological course. It was presented, if at all, in a fragmented manner, usually divorced from other tracts dealing with trinitarian, christological and sacramental questions. A treatment of the last things was something of an afterthought, to be addressed, if at all, once the supposedly more important doctrinal issues had been settled.

Developments in Church Teaching

There have been many developments since the Middle Ages, as we shall see. One such development impressively occurred in church teaching itself. The eschatological character of hope is a striking and indeed unprecedented dimension of the documents of Vatican II, especially *Lumen Gentium, Gaudium et Spes,* and *Nostra Aetate.* Before this, the history of official church teachings had been rather disjointed and episodic. It was pretty much confined to matters dealing with the fate of the individual (e.g., the beatific vision, the nature of purgatory, judgment, and so forth). The manner in which a new hopeful eschatological mood surfaced in the Second Vatican Council is suggested by in the following quotation from *Gaudium et Spes,* the Pastoral Constitution on the Church in the Modern World:

> We know neither the moment of the consummation of the earth or of human existence, nor the way the universe will be transformed. The form of this world, distorted by sin, is passing away; and we are taught that God is preparing a new dwelling and a new earth in which righteousness dwells, whose happiness will fill and surpass all the desires for peace arising in the human heart. Then with death conquered, the sons and daughters of God will be raised in Christ, and what is sown in weakness and dishonour will put on the imperishable: charity and its works will remain, and all creation which God made for human beings will be set free from its bondage to decay. (#39)

THE CONTEXT OF INTER-HOPE DIALOGUE

Vatican II thus opened hope to a much larger horizon. In its generous sense of the mystery of salvation at work in the world, it encouraged ecumenical and interfaith dialogue, along with dialogue with nonbelievers and atheists. It exhibits a positive recognition of the Holy Spirit's work in the world. As regards the salvation of all in Christ, it has this to say,

All this holds true not only for Christians, but for all people of good
will in whose hearts grace is invisibly active. For since Christ died for
all (Rom 8:32), and since all are in fact called to one and the same
destiny which is divine, we must hold that the Holy Spirit offers to
all the possibility of being made participants, in a way known only to
God, in the paschal mystery. (#22)

These words encourage what we called in the previous chapter "inter-hope"
dialogue. The wounds of the past and the problems of the present certainly
demand interfaith dialogue. Yet there is the often forgotten dimension of
hope, and along with that, "the way known only to God" of bringing all to
share in eternal life. Moreover, as already mentioned, the astonishing proportions of the universe establish a context of cosmic humility in which all
can meet.[10] Admittedly, classic Taoism and Confucianism show no special
interest in how the universe began or how it will end. Taoism is more focused
on the harmony and balance of all things in the cosmic order of nature and
one's attunement to it. Speculations about beginnings and endings appear
almost as distractions to the quiet demands of the philharmonic life. To that
degree, the classic Sinic vision is a counterweight to the biblical and Western
emphasis on history and human freedom. The great spiritualities originating
in India, Hinduism and Buddhism, have elaborate cosmologies, but these are
marked by a cyclical pattern or process. The universe contains many worlds
and states. Souls are caught up in a purifying cycle of rebirths. The cycle is
repeated indefinitely until the soul attains release, or *moksa*, and enters into
a pure spiritual consciousness of union with absolute Self, or attains nirvana
in an immortality untouched by suffering and disunion and decay. Again,
from this Indic point of view, the categoric ending of the physical cosmos can
never be the main issue. A larger universal process continues, governed by
spiritual progress alone. From the witness of this classic spiritual tradition,
all faiths can come to a deeper sense of the mystery of the multidimensional
universe in which we exist, and appreciate more keenly the spiritual depths
latent in the drama of human existence.

All this is in contrast to the emphasis embedded in the biblical view. From
the eighth century B.C.E. there arose a kind of cosmic hope. The creator would
bring creation to its fulfillment in which the just would share. Islam, inher-

---

10. In this context, see Keith Ward, "Cosmology and Religious Ideas about the End of the
World" in *The Far-Future Universe: Eschatology from a Cosmic Perspective,* ed. George F. R. Ellis
(London: Templeton Foundation, 2002), 235-48; and Jacob Neusner, Bruce Chilton, and William
Graham, *Three Faiths, One God: The Formative Faith and Practice of Judaism, Christianity, and Islam*
(Boston: Brill, 2002).

iting much of this Jewish sense of creation, is more explicit on the resurrection of the dead and on the continuing reality of hell or paradise. How much either of these Abrahamic faiths envisages the ending of the physical cosmos is a matter of surmise. The theocentric character of their trust in the faithfulness of the creator would not tend to make it a pressing issue. While the faith of Israel witnesses to the reality of creation and the continuing nature of providence, Islam invites us to that radical submission to the purposes of the Creator that will always elude human comprehension.

Christianity, on the other hand, has developed various kinds of explicit eschatology bearing on our human and cosmic future. The Christian Scriptures clearly exhibit many different and developing viewpoints.[11] But there is a special cosmic focus arising from the incarnation itself, the Word in whom all things are made himself becomes flesh and dwells among us (Jn 1:1-16).[12] In the risen body of Jesus, the transformation of the cosmically linked physical reality of humanity has already begun. In the developing vision of the early church, everything finds its source, coherence, reconciliation, and goal in Christ (Col 1:15-20). Through the eucharist, the fruits of the earth (nature) and the work of human hands (history and culture) have an essential place in mediating the reality of the One who has come and is to come as the fullness of God (Col 1:19) communicated to all creation. In this perspective, hope cannot ignore the fate of the universe already so intimately and comprehensively claimed by God as integral to the divine self-communication. How the end might be scientifically described is not the pressing issue, but that the end will reveal God as "all in all" (1 Cor 15:28) is of the essence of Christian hope.

While none of the partners in inter-hope dialogue is dependent on the new cosmological sciences, it is likely that each can experience a greater awe at the immensity and amazing fertility of the cosmos as current science sees it. It may prove, too, to be an occasion for each to express a more comprehensive and inclusive hope in the light of the providence that has brought us to this point.

This is especially the case when world history throws these different spiritualities and worldviews together and each is challenged by historical and cultural forces previously unknown. This point is intensified when the different cultural histories and even sense of self are being eroded. In the West, the individual, personal ego-self has long been under attack from Darwin, Marx, and Freud. In India, the transcendent self of the Brahman now has to

---

11. Compare, for instance, 1 Thess 4:13-5:11 and 2 Thess 2:1-3:5 to, say, Rom 8 and 11.

12. See Anthony J. Kelly and Francis J. Moloney, *Experiencing God in the Gospel of John* (New York: Paulist, 2003), 29-60.

contend with the modern reality of democracy, in which even the untouch-
ables have a vote and a *harijan* has been the prime minister. Clearly, too,
in China the Long March as a massive historical event has disrupted the
old patterns of cosmic harmony. Throughout the world indigenous peoples
are going through cultural dislocation in the postcolonial world, and all are
troubled by the technologically induced "consumer self" of the mass markets.
Hope is intensified when one's deepest identity is under pressure and potentially at least can expand in a new comprehensiveness. In a global world the
number of one's ancestors continues to increase!

Formal interfaith dialogue usually limits eschatological themes to topics
such as reincarnation, the role of Christ in the salvation of all, and the different meanings of salvation itself. Christian hope is, in many ways, the great
novelty. It includes the resurrection of the body and the transformation of all
creation in a horizon in which all are destined to share in eternal life. This
eschatological standpoint may provide the best resource that Christians can
bring to the great dialogue that has begun. In an atmosphere of all-inclusive
hope, Christian participants in the different forms of dialogue give expression to the conviction that all belong together in the communion of eternal
life in God.[13]

PHILOSOPHICAL INFLUENCES

But hope is not only a religious or ecclesial concern. In the face of the horrors
of twentieth-century European history, two remarkable philosophers have
had a great influence, especially in the domain of theology. As we mentioned
previously, these are Gabriel Marcel, a French Christian, and Ernst Bloch,
an East German Marxist.

Marcel's influential *Homo Viator: Introduction to a Metaphysic of Hope* was
a timely voice in a world that had been ravaged by two world wars to become
prey to that defiant existentialist despair exemplified in the writings of Jean-
Paul Sartre.[14] Marcel saw things otherwise: to be human was to be on a
journey, "on the way"—a *viator*, as in the title of his book. Hope is to human
consciousness what breathing is to the living organism. It is not, however, a

---

13. For a particularly promising area of dialogue, see Joseph H. Wong, OSB Cam, "Anony-
mous Christians: Karl Rahner's Pneuma-Christocentrism and an East-West Dialogue," *Theological
Studies* 55 (1994): 609-37.

14. See Jean-Paul Sartre, *Being and Nothingness: An Essay in Phenomenological Ontology*, trans.
H. E. Barnes (New York: Washington Square Press, 1969), 566.

wishful optimism; hope is always at its best when it has faced the temptation to despair.[15] Hope is most itself when it actively overcomes this temptation. It is ever breaking out of the self-imprisonment of the isolated ego,[16] to recover a sense of humility, patience, compassion, and love.[17] Hope acts prophetically. It contests any closed vision of human existence,[18] in the name of an ultimate and gracious mystery that can never be fully named or imagined.[19]

With a more social and historical emphasis, Ernst Bloch's monumental three-volume work, *The Principle of Hope*, locates the phenomenon of hope at the very heart of historical development.[20] Hope is related to the dream of the "New," the *novum*. It animates all the efforts of freedom to bring a new society into being. The hunger for the Not-Yet keeps history moving. It calls into question the present order of reality and inspires an awareness of the possibilities latent within it. It is always tending toward something yet to be realized. In this regard, hope is always "utopian." It is not, however, a vague aspiration but the active, realistic anticipation of new forms of just society. Though religious faith and especially Christianity are creative forms of hopeful imagination, "God," for Bloch, is simply a symbol for the as-yet-unrealized possibilities of human freedom.[21]

Clearly, these two philosophical approaches continue to be a great resource for Christian eschatology.[22] Marcel's approach is unashamedly that of a Christian philosopher, and so more direct and positive in its influence. Hope in the end is reliance on the Mystery for a fulfillment from beyond any human system. Bloch's contribution is more theologically negative, but healthily so.[23] Though he reduces God to a symbol of a more human future, he shows a noble humanist impatience with all forms of exploitation and oppression, and the ideologies that sustain them, religious or otherwise.

---

15. Gabriel Marcel, *Homo Viator: Introduction to a Metaphysic of Hope*, trans. E. Craufurd (New York: Harper & Row, 1966), 7, 10, 30, 32, 36, 41, 45.

16. Ibid., 36.

17. Kenneth T. Gallagher, *The Philosophy of Gabriel Marcel* (New York: Fordham University Press, 1962), 74.

18. Marcel, *Homo Viator*, 53.

19. Gabriel Marcel, *Being and Having: An Existentialist Diary*, trans. K. Farrer (Gloucester, Mass.: Peter Smith, 1976), 75, 79.

20. Ernst Bloch, *The Principle of Hope*, trans. Neville Plaice, Paul Knight, and Stephen Plaice, 3 vols. (Cambridge, Mass.: MIT Press, 1996).

21. Ibid., 3:1298.

22. See Jürgen Moltmann, *Theology of Hope*, trans. James W. Leitch (London: SCM Press, 1967) for an early critical theological engagement with Bloch's thought. Also J. Pieper, *Hope and History* (London: Burns & Oates, 1969), 61-76.

23. Bloch's views can be profitably related to Nicholas Lash, *A Matter of Hope: A Theologian's Reflections on the Thought of Karl Marx* (London: Darton, Longman & Todd, 1981).

THE THEOLOGICAL REDISCOVERY OF ESCHATOLOGY

Current eschatology looks back over a hundred years to Protestant bibli-
cal scholarship's rediscovery of the eschatological orientation of the New
Testament, above all in regard to Jesus' preaching of the Kingdom of God.
The story has been told many times, in which the contributions of Albrecht
Ritschl (1822-1889), Joachim Weiss (1863-1914), and Albert Schweitzer
(1875-1965) are given due recognition. They prepared the way for a more
critical, theologically comprehensive approach to matters eschatological.[24]
For a time, eschatology seesawed between the extreme transcendental
approach of Karl Barth and the more immanent existential presentation of
Rudolf Bultmann. Oscar Cullmann stressed the biblical notion of history as
a linear progress to its goal. For his part, C. H. Dodd represented a Christ-
centered "realized eschatology." The kingdom was already present and active
in Jesus and his mission.

The dialectic of conflicting aspects of biblical theology served to provoke
major achievements in theology.[25] A theological eschatology began to work
in a larger horizon that included a greater emphasis on the church's doctrinal tradition. Barth had already stressed that the eschatological was not an
archaic apocalyptic mind-set, but the horizon in which faith must be lived in
every age. Four other theologians continue to be powerful influences in any
current theology.

Wolfhart Pannenberg is remarkable for his eschatological approach to the
objectivity of human history as a whole. In the risen Christ, a real anticipation of divine revelation has occurred. The full meaning of this *prolepsis* must
await its cosmic manifestation at the end of time. But in Christ, the future
of God is already present in its active and attractive power, drawing history to its completion. Pannenberg grounds his eschatology in strong future-
oriented ontology.[26] No reality can be fully known save in terms of its future
realization.[27]

---

24. For an excellent historical overview, see Hans Schwarz, *Eschatology* (Grand Rapids:
Eerdmans, 2000), 107-209.

25. This is not to say that there have not been outstanding developments in biblical scholarship
in this whole area. For example, Dunn treats many eschatological themes that have a direct theological relevance: the Kingdom of God (*Jesus Remembered*, 383-488), the character of discipleship
(pp. 543-614), the self-understanding of Jesus (pp. 615-764), and his death and resurrection (pp.
765-880).

26. Ted Peters in *God—The World's Future: Systematic Theology for a Post-modern Era* (Minneapolis: Fortress Press, 1992) exploits Pannenberg's approach to impressive effect.

27. See Christiaan Mostert, *God and the Future: Wolfhart Pannenberg's Eschatological Doctrine of
God* (New York: T&T Clark, 2002), especially chapters 3 and 4 (pp. 55-126).

Jürgen Moltmann, influenced by Bloch, made a decisive contribution. In contrast to Pannenberg, Moltmann, in his *Theology of Hope*, puts more emphasis on subjective, and even apocalyptic, considerations. As the promised future, God continually contests every present, especially in a world of violence and injustice. What is to come can never be extrapolated from what is present. The eschaton remains always an open and indefinable reality. It judges the present, summons to action, but is never possessed or realized in any age.

Karl Rahner is the most eminent representative of the renewal of eschatology within the Catholic tradition.[28] He repeatedly emphasizes the interconnection of all the mysteries of faith in the one self-communicating reality of God. In such a context, he develops his influential hermeneutics of eschatological statements. For him, the future fulfillment in its individual and collective forms can only be read from what has already occurred in the incarnation, death, and resurrection of Christ. In this regard, he distances himself from any apocalyptic futurology. There is no way of already occupying some future point and, as it were, sending information back to the present. Rahner makes profound linkages between anthropology, the essential God-orientation of our free but mortal existence, and its definitive shape in death. In this light, he interprets the traditional themes of purgatory, heaven, and hell. An eschatological horizon is inscribed into every aspect of human existence.

Hans Urs von Balthasar, compared to Rahner, is less systematically hermeneutical. The Swiss theologian places greater emphasis on the contemplative and imaginative dimensions of hope. His theology of the *Mysterium Paschale* has been widely influential, in the context of his masterwork, *The Glory of the Lord*. His spiritual eschatology was distilled in one of his final works, *Dare We Hope 'That All Men Will Be Saved'?* It expressed in more accessible form the surprisingly hopeful standpoint of this great theologian usually known for his more conservative stance in doctrinal matters.

Liberation/Political Theology

Despite the variety of cultural, social, economic, historical, and political contexts, Liberationist theologies have insisted on the social and political productiveness of eschatological thinking. They witness to a new social and historical consciousness on the part of churches, which is fed by the social sciences and in no small way inspired by the original impetus of the Marx-

---

28. The best treatment of Rahner's eschatology continues to be Peter C. Phan, *Eternity in Time: A Study of Karl Rahner's Eschatology* (Selinsgrove, Pa.: Susquehanna University Press, 1988).

ist analysis of history, especially as carried forward in the writings of Bloch and in the analyses of the Frankfurt School. In this theological development, commitment to the ultimate in terms of Christian hope must have practical resonances in the penultimate areas of politics, economics, and social anthropology. No type of liberation theology denies the importance of individual freedom and destiny, nor the cosmic dimensions of salvation in Christ. But common to all types is the insistence that, to be authentic, hope must have a practical historical and political effect on structures that oppress human lives. It takes history seriously as the dramatic field of God's saving action, and so seeks to motivate an urgent involvement in the works of peace, justice, and reconciliation. It draws its inspiration both from the great biblical prophets and from Jesus himself as he identifies himself with the poor and the marginalized. In this manner, it seeks to voice the struggles and hopes of those who have suffered on the underside of history.

While hope announces the definitive coming of the Kingdom of God in Christ, it must also denounce everything that opposes the Kingdom by oppressing humanity and enclosing it in despair. True hope must be productive of a more just society and a more human world. Eschatological hope is not to be so spiritualized as to have no historical consequences. Liberation from injustice and oppression is an integral part of the history of salvation.[29]

In Latin America, theologians such as Gustavo Gutiérrez and Clodovis and Leonardo Boff repudiate any split between eschatological salvation and politico-social liberation.[30] Liberation theology is specifically linked to the conduct of solidarity with the suffering other.[31] It is less a theological construct and theory than a hope-inspired praxis. It meets the problem of evil with an eschatological hope certainly, but in such a way that Christian witness is energized to bring about a realistic anticipation of God's saving and life-giving will at a given historical juncture. The world to come and the suffering reality of this world are not to be kept apart. The forms of liberation by which Christians collaborate with God's saving purpose have what Leonardo Boff has called "a sacramental function: they have a weight of their own, but they also point forward, and embody in anticipation, what God has definitively prepared for human beings."[32]

---

29. Schwarz, *Eschatology*, 160-65.

30. See the classic exposition, Gustavo Guttiérez, *A Theology of Liberation: History, Politics and Salvation*, trans. and ed. C. Inda and J. Eagleson (Maryknoll, N.Y.: Orbis Books, 1973; rev. ed. 1988).

31. A basic reference is I. Ellacuria and J. Sobrino (eds.), Mysterium Liberationis: *Fundamental Concepts in Liberation Theology* (Maryknoll, N.Y.: Orbis Books, 1993).

32. Leonardo Boff, *Liberating Grace*, trans. John Drury (Maryknoll, N.Y.: Orbis Books, 1979), 152.

It has been objected that liberation theology places more emphasis on human action than on divine initiative, but that would be to overlook the "sacramental function" of the works of liberation. In the horizon of Christian hope, such actions on behalf of the poor are radically eucharistic. Just as the sacramental liturgy is in an obvious way a human function, it is only possible by invoking the transforming power of the Spirit, communing with Christ in his death and resurrection, and longing for his return in the fullness of God's reign. While aspects of social analysis might rely on a variety of Marxist categories for their expression, the theological and Christian dimension of liberation makes it clear that the action of God is the defining eschatological factor. Every effort to eliminate poverty and contest the exploitation of our fellow human beings is an anticipatory sign of the final Reign of God.

From the 1970s onward, this liberationist form of eschatological thinking has found applications far beyond the Latin American situation. A critical, socially responsible and historically attuned hope cannot bypass the problem of evil wherever it is found. On the European scene it has taken the form of political theology. Johann-Baptist Metz, along with such theologians as Jürgen Moltmann and Dorothea Sölle, is acutely aware of the reductive and domesticating influence of Western society on Christian hope. For that reason Metz sees the necessity for an "apocalyptic sting" in the Christian witness to hope in the actuality of history.[33] By acting in solidarity with the hopeless, the Christian must express the imperatives of hope in a particular lifestyle, bearing in mind the "dangerous memory" of the Crucified. In contradiction to liberal ideologies of social progress and a blind evolutionary optimism, hope must be productive of its own history, critical of the reductive force of the cultures in which it works. Metz, in a thesis on the place of liberation in theology, makes the point:

> Faith in a messianic God, a God of the resurrection of the dead and of judgment, a God before whom even the past is not safe, before whom past sufferings do not disappear subjectless into the abyss of an anonymous and endless dispassionate evolution, this faith is not an opiate in the histories of the liberation of humanity. Rather, it guarantees nonnegotiable standards in the unabating struggle for the dignity of all human beings as subjects in the struggle for universal liberation.[34]

In his *Passion for God: The Mystical-Political Dimension of Christianity*, Metz strikingly connects the Christian sense of God with a sense of solidarity

---

33. For a good overview, see James Matthew Ashley, *Interruptions: Mysticism, Politics and Theology in the Work of Johann Baptist Metz* (Notre Dame, Ind.: Notre Dame University Press, 1998).

34. As quoted in Schwarz, *Eschatology*, 152.

embracing those who bear the brunt of the problem of evil throughout human history.[35] For this German theologian, the focal experience is found in the horror of Auschwitz as a continual judgment on European history. In some inspiring pages, Metz gives an account of his own journey beyond a theoretical theology into the sufferings of history as the most provocative *locus theologicus*. Accordingly, he places special emphasis on "dangerous" or culturally unsettling recollection of the Crucified and the prayer of innocent sufferers. The "dangerous memory" of Jesus inspires the risk of individual and communal witness to the God of love who alone can bring history to its fulfillment. Hope finds no assurance in "aestheticizing" or spiritualizing suffering by projecting such evils onto God. In solidarity with suffering humanity, the Christian is rather "suffering unto God," in a Job-like experience, repressing nothing of the surd of evil, but affirming the dignity and inalienable value of the suffering other in a hope resolutely centered on the Love that alone can bring history to its conclusion.[36]

While hard and fast distinctions cannot be drawn between the tasks of reconciliation and economic, political, cultural, racial, gender, and postcolonial concerns in any given historical situation, the general orientation of liberationist theology has been extraordinarily productive in Asia. There it speaks in many other idioms and languages. The Vietnamese American Peter C. Phan is a leading theological commentator on this emerging new context.[37] He presents the history and foundational principles of this new discourse as a triple dialogue with the poor, with cultures, and with other religions. Drawing on abundant bibliographical references to this new form of "hopeful discourse" in the wake of Vatican II, he indicates the great plurality of voices speaking in the idioms of liberation in such countries as the Philippines, India, Japan, Indonesia, Taiwan, Malaysia, Korea, Pakistan, Thailand, and Vietnam.[38]

The complexity of the Chinese context is suggested in Choan-Seng Song's pioneering *Third-Eye Theology: Theology in Formation in Asian Settings*, especially his chapter entitled "A Political God."[39] Song speaks of "the barbarism of power" and challenges the Asian tendency to idolize authority. The liberationist witness of the gospel is subversive. He speaks of the

---

35. Johann-Baptist Metz, *A Passion for God: The Mystical-Political Dimension of Christianity*, trans. J. Matthew Ashley (New York: Paulist, 1998), 1-5.

36. Ibid., 1-5, 69-70, 119.

37. Peter C. Phan, *In Our Own Tongues: Perspectives from Asia on Mission and Inculturation* (Maryknoll, N.Y.: Orbis Books, 2003).

38. Ibid., 20-29, 204-14.

39. Choan-Seng Song, *Third-Eye Theology: Theology in Formation in Asian Settings* (Maryknoll, N.Y.: Orbis Books, 1979), 200-221.

politics of God as not only a politics that liberates an oppressed people from oppression and injustice, but also as liberating the oppressors from the false pretenses and acts of violence that keep them in power. In this regard, the politics of God contest the politics of make-believe: "for it confronts injustice with justice, deception with truth, bondage with freedom, and terror with love."[40] The participation of Christians in this politics of God is in fact the politics of the resurrection and ultimate hope, open to the radically new, and never foreclosing on the surprises of the Spirit.[41]

In the Indian and African situation, of central concern is inculturation, the continuing critical effort to communicate the gospel of hope not in its Western form but within the meanings and values, the symbols and rituals of the local or regional culture. It is not simply a question of liberation of the masses from poverty and exploitation, but something much deeper, namely, the affirmation of the cultural soul of the peoples concerned. This, in turn, has deep ecclesiological consequences. Here the influence of the Sri Lankan Jesuit Aloysius Pieris is especially notable.[42] He highlights the need for a more contemplative or spiritual approach if Christianity is to live in deep contact with the great spiritual paths of Hinduism, Buddhism, Taoism, and Jainism as these profoundly affect the Asian cultural milieu. Liberation from oppressive poverty is especially related to the spirituality of voluntary poverty. Interior liberation from "mammon" is a prized ideal in the cultures where the monk embodies this spiritual ideal. It is this spiritual energy that must be tapped in the service of those who have been victimized by the force of mammon and the gross materialism it represents. In consequence, "true inculturation is a rooting of the Asian church in the *liberative* dimension of voluntary poverty." Pieris, while giving a number of examples of communities who witness to this new inculturation of the hope of the gospel, summarizes his position:

> A church inculturated in Asia is indeed a church liberated from mam-
> mon, and is therefore necessarily composed of the poor: poor by option
> and poor by circumstances. In other words, inculturation is the eccle-
> siological revolution already initiated by basic human communities,
> with Christian and non-Christian membership, wherein mysticism
> and militancy meet and merge: mysticism based on voluntary poverty
> and militancy pitched against forced poverty.[43]

---

40. Ibid., 218; concerning Communist China, see pp. 246-52.
41. Ibid., 257-59.
42. Aloysius Pieris, SJ, *An Asian Theology of Liberation* (Maryknoll, N.Y.: Orbis Books, 1990).
43. Ibid., 22-23, 57.

Pieris thus uncovers a deeper dimension of the meaning of liberation, and with it a deeper understanding of the challenge of hope and the witness of church.

In the huge world of Africa with its many nations, peoples, and historical experiences, the problems caused by poverty, political oppression, and racial conflicts are, of course, not absent. But, in ways not dissimilar to the approach of Pieris, a genuinely African theology is looking for a new inculturation of the gospel in relation to vital aspects of popular culture. Clearly, Christian hope cannot be fully expressed in African cultures without a deeper valuing of their traditions of healing, leadership, ritual, dance, and ecstatic religiosity.[44] Categories of "liberation" and their relation to eschatological hope are given new significance in the emerging theologies of Africa. This will mean that Christian hope must critically denounce the cultural oppression of the African peoples in the colonial era—in terms of the consequent economic and "anthropological" or cultural impoverishment they have suffered—while at the same time announcing a new liberating hospitality to the full humanity of the African experience.

In these differing cultural contexts, feminist theologians (for example, the Filipina Sister Mary John Mananzan, María Pilar Aquino of the United States, and the Kenyan Teresia Hinga) quickly drew attention to the many ways in which women suffer oppression. The basic principle is clear: whatever degrades the full humanity of women is the contradiction of the hope that can be fully authentic only by promoting the full and free humanity of women. This principle has many applications.

In Asia, the evils of oppression are instanced in the tolerance of rape, incest, economic inequality, mail-order brides, prostitution, sex trafficking, along with the burden of poverty, which is disproportionately borne by women. The prevailing culture cannot be the all-deciding factor in matters associated with the necessity of dowries (India) and female circumcision (West Africa), for example. Hope must bring about a more humane and liberative form of culture. The path of hope is to release the ignored spiritual and theological potential of women in interpreting and communicating the tradition flowing from the Scriptures and the life of the church. Here the collective voice of women is important, promising a far more radical and far-reaching critique of culture than would be possible from any individual theologian, female or male. Such theology looks beyond itself to the concrete situation in which women work together in the solidarity of suffering and hope.[45]

---

44. For a useful overview, see Elochukwu E.Uzuku, CSSP, "African Inculturation Theology: Path of Liberation," http://www.theo.kuleuven.ac.be/dt/pub_uzukwu_text_1.htm.

45. For a concise account, see Tom Roberts, "Feminist Theology Must Lead to Action," *National Catholic Reporter*, December 17, 1999.

Allied to all this is another development that combines psychological, social, and cultural dimensions of Christian eschatology. It relies on the anthropological investigations of René Girard into the violence deeply embedded in the dynamics of human culture. The destructiveness of the violent mimesis is uniquely unmasked in the gospel, and above all in the cross. Writers such as Raymund Schwager, James Alison, and Gil Bailie are most noteworthy in this connection.[46]

Of its nature, Christian hope cannot be neatly synthesized. But each one of these theological influences must be respected if hope is to manifest the realism, the intelligence, and the practical concern that it demands.

DIALOGUE WITH SCIENCE

Eschatology, if it is to express hope in a realistic manner, must be elaborated in a scientifically attuned world, with its awareness of the unimaginable dimensions of space and time. While not allowing itself to be reduced to a one-dimensional scientific framework, a theological account of hope must give due weight to both the beginning and the end of the universe as science is envisaging it.[47] Again, dialogue is the key.[48] It is taking place on a variety of fronts. Chief among these efforts is the correlation of current astrophysics of the Big Bang with the theology and philosophy of divine creation. This includes questions concerning the significance of the emergence of human consciousness and the allied considerations of the human body-soul composite. It discusses, too, the implications of quantum physics for our experience of the space-time continuum, to raise new questions on the relationship of eternity and time, spirit and matter. Evolutionary models relating to life and the emergent cosmos demand fresh considerations of the

---

46. Raymund Schwager, *Jesus in the Drama of Salvation: Toward a Biblical Doctrine of Redemption*, trans. James G. Williams and Paul Haddon (New York: Crossroad, 1999); James Alison, *Raising Abel: The Recovery of Eschatological Imagination* (New York: Crossroad, 1996); James Alison, *The Joy of Being Wrong: Original Sin through Easter Eyes* (New York: Crossroad, 1998); Gil Bailie, *Violence Unveiled: Humanity at the Crossroads* (New York: Crossroad, 1997); see especially chap. 12, "It Is Accomplished" (pp. 217-33), for a profound reflection on Christ in the Gospel of John.

47. For a good overview, Arnold Benz, *The Future of the Universe: Chance, Chaos, God* (New York: Continuum, 2000).

48. An excellent example of this continuing dialogue is the collection of papers sponsored jointly by the Templeton Foundation and the Pontifical Academy of Sciences and the Vatican Observatory: George F. R. Ellis, ed., *The Far-Future Universe: Eschatology from a Cosmic Perspective* (London: Templeton Foundation, 2002). For evidence of a lack of dialogue, see McGrath's devastating critique of Richard Dawkin's ideological atheism, in Alister McGrath, *Dawkin's God: Genes, Memes, and the Meaning of Life* (Oxford: Blackwell, 2005).

divine mode of acting in the finite universe, and the nature of the divine creative act itself.[49]

Intriguing questions play around the incredible confluence of conditions that give rise to human consciousness and, in some sense, look to its emergence. These matters are crystallized in various forms of the Anthropic Principle.[50] Christian hope must also take into account the scientifically informed presumption that this universe is finite and will come to an end.[51] Human existence emerges not only within a genetically evolutionary biosphere but as the outcome of vast cosmic processes. New questions naturally arise. If human existence is embodied in this cosmic reality, how does hope for the resurrection of the body include the transformation of the material universe? To what degree, then, does hope extend to the cosmos? Or, at the other extreme, in what measure do cosmic conditions place limits on our hope?[52] Most of all, how are such doctrines as the incarnation and the resurrection relatable to contemporary scientific positions?

This new stage of dialogue between faith/hope and science presents a special challenge to eschatology. The word of hope is spoken within the unfolding of a cosmic story. It includes the explosive first instant (the Big Bang), the resulting emergence of nuclei of hydrogen and helium, and the formation of the atoms that constitute physical reality. It is set within the universal framework of the formation of galaxies and stars and the birth of our solar system. It leads to the particular story of planet earth, with the beginning of life in the prokaryotes and eukaryotes, and springing forth of

---

49. Ian Barbour's *When Science Meets Religion: Enemies, Strangers or Partners* (New York: HarperSanFrancisco, 2000) usefully documents the field of exciting recent questions. Closer to our theme are the papers edited by John C. Polkinghorne and M. Welker, eds., *The End of the World and the Ends of God* (Harrisburg, Pa.: Trinity Press International, 2000); see also Polkinghorne, *The God of Hope and the End of the World* (London: Yale University Press, 2002); Warren S. Brown, Nancey Murphy, and H. Newton Maloney, eds., *Whatever Happened to the Soul? Scientific and Theological Portraits of Human Nature* (Minneapolis: Fortress Press, 1998); Celia E. Deane-Drummond, *Creation through Wisdom: Theology and the New Biology* (Edinburgh: T&T Clark, 2000); and Denis Edwards, *Breath of Life: A Theology of the Creator Spirit* (Maryknoll, N.Y.: Orbis Books, 2004).

50. There are various versions of this principle. Basically, it presents the universe as not only hospitable to human life but in some extraordinarily precise ways so constituted as to favor the emergence of life and human intelligence. See Errol E. Harris, *Cosmos and Anthropos: A Philosophical Interpretation of the Anthropic Cosmological Principle* (Atlantic Highlands, N.J.: Humanities Press, 1991); and, more accessibly, David Toolan, *At Home in the Cosmos* (Maryknoll, N.Y.: Orbis Books, 2001), 173-77.

51. Neil A. Manson, ed., *God and Design: The Teleological Argument and Modern Science* (London: Routledge, 2003).

52. See George C. Coyne, SJ, "Seeking the Future: A Theological Perspective" in Ellis, *Far-Future Universe*, 12-22; and Robert John Russell, "Eschatology and Physical Cosmology: A Preliminary Reflection," in ibid., 316-54.

plant, animal, and human life. The marvel of the earth's biodiversity and ecological interconnectedness emerges as a subject for both wonder and deep moral concern in the human mind and heart, as we ponder anew our human responsibilities to both God and the creation of which we are a part.

ESCHATOLOGICAL POSITIONS

Here I wish to sketch some key positions affecting the eschatological elaboration of hope in what follows in later chapters.

The Language of Body and Soul

The language of body and soul will probably continue to be a vexed issue for a long time yet. Problems stem usually from two sources. One source of confusion is to think of the soul as independently and naturally immortal. This supposedly philosophical notion appears to be unrelated to the supernatural gift of eternal life and the resurrection of the body. It is as though the natural, spiritual component of the human makeup makes the supernatural gift of eternal life somewhat irrelevant. The other problem is a dualistic outlook. It imagines the body and soul as separate, independent entities, related only in an extrinsic manner. In death, the soul, leaving the body behind, continues on as the most important part of our personal existence.

Despite these problems, we would argue that it is impossible to speak of the totality of our human makeup as persons without invoking the primal spirit/matter or soul/body distinction in some way.[53] To speak of human existence purely in material terms would restrict hope to biological evolution or to the future of the material cosmos. On the other hand, if the human person is depicted only in spiritual, that is, nonmaterial, terms, that would leave out our immersion in history and community and would conceive of the person haunting the earth rather than inhabiting it. Since this body/soul distinction has application in many of the eschatological questions before us, a brief note is called for. It will emphasize, above all, the interdependence of body and soul, matter and spirit.

Inevitably there are terminological problems. It is not always clear just what particular authors mean when they use terms such as "matter," "body," "corporeality," "soul," "self," and "person." It reminds us of the struggle

---

53. For a searching consideration of the philosophical problems, see D. Braine, *The Human Person: Animal and Spirit* (Notre Dame, Ind.: University of Notre Dame Press, 1992).

of the Greek fathers in the fourth century to come to some agreement on the meanings of *ousia* ("nature") and *hypostasis* ("person"). Though the New Testament teaches that the dead live on with the Lord, and that the resurrection of the flesh occurs at the end of days, it is not concerned to communicate any clear definition of body or soul or how the two are related. Aquinas's theoretical elaboration of the unity of the human person, in which matter and spirit are co-principles, was the product of a long development, and is often not clearly grasped. For him, the human person is always more than the soul.[54] Later theological and philosophical language, in trying to give precise content to the primal duality of body and soul, often veers away from the *duality* of two related principles of human existence in the direction of *dualism*, that is, a separation of the two that allows for no essential correlation. As a result, there is a tendency to privilege one over the other. On a pastoral level, theology must take great care not to undermine the language of hope as we pray for the dead in funeral rites. Since a requiem Mass is not a theology seminar, the needs of realistic pastoral communication must be respected. The mortal remains of the deceased lie in the coffin while the church prays that he or she will be received by God into eternal light. That being said, theology, taking its lead from the praxis of faith and hope, is free to pursue its own kind of explorations. Consequently, I would emphasize the following points.

One of the enduringly valuable insights of Thomistic anthropology is the understanding of the soul as essentially the "form of the human body." Only as a body-soul or, more accurately, a matter-form composite, can we refer to the human person as a living, existing personal subject. For Aquinas, the "formal" spiritual principle is always and essentially related to the physical-material principle in the constitution of the being. From different perspectives, we can say that the human person is both an animated body and an embodied spirit, a *somebody*—for the human soul is intrinsically related to matter. The whole thrust of its being is to be embodied and expressed in matter. As the scholastics would say, the form—that is, the soul—exists in a "transcendental" relation to its material principle. In death, a fundamental rupture in human existence occurs. The soul ceases to be embodied in the manner that served biological life. Some suggest that the soul, after death, because of its intrinsic relationship to matter, enters into some other form of embodiment immediately. Consequently, the traditional doctrine of the soul waiting for its completion in the "resurrection of the body on the last day" is a mythological mode of expression. After all, the full-bodied resurrection of

---

54. See, e.g., *STh* 1, q. 2, a. 9 ad 5 (note: "ad 5" is Thomas's response to the fifth objection); 2-2, q. 83, a. 11.

Jesus is a clear scriptural and doctrinal teaching. Moreover, Catholic tradition includes the doctrine of the assumption of Mary. She has been "assumed," body and soul, into heaven, as the mother and exemplar of the church.

However we probe such issues, we must bear in mind two related kinds of totality inscribed into human existence. Given the whole panoply of divine creation, the human being is a microcosm. It combines in itself material and spiritual dimensions of the universe. This is a favorite theme of, say, Maximus Confessor and looks back to Plato's *Timaeus* for its origins.[55] Today we can take this idea further. As embodied in the material and physical cosmos, the human being is immersed in the whole dynamic network of material creation. The body is not simply contained by its skin. In the one web of evolutionary life, human beings are related to all other living beings on this planet. Moreover, there is the much greater cosmic connection. We are made of stardust. In physical and chemical constitution, our bodies and brains owe their origins to vast cosmic occurrences billions of years ago that formed the hydrogen and carbon that are the basis of all biological life.

The spiritual dimension of human existence is related to the soul. In Aquinas's oft-repeated phrase, the human spirit is "in some measure all things," *quoddamodo omnia*.[56] This overture of the spirit to the whole universe arises out of the distinctive experience of human consciousness as it transcends that range of material and purely physical reality. Human consciousness, for example, experiences itself as being able to reflect on itself reflecting. Nothing is in principle beyond the ambit of its explorations, be it spiritual, material, or the divine mystery itself. The spiritual phenomenon of consciousness is of universal significance. However inchoately, in the human mind the cosmos awakens to itself as an expanse of wonder. Through human intelligence, the whole of existence can be experienced as an uncanny gift. Through the reach of the human spirit, creation awakens to give thanks to the Source of all that exists and to understand the universe as a divine creation.

The awareness of these dynamics and dimensions written into human nature caused Goethe to observe, "Man is the first conversation that nature holds with God."[57] Long before him, Maximus Confessor considered that, "the human person is the laboratory in which everything is concentrated and itself naturally mediates between the extremities of each division, having been drawn into everything in a good and fitting way through becom-

---

55. Lars Thunberg, *Man and the Cosmos: The Vision of St. Maximus the Confessor* (Crestwood, N.Y.: St. Vladimir's Seminary Press, 1985), 71-92.

56. *STh* 1, q. 14, a. 1; q. 16, a. 3; 1-2, q. 80, a. 2.

57. Quoted by Gabriel Daly in his stimulating *Creation and Redemption* (Dublin: Gill & Mac-Millan, 1988), 116.

ing."[58] The point is that the human being exists within a dynamic field of interconnections and inter-relationships. It is potentially open to everything within the universe. Its spiritual scope reaches beyond even this, to the abiding source and goal of all existence.

Now we come to what today are more controverted matters. Can the material cosmos alone explain the spiritual capacities of the human person? Clearly, our bodily constitution is the outcome of cosmic physical, chemical, and genetic forces of unimaginable complexity. All this structures and energizes the life of our bodies and wondrous workings of our brains, the most complex system in the natural world. Each of the brain's hundred billion neurons is connected with hundreds of thousands of others, resulting in a possible hundred trillion synaptic connections. But matter alone cannot explain the genesis of the human spirit. What we call the "soul" pertains to what is deepest in the universe as God's personal creation. However mysteriously and however intimately connected with evolutionary dynamics, only God can create.[59] On the one hand, the human spirit is embodied in the totality of the created universe. On the other hand, it is immediately created by God to exist in a dialogical relationship with its Creator. It is the created foundation for a relational God-ward-ness. Through this spirit we are "faced" with God, at every stage of existence, whether in the present space-time structure of biological life, or after death. In this regard, the soul is a principle of continuity in the identity and history of the human being: whatever the human state—living, dying, dead—or in some state beyond (such as purgatory, hell, heaven, or full bodily resurrection), it is one and the same person created by and for God. The whole mystery of salvation is oriented to bring to completion the living dialogue with God that is the basic feature of our being. Though we coexist or "in-exist" within material creation, we are more. We "ex-ist," that is, we "stand out" from material creation in an immediate relationship to God. This is what distinguishes the human creature from all else in the material universe. To be human is to be beholden to the "No-thing" that is outside all creation. It is to be faced with the "No One" that is like no one else. For the spirit inhabits a limitless "Nowhere" beyond all boundaries and locations. It touches on the "No Time," the eternal, which gives meaning and direction to all our days. It is a living relationship to the utterly transcendent and unimaginably immanent "Other," who is the source of all being.

---

58. Difficulty 41, 1305B as translated in Andrew Louth, *Maximus the Confessor* (New York: Routledge, 1996), 157.

59. *STh* 1, q. 90, a. 3; *Summa Contra Gentiles*, book 2, chapter 87. Hereafter, cited as *SCG* 1. 2, c. 87.

The relational consciousness, the spiritual depth and Other-ward orientation of our being, gives rise to the language of self-transcendence. Human consciousness is ever on the move. It unfolds in wonder, love, and exploration. It grows in answerability. It expands through art and contemplation. It is hidden in the daily round of the lives of innumerable good and decent people. It animates the great religious traditions and spiritualities that have formed human history. The dynamics of this spiritual consciousness work as a deep undertow in our supramaterial existence. Various theologies suggest that it is released to its full range in the experience of death. In our passing from this world, our radical God-orientation is revealed for what it is. Even in "the souls of the damned," however we might conceive of that possibility, the radical God-ward-ness remains.

Holding to the immediate creation of the soul by God does not mean regressing to a pre-Christian view of things. It is rather a matter of appreciating the depth dimension of creation itself. Embodied in the physical and biological world, the human being alone is summoned, "called forth" into existence by God's immediate creation of each human soul. In each instance, creation opens to its original and final mystery.

This perspective opens the way to a deeper understanding of eternal life. It is not as though God looks down from heaven and decides to save souls. The deepest truth is that everything emanates from the love of God: the world is good and related to God in a particular way through the human spirit. In the words of Aquinas, "the love of God is [ever] infusing and creating the goodness of reality" (*amor Dei infundens et creans bonitatem in rebus; STh* 1, q. 20, a. 2). Scientists are searching for a "Theory of Everything" (TOE) to explain the immense interactive field of the emergent cosmos. But in the universal domain of God's creation, only the original love of God is the ultimate explanation. It is a love desirous of communicating itself to a creation capable of receiving it. God created matter to ground the spiritual, and created the spirit or soul to render that created universe capable of receiving its crowning gift. Through the dialogical openness inscribed into human existence, the human being emerges as the creature capable of receiving God's ultimate communication.[60]

The theologian John Polkinghorne brings a recognized scientific expertise into dialogue with the theological tradition. In his treatment of the soul, he picks up the Thomistic point that the soul is the form of the body. In a more contemporary idiom, he modestly but astutely suggests that the soul can be understood as the information-bearing pattern perduring through the space-

---

60. See Alison, *Joy of Being Wrong*, 287–89.

time-energy manifold of the metabolic history of the body. When this link is definitively severed in death, the soul-pattern endures not as a reality in itself but only in the memory of God.[61] I would suggest that this is not realistic enough. It is not as though God has to remember what he has definitively created, in order to reconstitute it in a new form. Divine faithfulness is manifested not in terms of having a good memory of the personal pattern each of us once was but in actualizing the potential of the already existent spiritual reality we are. For the spiritual form of the human person is a God-willed and God-wrought dimension of creation itself. It was always more than a tenuous information-bearing pattern, limited to a particular embodied unit of being. As form, it is intrinsically related to matter, with its specific and individual limitations. But as spirit, it is intrinsically open to the infinite, so constituted as to express itself in a dialogical relationship with God. Certainly, it informs matter, now and in some future mode of embodiment. But, even though incarnate in matter, the soul is the subsisting God-created capacity for dialogue with the creator. In its God-relatedness, it is not reducible to an information-bearing pattern that ceases in death. It is rather a continuing openness, in every phase of its being, to the infinite mystery. Through it, creation is made receptive to God, *capax Dei*.

An adequate account of Christian hope presupposes the language of the soul and its immediate creation. The reality of the soul is the elemental promise inherent in our existence that is destined to be kept. The idea of the God-created spirit makes space for a more comprehensive understanding of the process through which the Holy Spirit leads history and the universe to its goal. The life-giving Spirit, through the immediate creation of each human spirit, breathes into the universe the promise of life to the full. Far from diminishing the reality of "the resurrection of the body," the reality of the soul enhances it. For in the resurrection, the human spirit, in its dialogical fulfillment in God, will be embodied in a universe transformed in its every aspect by the Spirit. In this way, the spiritual openness of the soul is joined to the material relationality of the body. Both are aspects of the milieu of ultimate communion with the Trinity and with all creation as it is conceived in the heart of God.[62]

Reducing the God-created and God-oriented openness of the human spirit to the capacities of matter has consequences. It can take the form of a crude materialistic form of reduction. This would argue that the human being is nothing but a concentration of chemicals, or a particular genetic instance in the wider web of evolving life. The experience of the spiritual dimension

---

61. Polkinghorne, *God of Hope*, 103-13.
62. See also Polkinghorne and Welker, *End of the World*, 39-40.

would be simply an epiphenomenon of our purely physical-chemical constitution. Soul is merely an ethereal aura explicable in terms of brain waves or particular cerebral states. But there is also a more benign sense of materialistic reduction. It is motivated by a concern to give a more holistic sense of the emergence of human consciousness. What is termed "spirit" or "soul" emerges from God's working through the complex biological and evolutionary influences at work in the occurrence of life on this planet. God, in this case, uses finite material agencies to produce the soul and its transcendent capacities. The more traditional conception of the soul being immediately created can be abandoned in the interests of a more holistic sense of divine activity. God "creates" or forms the soul through the mediation of finite, material agencies.[63] Such discussions are usually focused on the extraordinary neural complexity of the human brain, a wonder of nature to an astonishing degree.[64]

Both cases of reduction of the spiritual to the material prove unsatisfactory. If science is limited to what can be seen, weighed, measured, and in some degree controlled, no amount of observation, measurement, and intervention is going to demonstrate a spiritual component—except in the intelligence of those who perform such activities. It would be like saying there are no birds to fly because they are not found on the ocean floor. Spirit and consciousness are of a different order of reality compared to the material. This other dimension is experienced, perhaps in a disconcerting fashion, in the imperative registered in the mind and the heart of even the most materialist-minded scientist. The demands of honesty, truthfulness, thoroughness, and responsibility in the conduct of their research are unavoidable. In other words, the drive to understand, the demands of truth, and the workings of conscience generally, are not irrelevant data: they form the mind of the scientist at work. This kind of data also demands an explanation; and no amount of computerized calculation and sense-based empirical method offers it.

There can be no argument against the creative Spirit of God working through the mediation of innumerable, finite physical and genetic influences to summon the embodied human person into existence. In this perspective, the critically established findings of the cosmological and evolutionary sciences are entirely acceptable. Still, the point remains. While interweaving cosmic and biological factors "cause" the human body, only God creates the soul. The spiritual form, or soul, of the human person, cannot be educed from matter. Nor can matter, in whatever form, however manifold and complex its

63. See, e.g., Brown et al., *Whatever Happened to the Soul?*
64. See A. Ganoczy, "Cerveau et conscience en anthropologie théologique," *Recherches de Science Religieuse* 92, no. 3 (2004): 349-81.

causality, create spirit. Only the creative Source of both matter and spirit can summon the embodied spiritual person into existence. The reality of spirit is not a form of tenuous matter. It belongs to a different order of reality, activity, and relationship. Because of its limitless overture to all truth, goodness, and being, the spiritual soul can be summoned into existence only by the One who is the Truth grounding all truth, the Good from which all goodness flows, the limitless act of "Be-ing" that is the source of all finite being.

We have dwelled on this point because any position on the God-created reality of the spirit and soul has important consequences for eschatology. For instance, the notion of the soul/spirit as immediately created by God is of great relevance to the dialogue of hope with people of faiths and spiritualities that differ from Christianity. Meeting with the other becomes a moment in the shared experience of being created by and for the infinite mystery that can never be fully named or known. On the other hand, the spiritual reality of the soul, especially when understood in its intrinsic relationship to matter, opens the way to a richer communication about what hope for the fullness of life might mean. The notion and reality of the God-created soul suggest the coexistence of all, not only in the wonder of the physical cosmos but in the transcendent reality of a divine creation. It is not clear how a reductively materialist account of spirit can be related, say, to Buddhist liberation in an enlightenment beyond all fixation in finite or limited desire. Nor is it immediately hospitable to the Hindu notion of self-realization in the infinite bliss of the Brahman, beyond all the appearances of the empirical ego. Likewise, Islam, with its unconditional submission of the self to the will of Allah, testifies to a self-surrender that cannot be conveyed in materialist terms.

This is to say that the multidimensional universe of God's creation is not limited to scientifically observable material universe. There is the dimension of spirit. This is not accessible through data of the senses, but relies on the data of consciousness. This consciousness expands as we wonder about why there is anything at all; it expands in the unrestricted drive to explore and understand, in the manner in which we live under the sway of truth. It is intensified in the ways consciousness becomes conscience in acknowledging the burdens of moral responsibility. It finds a special peace and even joy in prayer, thanksgiving, and adoration.

The rapidly developing brain-science of our day reveals many wonders. Though the human brain is a neurophysical organ of incredible complexity necessary for our embodiment in the life of this planet, it is not a personal subject. Physically speaking, the brain is an observable organ of a certain size and weight located in the human head. Scientifically speaking, it is a theoretical construct, approachable through different models of experimentation and research. Paradoxically, the brain as such is never directly experienced in consciousness, even when the astonishing reality of its neural networks is being increasingly explored. What is immediately evident to consciousness is the variety of intentional acts (observing, recording, interpreting, imaginative modeling, weighing the evidence, and so on) employed in exploring it. In short, the mystery of the person is more than its brain. Since it would take us too far afield to discuss further mind–brain–body interconnections, we can simply record our agreement with the remark of Sir John Eccles, Nobel laureate:

> Let us be quite clear that for each of us the primary reality is our con-sciousness—everything else is derivative and has a second order reality. We have tremendous intellectual tasks in our efforts to understand baffling problems that lie right at the center of our being.[65]

In the compact exploration of "the primary reality of consciousness," explorations can occur "from below upward." Science observes, records, generalizes and extrapolates from its empirical data. In this case, the human brain is located within the web of physical, chemical, biological, and genetic factors that govern our embodied existence. Yet there is also a "from above downward" kind of exploration. In this case, we seek an explanation of the human spirit and its origins in the transcendent creative causality of God. Yet the soul is the form of the material body, and the body is the cosmic expression of the soul. The brain serves the activity of the spirit, and the spirit calls forth, in a sense, the structure and functioning of the brain. Spirit and matter are interrelated: matter serves the spirit and finds its highest complexity in union with it. But the spirit needs matter to express itself in a world. The creative Spirit of God, reaching deeper than anything we consider "from below," and operating higher than anything we consider "from above," summons the whole human person into existence.

If, however, the soul is interpreted as a function of matter, then the realm of spirit is closed off from reflection. Eschatology is skewed from the beginning. Hope is constricted to the ultimately doomed physical cosmos as we know it. If hope is not to be limited to the material cosmos, then God has either to perform the function of the soul, or to act as some universal principle of potentiality, not unlike an Aristotelian version of prime matter. In contrast, the God of creation is the continuing sustaining source of all that is. The Spirit of God is actively working in all causes and conditions of the

---

65. J. C. Eccles, *Brain and Conscious Experience* (Berlin: Springer Verlag, 1962), 327.

material and spiritual universe. If the goal of the universe is union with God, the divine mystery must act to create the human soul. If our God-given destiny is to share in the divine life, then the human person must have the spiritual capacity to receive this final gift.

Further, not to admit the existence of the spiritual reality of the human soul is to live in a peculiarly isolated existence. If human beings are purely material, purely bodily, then only God is spirit. If, however, the Holy Spirit creates spirit as well as matter, then the way is open to retrieve many aspects of the biblical tradition that have been neglected. For the biblical tradition, and the liturgical consciousness it inspires, assumes that the human is not the only form of spiritual existence. The universe includes other forms of intelligence, unlimited by matter, namely, the angels. The universe includes innumerable beings of pure spirit, each one of which is a separate species, as Aquinas reasons,[66] manifesting the superabundant creativity of God and the vast cosmic communion of life in the Spirit.[67] Humanity joins with them in manifesting the infinities of God's creative love. An eschatology that closes its eyes to this other personal dimension of existence is impoverished, just as any view of evolutionary biology limited to humans or koalas would be deficient.[68]

Given the size and wonderful productivity of the cosmos, we have often been led to ask, Do we have a big enough God? But once we come to some sense of the infinite creativity of God manifested in the realm of the angels, another question arises. If a whole dimension of created reality is dismissed or repressed, leaving only the human in possession, do we have a big enough universe? Human self-centeredness is not the best measure of God's creative power.[69]

Time and Eternity

A further crucial question for eschatology is the relationship between time and eternity. The current knowledge of the time-structured material uni-

---

66. See *SCG* l. 2, c. 93. For a specialized study, see David Keck, *Angels and Angelology in the Middle Ages* (New York: Oxford University Press, 1998).

67. See further, Grenz, *Theology for the Community of God*, 213-42; and Amy Plantinga Pauw, "'Where Angels Fear to Tread,'" *Modern Theology* 16, no. 1 (January 2000): 39-59; Robert Ombres, OP, "God, Angels, Us," *New Blackfriars* 86 (January 2005): 48-61. For a brief study of the patristic tradition, see Jean Daniélou, SJ, *The Angels and Their Mission*, trans. David Heimann (Allen, Tex.: Newman Press, 1957).

68. See C. Schönborn, *From Death to Life: The Christian Journey*, trans. B. McNeil (San Francisco: Ignatius, 1995), 95-97.

69. See Alison, *Raising Abel*, 193-94.

verse makes this an especially difficult question. It is related to the processes of change and succession. Then there are further questions concerning our consciousness of time and the standardized measurements of time in relation to a universe of Einsteinian relativity. Here we would distinguish between public time of quantitative measurement and the qualitative time related to psychological experience.[70] What all these apprehensions of time have in common is the recognition of a changing universe. Dimensions of past, present, and future interweave. There is a before and an after in reference to both quantity and quality in the contexts of growth and development. Most obviously there is the contrast between a time of pure potential and times of actualization of what was previously simply a possibility.

Eternity, in contrast, is properly a divine attribute. God is the utter plenitude of Be-ing. In the divine "To Be" (*Ipsum Esse Subsistens*) there is no potency or time-structured incompleteness. All that God infinitely *is*, is a present actuality. This notion of divine eternity makes the hermeneutical space, as it were, in which the utter transcendence of divine love and mercy can be more adequately understood (*STh* 1, q. 10, a. 2 ad 3). Though God is the creator of the time-structured universe, God is not in time; and there is no time in God, no development in the sheer self-present actuality of divine Being. Because this infinite plenitude of life implies no limits or potentiality, God is in no way measured by, or subject to, "before" and "after," as in worldly time. At every moment of time, God is the one who is, who was, and who is to come. This suggests two dimensions of creation's relationship to the eternal God. The first looks to our place in time. The second looks to God's coming to meet us in time.

First, we live in time. Creation in its every instant is related to the creator. Without this ever-originating relationship nothing would exist. The duration of the universe can be scientifically described, say, as originating in the Big Bang and eventually leading to a "big crunch," an entropic cosmic collapse, or even as an endless oscillation between both states. Theologically, however, it is still completely dependent on God for its being in its every state.[71]

Second, Thomas Aquinas allowed that, as far as philosophy could determine, creation could have been of eternal duration. But he believed, on the grounds of revelation, that creation took place in time. Recent theology, especially through the influence of Wolfhart Pannenberg and Karl Rahner,

---

70. William Norris Clarke, SJ, *The One and the Many: A Contemporary Thomistic Metaphysics* (Notre Dame, Ind.: University of Notre Dame Press, 2001) contains a searching exploration of the meaning of time (pp. 161-77).

71. Kathryn Tanner, "Eschatology without a Future?" in Polkinghorne and Welker, eds., *End of the World*, 222-37; see especially 224-26.

while not denying the essential relationship of creation to the creator, has introduced another dimension. It underscores the positive significance of the future for human time. History in its entirety is the history of salvation in Christ, the alpha and omega of all creation. Time unfolds in a goal-oriented dynamism. As created by God and for God, it has eschatological value. Through freedom and hope, our time-structured human existence collaborates with what God is bringing into being in the fullness of time.

While we are destined for eternal life with God, hope inhabits history. It is the virtue of finite creatures living in time. Human fulfillment is given in the course of time. The summons to eternity resonates through the course of a lifetime, through the history of all lifetimes, through the history of the cosmos itself. Though eschatological salvation exceeds all time-bound human capacities to bring it about (*STh* 1, q. 10, a. 3; ad 1 and ad 2), human freedom must still work out its salvation in time. The created, finite human person is given time and must take the time that is given, in order to come to the fullness of life which transcends our present experience of time.

In other words, God creates the material universe as cosmic space-time manifold. Since human existence is embodied in its materiality, time and space are necessary dimensions of what we are. Time is the gift in which we live out our dialogical relationship with the eternal God. In time, we meet God, who comes in time "for us and our salvation." Though God is essentially outside of time, the self-giving love of the Trinity has time for creation and makes time for history and its full unfolding. In this regard, God, eternal in love, is at both the beginning and goal of time. The love of God neither lags behind our times, nor runs ahead. It is the eternal depth of grace and meaning in our every moment. Our imaginations are inextricably time-structured. Our languages cannot do without a past, present, and future tense. It is impossible to have a direct apprehension of the eternal "now" of God's creative action. Inevitably we project our experience of time onto the eternity of the divine consciousness. Still, from the depths of that eternity, the creative love of God gives time and gives into its every moment the promise of what is to come.

In the perspective of Christian hope, time is a gift, a goal-oriented journey into eternal life. We are creatures of graced time in a temporal universe. Time, deriving from God's eternal love, is not a succession of meaningless instants but a pilgrimage intent on a final goal. Compassion and intercession unite all in our common journey through time. In hope, time looks beyond itself to purgatorial integration of what previously we had no time for because of the deferrals and distractions that clouded our paths. Most of all, it looks to the bliss of vision in which the sacred depth of all history will be revealed in the eternity of God's vision.

Second, God meets us in time. God's entry into the time-structured world is classically articulated in terms of the divine missions of the Word and Spirit. The eternal processions of the divine persons are projected into time to give it meaning and direction. Through the "invisible missions," the Word and the Spirit are sent to inhabit the depths of human consciousness as it unfolds throughout history. Even if unnamed or unknown in an explicit sense, the Word illumines the minds of all genuine searchers for wisdom, just as the Spirit intimately enkindles a love for God and neighbor in the lives of all good people. For St. Thomas the beneficiaries of the invisible missions were especially the patriarchs and saints of the Old Testament. But this invisible gift can be understood as extending to all people of all times and places and religious traditions as they seek the path of true life.

The "visible missions" are related to the incarnation of the Word at a specific time and place, and to the Holy Spirit poured out at Pentecost to animate the Christian community in its vocation to witness to the universal mystery of salvation. The Word and Spirit are thus "sent" in time to lead human beings through time to its completion in the vision of the Father.

Thinkers such as Pannenberg give valuable clues as to how the tradition can be extended through a more future-oriented sense of being.[72] Pannenberg would argue that, in contrast to more abstract versions of reality, the truth of anything is not pinned down as a timeless essence. It can be disclosed only in its orientation to the future. Only in the course of time will the full truth be manifest. Reality is most truly evident only in relation to the future. Traditionally, and with good biblical warrant, we think of God as the one who is, and was, and is to come. There is a deeper perspective, however. The fullness of the divine mystery can be most fittingly understood by privileging the future dimension. God is the One who is to come. In this respect, God can be most fully known only in a "proleptic" manner. The word suggests a mode of knowing and a sense of reality that focus above all on what is coming to be. As our creator and redeemer, God is thought of as acting in the past and continuing to act in the present. But the full meaning of the creation, the incarnation, the resurrection, and the outpouring of the Spirit cannot be fully realized until the end of time. In this way, God's past and present dealings with us in time can be understood as the presence of the absolute future. This is to say that God is coming forward to meet us as the absolute future that gives time its meaning and direction. The end of time

---

72. See Wolfhart Pannenberg, *Systematic Theology*, volume 3, trans. G. W. Bromiley (Grand Rapids: Eerdmans, 1998), 595-607: "The relation between time and eternity is the crucial problem in eschatology, and its solution has implications for all parts of Christian doctrine" (p. 595). See also Mostert, *God and the Future*, 141-61.

will be an epiphany, a "shining forth" of the divine future that was coming to meet human freedom in every moment. In that fullness of time, we finite and temporal beings, although already participating in the divine life, will enter into "eternity," which has already entered history. God is the One who has come, who is, and who is to come.

From this future-oriented or proleptic point of view, time is not a neutral measurement of repetitious events. It has an eschatological significance. It is a future-charged course terminating in the full epiphany of God within finite creation. The One who is to come is the one who has come, who has had time for the whole of human history to awaken to its freedom.

The positions outlined above will receive more specific treatment as we consider particular eschatological questions relating to the resurrection of Jesus, purgatory, heaven, and so forth. Here our aim was to sketch some of the issues inherent in any account of Christian hope.

3

The Intelligence of Hope

THERE IS AN ESCHATOLOGICAL DIMENSION inherent in every aspect of theology. The *logos*, "the meaning," of both *Theos*, "God," and the *eschata*, "the last things," is necessarily a field of interconnections. Every moment of theology is eschatological. Yet no theological eye is able to look into the face of God. No theological ear has yet heard the whole truth of the Word. No theological imagination can match the transformative power of the Spirit. For this reason, theological exploration, however eschatological its intent or refined its methods, cannot occupy that future that only God can give. It can never send back information from a future standpoint. As Karl Rahner insists, there is no way of thinking about the future as God will determine it except in ways inspired by the present data of faith.[1] These *data*, literally, the "givens," are in fact the *dona*, "the gifts," the "grace" of the self-giving God. This divine self-giving is the determining feature of all theology. The Father has given what is most intimately his own, namely, the Word and the Spirit, into human hearts and history. From such data, eschatology works out its account of hope. And so it reaches toward the future hidden in God by extrapolating from what is already present. A properly hopeful theology humbly locates itself on the ground of the present moment of God's grace. The gifts of God have shaped the history of faith. Within that history of grace and blessing, hope is drawn to consider what is to come, in the time and form determined only by God alone.

St. Anselm famously described theology as "faith seeking understanding" (*fides quaerens intellectum*). He had in mind especially the existence and nature of God and the reasons for the incarnation and redemption. In seeking to explore the future bearing of such mysteries, it is appropriate to reexpress the Anselmian adage as "hope seeking understanding," *spes quaerens intellectum*. The love that inspires the search of faith for further intelligence

---

1. Karl Rahner, "The Hermeneutics of Eschatological Assertions," in *Theological Investigations*, vol. 4, trans. Kevin Smyth (Baltimore: Helicon Press, 1966), 323-46. For the larger context, see Peter C. Phan, *Eternity in Time: A Study of Karl Rahner's Eschatology* (Selinsgrove: Susquehanna University Press, 1988), 64-78; and Wolfhart Pannenberg, *Systematic Theology*, volume 3, trans. G. W. Bromiley (Grand Rapids: Eerdmans, 1998), 542-46.

of what God has done "for us and our salvation" is the same love that inspires hope to consider the fulfillment of the promise contained in what God has already done.

However confident and courageous hope might be, it has to move forward without any controlling vision of what is to come. Paul is quite clear on this. He writes, "Now hope that is seen is not hope. For who hopes for what is seen? But if we hope for what we do not see, we wait for it in patience" (Rom 8:24-25). It would seem that the more hope is focused on the risen Christ, the more it moves in a certain darkness. It would be presumptuous for theology to want too much light too soon. That would be a failure in patience. The future of "what God has prepared for those who love him" is not as a simple, homogenous extension of our present limited understandings or expectations. Hope relies on God alone to reveal the final evidence of love at work in every moment of history. Eschatology must defer to the unimaginable "otherness" of infinite mystery. In this regard, hope has to look beyond the repetitious sameness of our notions of either God or ourselves. The First Letter of John makes the point: "What we shall be has not yet been revealed. What we do know is this: when he is revealed we shall be like him, for we shall see him as he is" (1 Jn 3:2).

THE *VIA NEGATIVA* OF HOPE IN THE NEW TESTAMENT

Current philosophies of deconstruction insist that there is no totalizing system that exhausts the meaning of events.[2] The more significant the reality, the greater the play of possible meanings. A related theme in recent reflection has been meaning and the possibility of a true gift.[3] There is a kind of eschatological indefinability inherent in a genuine gift if it is not to be reduced to calculations of mere exchange or manipulation. In our investigation of hope, let us then consider some biblical evidence of the way Christian hope is formed by the indefinable and incalculable otherness inherent in God's self-giving in Christ.

It is one thing for Christian hope to rejoice in the risen Christ and to anticipate an ultimate fulfillment of the divine intention "that God may be all in all" (1 Cor 15:28). It is another matter to attempt to fill this horizon of expectation with definite objects of shape, color, and temporal sequence, and

---

2. See especially Kevin Hart, *The Trespass of the Sign: Deconstruction, Philosophy and Theology* (New York: Fordham University Press, 2000); and my "Blessed Negativities: The Contribution of Deconstruction to Theology," *Australian EJournal of Theology* 2 (February 2004).

3. Robyn Horner, *Rethinking God as Gift: Marion, Derrida and the Limits of Phenomenology* (New York: Fordham University Press, 2001).

then to describe them in the language and imagery of a provisional world. For all the explicitness of their promise of eternal life, for all the variety of images they employ, the scriptures in fact exhibit a marked reserve in describing the realities to which they most witness. Biblical faith is familiar with the double silence in the narrative of its hope: the dark silence of the dead body of Jesus on the cross, and the luminous silence of the resurrection, in which faith trembles at the dawn of the new creation.

Here Christian hope learns from the history of Israel. The chosen people always maintained a sense of the uniquely gifted origins at the key points of their history (Gen 12-36; Ex 1-15; Ps 78:67-71 [143-44]).[4] At dire moments of exile, Israel reaches a nadir that can only be expressed in communal lament (Jeremiah's Book of Lamentations; Psalms 44, 74, 79, 137). Still thanksgiving and trust continue in the recognition that God's fidelity and purpose are outside any economy of human calculation and exchange. God's faithfulness always leads to renewal and homecoming. Each saving event leads to an ever-larger sense of the universal activity of God working in all times and in all peoples (Jer 30-31; Ezek 33-48, especially 37:1-14; Isa 40-55).[5] These antecedents in the history of Israel's hope must never be forgotten in any Christian theology. They serve to remind theology that the ways of God are never designed to fit into human calculation. Take the case of the earliest witnesses to Christ. After his crucifixion and death, Christ "had presented himself alive to them by many convincing proofs" (Acts 1:3). Yet they could still ask, "Lord, is this the time when you will restore the kingdom to Israel?" (Acts 1:6). Jesus' answer is instructive: "It is not for you to know the times or the periods that the Father has set by his own authority" (Acts 1:7). These disciples are commissioned to witness to Christ, "in Jerusalem, in all Judea and Samaria, and to the ends of the earth" (Acts 1:8). Yet they are clearly not given an all-controlling knowledge of what is to come. Let us take a number of other instances.

Paul's Negations

For Paul, the death and resurrection of Jesus constitute the absolutely basic factor in determining Christian existence. Nonetheless, it takes none of the

---

4. It would take us too far afield to survey the entire Old Testament in this regard. Here I refer mainly to an excellent article by Walter Brueggemann, "Faith at the *Nullpunkt*," in Polkinghorne and Welker, eds., *The End of the World*, 143-54. Good general treatments are Zachary Hayes, *Visions of a Future: A Study of Christian Eschatology* (Wilmington, Del.: Michael Glazier, 1989), 15-42; and Philip S. Johnston, *Shades of Sheol: Death and Afterlife in the Old Testament* (Downers Grove, Ill.: InterVarsity Press, 2002).

5. Brueggemann, "Faith at the *Nullpunkt*," 150.

waiting or darkness out of our hope. In reference to Isaiah, Paul writes, "Eye has not seen nor ear heard nor the heart of man conceived what God has prepared for those who love him" (1 Cor 2:9). Compared to human perceptions, the ways of God remain inscrutable, and divine judgments are unsearchable (Rom 11:33). In the expression of his hope, Paul alludes to the oldest recorded prayer in the New Testament, "Maranatha! Our Lord, come!" (1 Cor 16:22; cf. Rev 22:20). He prays for the Lord to "come" since his coming among us is not already complete. Any expression of the future is more like a description of what is being left behind. To use a modern metaphor, it is seen only through a rearview mirror. There is no clear map of what lies ahead. Paul's impatient reply to a Corinthian query is noteworthy: "How are the dead raised? With what kind of body do they come?" (1 Cor 15:35). He answers in predominantly negative terms. The risen body is contrasted to what is "perishable, dishonorable, weak, physical" (1 Cor 15:35) in our present experience. Yet hope anticipates that, through the creative power of the Spirit, the risen body will become "imperishable," "glorious," "powerful," "spiritual" (1 Cor 15:42-44). In this significant instance, hope for a risen existence reaches beyond any capacity to understand, present, or represent the future. It awaits a fulfillment in the God who, "by the power at work within us is able to do far more abundantly than all we ask or think" (Eph 3:20). Paul confronts any straining for a controlling knowledge of the future with the transcendence of God's wisdom. Here he quotes both the prophet (Isa 29:14) and the Psalmist (Ps 33:10): "I will destroy the wisdom of the wise and the discernment of the discerning I will thwart" (1 Cor 1:19). He goes on to say, "For since in the wisdom of God, the world did not know God through wisdom, God decided through the foolishness of our proclamation to save those who believe" (1 Cor 1:21). He points to the source of true wisdom as being beyond all human measure and control: "And we speak of these things in words not taught by human wisdom but taught by the Spirit, interpreting spiritual things to those who are spiritual" (1 Cor 2:13).

A certain negation or "deconstruction"—at least in a general sense—is demanded. The ever-new gift is not a simple datum. It cannot be represented in accord with the calculations and categories of present experience. If "the Jews demand signs and the Greeks desire wisdom" (1 Cor 1:22), the cross will be a stumbling block to the expectations of the traditional religion, just as it will appear to the philosophers as an extravagant folly: "For God's foolishness is wiser than human wisdom, and God's weakness is stronger than human strength" (1 Cor 1:25). Even though Paul himself is justified in invoking the riches of the tradition of Israel as his own—"a Hebrew born of Hebrew, as to the Law, a Pharisee . . . " (Phil 3:4-6), he has come to regard all this as "loss" (Phil 3:7) and "refuse" (Phil 3:8) that he might gain Christ and find justification in him alone (cf. Phil 3:7-11). Hope in Christ has meant for him a "deconstructed" life, intent on the ways of God rather than any intellectual or religious assurance.

Hope is not allowed to rest in any imagination drawn from the present sphere of human experience: "hope that is seen is not hope" (Rom 8:24). It expands to its proper proportions only by yielding to what only God can bring about. Even praying for the fulfillment of hope lacks clear objects. Such prayers need the guidance and direction of the Spirit: "for we do not know how to pray as we ought, but the Spirit himself intercedes for us with sighs too deep for words" (Rom 8:26). Christian hope must learn to live with not only not-understanding and not-representing but also with a certain not-willing. It must yield its mundane desires and expectations to the incalculable dimensions of the Spirit. A Buddhist or Hindu exegesis in terms of detachment from the desires of the ego would be valuable.

Synoptic Negations

The Synoptic Gospels do nothing to lessen this distinctive Christian sense of negativity and provisionality. Despite the evidence that the Gospel writers were certain of the all-deciding event that occurred in Christ, they left plenty of room for what is yet to be revealed. There is no question of simply appealing to the arrival of the Reign of God for information about what is still to come. The growth and seasons of the Kingdom are not in human hands, nor subject to human law or prediction (Mk 4:26-29). Moreover, the scope of God's reign allows for wild aspects of undecidability. It nets fish of all kinds and qualities (Mt 13:47-50) and permits the weeds to grow alongside good grain (Mt 13:24-30). To enter into this Kingdom is to treasure new things and old in a proportion that remains unclear (Mt 13:51-52). For Luke especially, it means refraining from judgments and the condemnation of others, if one is to be included in the incalculable field of God's mercy (Lk 6:37-42). The true relatives of Jesus are not those represented by blood relationships but those who do the will of God (Lk 8:19-21). Most notably, the separation of the sheep and goats in Matthew 25 is disconcerting to all believers—and nonbelievers too—who have allowed a cultural form of religion to obfuscate the inclusiveness of God's Kingdom (Mt 25:31-46).

A telling metaphor for the distinctive intentionality of Christian hope speaks of putting the fresh wine of revelation into fresh wineskins (Mt 9:16-17; Mk 2:21-22; Lk 5:36-39). Old wineskins are always available; and the old garments can be patched with new cloth. But neither meets the new situation in which old skins would burst and old cloth would tear. The surpassing newness of what God is bringing about, even if, in some ways, it is a continuance and fulfillment of the old, must be left free to be itself. The otherness of an infinite love has entered our world.

Negation in John

Then there is the Johannine perspective. Even while encouraging the disciples to accept his word, Jesus acknowledges that they cannot, in their historical present, bear the full reality of what is being revealed: "I still have many things to say to you, but you cannot bear them now" (Jn 16:12). His followers must go beyond their present apprehension to await an as-yet-inexpressible future: "When the Spirit of truth comes, he will guide you into all truth . . . and will declare to you the things that are to come" (Jn 16:13). Earlier in the Gospel, Jesus declared to the Samaritan woman, "you will worship the Father neither on this mountain nor in Jerusalem" (Jn 4:22). The true worship of God is not tied to sacred sites but is to be conducted "in spirit and in truth" (Jn 4:23-24). The horizon of hope is, therefore, neither geographically nor ethnically bounded. It opens onto the indefinable reality of the Father himself.

In the Johannine writings, confidence in the continuing revelatory power of the Spirit is compatible with a warning against believing every kind of spirit. The First Letter of John advises such caution. That early community, undergoing the conflicts and temptations inherent in its special history, is advised: "Beloved, do not believe every spirit, but test the spirits to see if they are from God . . . By this you know the Spirit of God: every spirit that confesses that Jesus Christ has come in the flesh is from God" (1 Jn 4:1-2).[6] Such a demand for discernment is not without its difficulty. It entails holding together in some way the truth of God's self-giving love and the human character of its revelation. But once intelligence tries to come to grips with the elusive and opaque human reality of "the flesh," discernment becomes complex. Only to a lofty gnostic system is everything clear and pure, untroubled by the presence of the utterly Other. But the true discernment points in another direction: "We know love by this, that he laid down his life for us— and we ought to lay down our lives for one another" (1 Jn 3:16). This demand is insistent: "for those who do not love a brother or sister whom they have seen, cannot love God whom they have not seen" (1 Jn 4:20). John's letter has

---

6. See Christopher Morse, *Not Every Spirit: A Dogmatics of Christian Disbelief* (Valley Forge, Pa.: Trinity Press International, 1994).

a stark but not altogether surprising conclusion: "Little children, keep your-selves from idols" (1 Jn 5:21). Some kind of orientation beyond neat religious notions or consoling interpretations seems to have been envisaged all along: "let us love, not in word and speech, but in truth and action" (1 Jn 3:18). This is the original emphasis of the Gospel itself. To know God is not a matter of "seeing" the divinity in some immediate gaze. A commitment to following the other-directed "way" of Jesus (Jn 14:6) is the essential point, for "no one has ever seen God; it is the only Son, who is turned toward the Father, he has made him known" (Jn 1:18). Believers are reminded not to settle for any provisional version of human identity, no matter how secure the promise of eternal life, for "it has not yet appeared what we shall be" (1 Jn 3:2). Though Jesus is "the resurrection and the life" (Jn 11:25), the risen Lord is never an object of matter-of-fact description. Experiences of presence and absence interweave in the lives of these early witnesses to hope (cf. Jn 20:29-31).

Conclusion

More radically still, the demand for a complete self-dispossession pervades the New Testament. Only by losing one's life for the sake of the gospel can one truly save it (Mt 16:24-25; Mk 8:35; Lk 9:24; Jn 12:25). The moral and spiritual implications of this radical demand have, rightly enough, been the focus of the Christian tradition. But there are also implications of a more intellectual character. Hope-inspired thinking seeks to go beyond the pre-tensions of all theoretical systems. In their inability to allow for "God's foolishness," these systems tend easily to become idolatrous. In contrast, the biblical authors show an eschatological reserve. They defer to a fulfillment and justification that only God can give. In doing so, they also exhibit a deliberate "unknowing." It is embedded in its most confident testimony. Par-adoxically, the very confidence of their witness calls forth the expressions of negation, dispossession, reserve, and waiting that we have summarily cited. The various theological and spiritual traditions of "negative theology" in, say, the mystical writings of Pseudo-Dionysius or John of the Cross, clearly stem from the New Testament itself.

DIMENSIONS OF GOD'S LOVE

However varied accounts of hope might be, and however much the New Testament bristles with negations, there are clear constants that any authen-tic eschatology must respect. The constants reduce to two: first, the grace, the overwhelming "given-ness" of the mystery of Christ; and, second, the questing, ever-unfinished tending of our lives toward an ultimate wholeness and a final homecoming. At every stage of history, theology must attempt to give a more or less adequate expression of hope, focused in "Christ, in you, your hope of glory" (Col 1:27). In such a horizon, "human time is wrapped in eternal love," to repeat Brian Daley's beautiful phrase quoted in the previous chapter. Admittedly, the word "love" is not explicitly mentioned in any nonbiblical creedal formula. Yet the most fundamental of all "articles of faith" can be found in the Johannine affirmation "God is love" (1 Jn 4:8, 16). Not only the Johannine writings, but the whole of the New Testament and the creeds formed in the centuries to follow,[7] are expressions of a hope that wholeheartedly celebrates the reality of such love, surrenders to it and cooperates with it.[8]

Whatever form the account of Christian hope might take, its vocabulary necessarily includes seven key terms in the narrative of how God is love. The symbolic term "Father" suggests that God is love as primordial freedom. "Son" indicates the extent of God's personal self-giving, while the "cross" and "resurrection" point respectively to the unconditional character of God's love and its transforming power. The "Spirit" reveals the creative communication of love working in all times and places, just as "the church" expresses its identifiable sacramental actualization in history. "Eternal life" or "heaven" indicates the transcendent consummation of love in a transformed universe. While these seven terms, or their equivalents, can be presented in different sequences, none of them can be omitted without mutilating the eschatological message of the gospel or diminishing the range of hope it inspires. Each of these terms must figure in anything that would claim to be a full "accounting of the hope that is within you" (1 Pet 3:15).[9] In these seven key terms we have a checklist, as it were, for the development of a critically comprehensive eschatology. A brief word, then, on each of them.

The Father: Love as Origin

"God is Love" in terms of the divine originality and initiative of the Father. All is given, and is to be received, as "the gift of God" (Jn 4:10): "In this is

---

7. Reading Jaroslav Pelikan's magisterial *Credo: Historical and Theological Guide to Creeds and Confessions of Faith in the Christian Tradition* (New Haven: Yale University Press, 2003) from an eschatological perspective would prove a valuable exercise—even if it is outside the scope of this present work.

8. See Christoph Schwöbel, "Last Things First?" in *The Future as God's Gift: Explorations in Christian Eschatology*, ed. David Fergusson and Marcel Sarot (Edinburgh: T&T Clark, 2000), 219-41.

9. For a comparatively brief account of his distinctive love-oriented theology, see Hans Urs von Balthasar, *Love Alone*, trans. and ed. Alexander Dru (New York: Herder & Herder, 1969).

love, not that we loved God but that he loved us and sent his Son . . ." (1 Jn 4:10). God exists and loves as the absolute "beginning." Divine love precedes all creation, all time, and all human action. As the Gospel repeatedly stresses, the Father acts as the generative initiative involved in the life, action, speech, and mission of Jesus himself.[10] In the Gospel of John, Jesus speaks of himself as light (8:12; 12:46), life (11:25; 14:6), and truth (14:6). But the First Letter of John, by following the logic of the Gospel, refers everything that Jesus embodies back to the Father, the source from which all gifts flow: God is love as the light (1 Jn 1:5), and as "true God and eternal life" (1 Jn 5:20). Because of the absolute originality and initiative of God, Christian experience must look, beyond everything that restricts or diminishes its confidence, to the one who "is greater than our hearts" (1 Jn 3:20; 4:4, 18; 5:4, 9). The horizon of Christian hope is filled with a gift from beyond this world.

For Paul, the "Father of our Lord Jesus Christ has blessed us in Christ with every spiritual blessing, just as he chose us in Christ before the foundation of the world" (Eph 1:3-4). This "God, who is rich in mercy, out of the great love with which he loved us even when we were dead through our trespasses, made us alive together with Christ . . ." (Eph 2:4-5). For "we are what he has made us, created in Christ Jesus for good works, which God prepared beforehand to be our way of life" (Eph 2:10). The Father is the source of the creative and redemptive love that is at work. It looks to the future when "God may be all in all" (1 Cor 15:28). In recognition of this original and fulfilling character of God's love, the "Our Father" prays that the Father's name will be hallowed, that his Kingdom will come, and that his will be done, on earth as it is in heaven. Likewise, Jesus prays for his disciples that they may see his glory—which the Father had given him "because you [the Father] loved me before the foundation of the world" (Jn 17:24).

God enters our world as pure gift. The love that is the source of this giving is not compromised by human lovelessness and despair: "God showed his love for us, in that while we were yet sinners, Christ died for us" (Rom 5:8). God's all-originating gift is the source of our knowledge of the Father as love. It wells up out of the innermost depths of divine freedom, in the Father's eternal self-determination to be "our God." Paul exults, "O the depths of the riches and knowledge of God. How unsearchable are his judgments and inscrutable his ways . . . Who has given him a gift that he might be repaid?" (Rom 11:33-34). Hope, then, unfolds in praise and in thanksgiving to Father, the original and engendering love that has brought the universe of nature and grace into existence.

---

10. For example, Jn 1:18; 3:16, 35; 4:23, 34; 5:18-21, 26-28, 30, 36-37; 6:32-33, 37-40, 44-45, 57, 65; 7:16.

The Son: Love as Self-Giving

The originating, engendering love of God is uniquely self-giving. The Father gives what is most intimate to himself, his "only Son," into the darkness and disgrace of the world: "In these last days he has spoken to us by his Son" (Heb 1:1-2). This unique, intimate, and unreserved communication is summed up in the Johannine statement, "God loved the world so much as to give his only Son . . . that the world might be saved through him" (Jn 3:16). The sending of the Son is the evidence of the divine extent of the Father's self-giving and self-expressiveness.[11] So intimately connected is the Son to the Father's self-revelation, that 1 John can state: "No one who denies the Son has the Father; everyone who confesses the Son has the Father also" (1 Jn 2:23). The self-communication of God draws the believer into the intersubjective communion that exists between the Father and the Son. It enfolds the community of believers into a divine milieu of unity (Jn 17:20-24). To believe is to be in communion "with the Father and with his Son Jesus Christ" (1 Jn 1:3). In this primal experience of divine love, the Son is the unique self-expression and self-gift of the Father: "God's love was revealed among us in this way: God sent his only Son into the world so that we might live through him" (1 Jn 4:9). Christian existence finds its focus in the unreserved personal self-communication of God to the world. It is a form of self-giving and self-expression so radical that it is possible only to God. The Word who is what God is, is made flesh; and so enters into the conversation of human history.

The Cross: Love as Unconditional

God is love as an original self-giving but also to an unconditional extreme. Love is not frustrated, diminished, or changed into something else in its confrontation with evil. Through the cross, the love that God is, is exposed to the maximal experience of the world's evil. The Son encounters a form of rejection so violent that it leads to his execution. But this love keeps on being love, "to the end" (Jn 13:1b). It is not changed into violence or vengefulness. Rather, it outstrips and outwits all human limits and contrary forces. The light of love is not overcome by the darkness of evil (Jn 1:5). As love remains love ever at this dark point, it exposes the power of evil for what it is. The excess of evil is met with the "ever greater" excess of love.

---

11. See Jn 1:18; 3:16; 8:19, 38; 10:17, 30; 12:45, 50; 14:7, 10-11; 16:28.

In the mystery of the cross, love makes death its own. Because love so absorbs the destructive menace of death into itself, death no longer appears as a dreaded limit blocking our relationship with God. Death is not the defeat of God's communication with the world but the extreme to which God's love has gone. Death is thus transformed into a revelation of love. It summons believers into a life of limitless loving: "We know love by this, that he laid down his life for us—and we ought to lay down our lives for one another" (1 Jn 3:16). By being exposed to the power of evil and not being overcome by it, the "Lamb of God takes away the sin of the world" (Jn 1:29). The Lamb who was slain (Rev 5:7) has become the "atoning sacrifice for our sins . . . but also for the sins of the whole world" (1 Jn 2:2).

Through his self-giving death, a great reversal in the vicious circle of self-destruction begins in human history: "If anyone does sin, we have an advocate with the Father, Jesus Christ the righteous" (1 Jn 2:1b). Through its intimate familiarity with the conflict between an ever-vulnerable love and the violence of human selfishness, a sober realism is woven into the texture of Christian experience. Still, the love manifested in the "lifting up" of the Son on the cross remains an immeasurable excess. Unconditional love swallows up all human conditions: "we will reassure our hearts before him whenever our hearts condemn us; for God is greater than our hearts" (1 Jn 3:19-20).

In other words, love keeps on being love even at this darkest point. The "weakness of God" is the refusal of the mystery of love to be anything but itself when confronted with violent rejection. A divine folly of unconditional self-giving works to undermine the self-centered calculations of human wisdom (1 Cor 1:21).

The Resurrection: Love as Transforming

God is love in its power to transform—first, with regard to Jesus himself and then for the disciples themselves. Love has not been defeated. In the emptiness of the tomb, divine love is revealed in its world-transforming power. Without its outcome in the resurrection, Paul would consider that love would be defeated, God would be misrepresented, Christian preaching would be in vain, faith would be futile, and hope would be an illusion—"you are still in your sins" (1 Cor 15:12-19). But because the love of God has attained a transformative victory over evil, the resurrection of Jesus is the focus of eschatological hope: "But in fact Christ has been raised from the dead, the first fruits of those who have fallen asleep . . . as in Adam all die, so also in Christ shall all be made alive" (1 Cor 15:20-24). A divinely wrought transformation has taken place in human history. It promises the ultimate triumph of God's saving will as "when all things are subjected to him, then the Son himself will be subjected to him who put all things under him, so that God will be all in all" (1 Cor 15:28).

Jesus has returned to his own as "the resurrection and the life" (Jn 11:25). He comes to give his peace and joy and to communicate his victory over the world, as the way to "my Father and your Father" (Jn 20:17). The crucified and risen Jesus is the revelation of the divine glory. He introduces his disciples into the communion of life and love that unites the Father and the Son. Transformed himself and transforming others, Jesus is "the word of life," of the "life [that] was revealed," "of the eternal life that was with the Father and was revealed to us" (1 Jn 1:1-2). God is love, as the life-force that rolled back the stone from the tomb of human defeat. The wounds still marking the body of the risen One are emblems of love's life-giving power.

The Holy Spirit: Love as Communicative

Neither the Father's loving originality nor the cross and resurrection of Jesus are events isolated in the past. God's loving is communicative. It reaches into all times and touches every dimension of our individual and corporate existence. In this regard, the Spirit is the ongoing, outgoing agent of God's love. The divine witness gives testimony to all believers throughout history of the victory of Christ. In Acts, this Spirit comes to the disciples after the ascension as a baptism and power, directing the church in its mission to the world (Acts 1:1-11; 2:1-47). For Paul, the Spirit is a divine field of energy. It pours forth the love of God in our hearts (Rom 5:5) and is the assurance of resurrection for all who believe (Rom 8:11). Forming the followers of Christ into a free, fearless relationship with the Father (Rom 8:14-17), the Spirit aids human weakness and expands Christian hopes "with sighs too deep for words" (Rom 8:26). Paul prays, "May the God of hope fill you with all joy and peace in believing, so that you may abound in hope by the power of the Holy Spirit" (Rom 15:13).

In a Johannine perspective, God gives into human history the permanent presence of the "Spirit of Truth." The Spirit is intimately connected with the presence of the Son, who is the incarnate "Way" to the Father. John the Baptist had testified to this Spirit descending from heaven and remaining on Jesus to be the medium with which he would baptize (Jn 1:32-33). Accordingly, in the experience of God's love, the Holy Spirit is a living stream emanating from the glorified Christ (Jn 7:37-39). The coming of the Spirit is the "advantage" that would follow the departure of Jesus from the earthly scene

(Jn 16:7). The gift of the Spirit is revealed as the last breath of the Crucified (Jn 19:30) and the first breath of the risen One (Jn 20:22).

Emanating from Jesus, the Spirit always connects Christian God-consciousness back to the form of love incarnate in the life and death of the Son (Jn 16:14; 1 Jn 4:2-3; 2 Jn 1:7). The Advocate, the Holy Spirit, guides those who follow the way of Christ into an ever fuller realization of the form of true life (Jn 14:26). This Spirit is the God-given witness to Christians. The Paraclete strengthens them in the midst of a world in which the excess of love is experienced as merely a threat to its self-enclosure. The historical community of witnesses, despite their weakness, will not lack *this* witness, the ever-greater testimony of God (1 Jn 5:9) in regard to what God has revealed through the incarnation of his Word. "By the Spirit that he has given us" (1 Jn 3:24; 4:13), those who have "this testimony in their hearts" (1 Jn 5:10) are conscious of living from a new center focused on the love that God is. They abide in God and God abides in them (1 Jn 4:13). This holy Breath of Life sustains Christian experience throughout history.

The Community/Church: Love as Sacrament in History

The love of God is expressed in a historically identifiable embodiment. It forms the church as the community of mutual love and shared mission. The Holy Spirit animates the community of faith, manifesting itself in all the variety of spiritual gifts (1 Cor 12:1-14). Participating in God's love, believers themselves live a love that "bears all things, believes all things, hopes all things and endures all things" (1 Cor 13:4-7). The Christian community already enjoys freedom through union with Christ and brings forth the fruits of the Spirit as "love, joy, peace, patience, kindness, goodness, faithfulness, and self-control" (Gal 5:22-23).

The gathering of believers, identified by their celebration of baptism and the eucharist, is sent into the world with its own distinctive mission. It thus continues the mission that Jesus himself has received from the Father (Jn 20:21). The primordial love that is the object of Christian witness is inherently bound up with the practical realization of such love in the mutual relationships of the members of the community and in its outreach to the world.[12] As the unity of believers participates in the expansive unity of the Father and the Son, it witnesses to the world the love that has been made known (Jn 17:23, 26). The Christian community, therefore, and the community of communities that is the church exist in the world which is the object

---

12. Jn 13:14, 34-35; 15:12-13; 1 Jn 2:7-11; 3:10-18; 4:7-8, 11, 20; 5:1-2, 16; 2 Jn 1:5; 3 Jn 5-8.

of God's love (Jn 3:16). In this regard, the church is that part of that world which has come alive to the extent of God's gift.

Eternal Life: Love Consummated

The love of God promises an eschatological consummation, even though the stream of eternal life has already begun to flow. The gift of God is irrevocable. The resurrection has happened. The Spirit is poured out. Believers are already the children of God (1 Jn 3:2). Yet the groaning ambiguities and tensions of this present existence remain. In Paul's idiom, the outward groanings of creation and the inward groanings of the Christian are supported by the deepest groanings of the Spirit, in expectation of the fullness of revelation: "In this hope we are saved . . . we wait for it with patience" (Rom 8:18-25). At present, hope can claim only the firstfruits of the Spirit. The full harvest is yet to grow and be gathered.

The prayer of Jesus is still to be answered: "Father, I desire that those also whom you have given me, may be with me where I am, to see my glory . . ." (Jn 17:24). The world as loved by God (Jn 3:16) is the world into which Jesus has come as its savior (Jn 4:42; 1 Jn 2:2). Yet that world is yet to respond to the love that has been shown it: "so that the world may believe that you have sent me" (Jn 17:21). Even though believers are already "God's children," it remains that "what we will be has not yet been revealed" (1 Jn 3:2a). Fulfilling our present relationship to God is a promised future revelation: "What we do know is this: when he is revealed, we will be like him, for we will see him as he is" (1 Jn 3:2b). The courage of believing in Jesus' victory over the world (Jn 16:33) manifests itself in a hope that this cosmic triumph will be fully displayed (1 Jn 5:4-5). Though faith can locate itself under the opened heaven (Jn 1:51), the world as a whole has yet to lift its gaze to the glory that has been revealed. Only when the word of Jesus is fully kept will the love of the Father be manifest—"And we will come to them and make our home with them" (Jn 14:23).

This final dwelling of God among us is strikingly expressed toward the end of the Book of Revelation:

> See, the home of God is among mortals. He will dwell with them as their God, and they will be his people, and God himself will be with them; he will wipe away every tear from their eyes. Death will be no more; mourning and crying and pain will be no more, for the first things have passed away. (Rev 21:3-4)

The self-giving love of God looks to a final consummation.

The eschatological dimensions of the affirmation "God is love" can be conveniently expressed under the seven headings given above. They serve as signposts guiding a continuing exploration of "the breadth and length and height and depth" (Eph 3:18) of the love on which hope relies as the first and last thing in every moment of Christian existence.

DEVELOPING ESCHATOLOGY

So far we have drawn attention to the negativity inherent in the expression of hope. More positively, we listed seven terms indicating the necessary dimensions of an adequate eschatology. Yet further understanding is possible. Here we can usefully refer to three traditional theological techniques as they are concisely expressed in Constitution on Divine Revelation (*Dei Filius*) of the First Vatican Council in 1870:

> If reason, illumined by faith inquires in an earnest, pious and sober manner, it attains by God's grace a certain understanding of the mysteries, which is most fruitful, both from the analogy with the objects of its natural knowledge and from the connection of these mysteries with one another and with our ultimate end. But it never becomes capable of understanding them in the way it does the truths which constitute its proper object. For divine mysteries by their very nature so excel the created intellect that, even when they have been communicated in revelation and received by faith, they remain covered by the veil of faith itself and shrouded as it were in darkness as in this mortal life we are "away from the Lord; for we walk by faith, not by sight" [*2 Cor 5:6-7*].[13]

In its concern to achieve some balance between the extremes of post-Enlightenment rationalism and a dogmatic traditionalism, this council maintained that theological intelligence, operating with due reverence and discretion, can come to a limited but fruitful understanding of the truths of faith in three ways. Theology can employ analogies drawn from human experience. It can view the mysteries of faith in their interconnections within the one divine economy of salvation. And it can consider the analogies and interconnections it elaborates in relation to what is ultimate in human des-

---

13. H. Denzinger, *Enchiridion Symbolorum, Definitionum et Declarationum de Rebus Fidei et Morum*, rev. A. Schönmetzer (Freiburg: Herder, 1965), n. 3019. Hereafter, *DS*.

tiny. While this last suggests a more eschatological emphasis, it can never be separated from the other two.[14] A brief word on each of these theological techniques will assist in pointing the way to a further exploration of the main themes of eschatology.

The Way of Analogy

In the most general sense, analogy seeks to clarify one thing in terms of another. For example, we come to some understanding of the love of God by considering various instances of love more directly accessible to our human experience, such as the love of parents, spouses, friends, and, indeed, in our love for the beauty and wonder of creation itself. But the theological use of analogy goes beyond any philosophical or literary theory. It works in a field of meaning that has a theological coherence. For God, being the creator of all that is, is the source, ground, and goal of the one universe of creation. In its radical relationship to God, everything is related in this one created reality, as it manifests the divine mystery and relates to the wholeness of the divine design.

Analogy has an even more explicit basis in the incarnation. The Word in whom all things came into existence himself was made flesh and enters into the fabric of the world. Thereafter, all reality has a consistency and a coherence in him in whom "all things hold together" (Col 1:17). Christ illumines the reality of creation, and each aspect of creation throws light on the inexhaustible significance of Christ. The Word became flesh and dwelt among us. In his death and resurrection, he embodies creation redeemed, transformed, made new. Consequently, the body, flesh, love, birth and death, and life in all its stages and transformations can offer analogies for a deeper understanding of the mystery of Christ, just as any fuller penetration of the same mystery will throw light on these fundamental dimensions of existence.

In its account of hope, an eschatological theology must search out relevant analogies in our experience of this created and redeemed world. Traditional analogies pass almost unnoticed, as when we speak of revelation, fulfillment, vision, communion, judgment, being saved, rising, life to the full, and so forth. Yet fresh analogies are available, as when we speak in terms derived from recent findings in the physical, cosmological, and biological sciences.

---

14. For an excellent overall treatment, see Anne Hunt, *Trinity: Nexus of the Mysteries of Christian Faith* (Maryknoll, N.Y.: Orbis Books, 2005), above all the chapter entitled, "Trinity and Eschatology," 200-215.

Likewise, fresh psychological and sociological insights into social and interpersonal communication and personal development offer new material for analogical thinking.[15] The same goes for rapidly developing communication technologies. Our understanding of matter and energy, space and time, and the web of relationships in which we exist has significantly developed. From all such sources, new analogies can be drawn for an exploration of "the things that are to come" (Jn 16:14).

For example, a broader and deeper exploration of the meaning of "the resurrection of the body" is made possible. Aquinas, for instance, was necessarily constricted to now discarded cosmological views of the celestial spheres and so on. Yet he was an eminent practitioner of analogical thinking in ways that continue to be productive, as with his psychological analogy of the Trinity and the analogies he employs in such themes as grace, the beatific vision, redemption, and sacraments. Nonetheless, new forms of analogies drawn from current experience will be programmatic for the ongoing development of eschatology for the years to come. Note, too, that analogies drawn from the human experience of hope as explored, for instance, in the writings of Gabriel Marcel, Ernst Bloch, or William F. Lynch are of great importance, as is clear from preceding chapters.

Interconnections

The technique of interconnecting or interrelating various theological themes presupposes a sense of the whole history of salvation. It sees each particular theme as part of the whole and the whole as positioning each theme in a larger field. It is not unlike a holographic view.[16] True, a definite sequence is firmly in place in the format of the creed. It begins usually with "God, the Father almighty" and ends professing "the resurrection of the body and the life of the world to come." There is a commonsense realism in placing eschatological hopes only after God, creation, the incarnation, and the unfolding of salvation through the gift of the Spirit and the reality of the church have been named. The impression is that what is most obvious and definite constitutes the body of the creed, while it ends with what is more mysterious, namely, "the last things." But the sequence determining our ways of understanding—what is first, last, and in between—must not be projected onto

---

15. I have in mind developmental psychologists such as Jean Piaget, Erik Erikson, Lawrence Kohlberg, and James W. Fowler.

16. This reference to the hologram is itself an analogical way of thinking, drawing on the recently developed techniques of lens-less photography.

God. The divine intention to be "all in all" (1 Cor 15:27) is first, determining all else. For instance, it is not as though God creates the world and then decides to offer it a further participation in the divine life. Rather, because God intends all along to give himself for the life of the world, God creates the world so that the divine gift can be received and appreciated. Hence, as suggested above, the articles of the creed are best read as a hologram, for they interweave and throw light on one another. At every stage, the glorious consummation of the divine design is primary in God's intention; it is at work in every moment and phase of creation and redemption. Every article of the creed—whether it deals with creation, the incarnation, the cross and resurrection, the gift of the Spirit, or the church—looks to a future fulfillment.

This present study of eschatology, for instance, necessarily follows a certain linear sequence marked by chapters and major divisions within them. But, in fact, all the different themes are constantly interweaving. The life of hope cannot be understood apart from God's trinitarian self-giving love. Such love cannot be considered apart from its historical actualization in the life, passion, death, and resurrection of Jesus. In the eucharist, the mystery of God's self-giving is celebrated and communicated to the believing community as its food and drink. In such "interconnected" or holographic theology, the great modern masters are Karl Rahner, with his emphasis on the one mystery of God's self-communication, Karl Barth, who centered everything in the divine self-revelation, and Hans Urs von Balthasar, who found his distinctive focus in the paschal mystery. Different theologies and eschatological emphases flow from such positions. But clearly eschatology could have little to say about the future if it failed to exploit the "interconnection of the mysteries" to enrich hope in its every dimension.

Reference to the Ultimate

There is an obvious sense in which eschatology is most concerned with this technique, namely, understanding every aspect of faith in terms of its eschatological fulfillment. This is clearly exemplified in the particular themes of death, purgatory, judgment, heaven, and hell. But in many different methods and emphases, current theology has become a theology of hope. It reflects on future fulfillment in a personal and collective sense. It places such considerations in the context of the consummation of all history. Wolfhart Pannenberg's future-directed ontological approach, the prophetic negativity of Jürgen Moltmann's writings, and various versions of liberation and political theologies are all strongly eschatological in emphasis. Furthermore, by directly addressing scientific and cosmological questions, as in *The Ends of God and the End of the World*, the title of a recent influential symposium,[17] theology attempts to locate Christian hope in its largest cosmic setting. Such is theology "in the future tense." It looks beyond particular theological contexts and particular doctrinal and moral perspectives in order to turn to the all-inclusive horizon of the saving will of God, who "wishes all to be saved and to come to knowledge of the truth" (1 Tim 2:4). The key biblical symbol is the Reign of God as Jesus proclaimed it.

In liberation theology, eschatology appears in its most dramatic and engaged form. It shows not only an eschatological emphasis but manifests an eschatological conscience. As Gustavo Gutiérrez, for example, explains: "eschatology is . . . not just one more element of Christianity, but the very key to understanding the Christian faith."[18] When confronted by the institutionalized economic and political violence that keeps millions in poverty, Christian hope is deeply challenged. A note of urgency and somber realism is heard in theology when those who are most involved in the struggle for a better world are assassinated, tortured, imprisoned, or exiled. Naturally, a theology born out of such experience has little use for any conception of a distant heaven that would distract from a present commitment to one's suffering neighbor—or any idea of an eventual hell that fails to recognize the infernal character of present social conditions. Hence, the urgent concern of liberation theology is to make eschatological hope an effective force in inspiring solidarity with those who are consigned to the underside of history as casualties to progress. To act in hope means being exposed to lethal reactionary forces defending the way things are. Still, the imperative of loving one's enemies and forgiving injuries seems to put hope at a severe disadvantage when it comes to resisting the evils of the present. How Christian dare our hopes be?

In the meantime, martyrs have given their lives in the service of great human causes. In the most challenging register, they speak with St. Paul, "If for this life only we have hoped in Christ, we are of all people most to be pitied" (1 Cor 15:19). Yet the questions remain: How does such hope find its most telling and practical expression in the political and cultural situations of our day? How does Christian hope embody an anticipation of the Kingdom of God?[19]

---

17. J. C. Polkinghorne and M. Welker, eds., *The End of the World and the Ends of God* (Harrisburg, Pa.: Trinity Press International, 2000).

18. Gustavo Gutiérrez, *A Theology of Liberation: History, Politics and Salvation*, trans. and ed. C. Inda and J. Eagleson (Maryknoll, N.Y.: Orbis Books, 1973; rev. ed. 1988), 162.

19. The answer to this question is tellingly presented in James Alison, *Raising Abel: The Recovery of Eschatological Imagination* (New York: Crossroad, 1996), especially in the concluding chapters.

CONCLUSION

The living, practical imagination of hope both inspires and profits from eschatological thinking that unfolds by way of analogy, interconnection, and anticipation of the future. Though hope moves in darkness, the Word of God still resonates and Spirit inspires Christian witness in all its variety, despite the enigma and obscurity of life. Yet hope takes time to express itself in the most telling way. Its language allows for different styles and tones. It would sound hopelessly optimistic if what a situation most desperately needed was a strong prophetic word of judgment to expose the entrenched evils of selfishness and violence. On the other hand, if that were the only message, hope would lack the ecstasy of its surrender to the infinite creativity of the Spirit. As a witness to this complexity, Paul exhorts his readers "to work out your salvation with fear and trembling" (Phil 2:12). But John assures his isolated, troubled, and divided community, "there is no fear in love, but perfect love casts out all fear" (1 Jn 4:18).

Hope is no optimistic construction placed on life, for it must confront the inescapable tragedy of death. Hope is never part of a system. But it does have a center, namely, Christ in his death and resurrection. Beginning from that center, it can expand to limits that only God can measure.

4

The Parable of Hope

The Paschal Mystery

HOPE LIVES IN "THE TIME AFTER EASTER." It stands in the open space of the ascension and breathes the ever fresh air of Pentecost as it celebrates all the feasts and seasons that follow. This annual round can be experienced as a routine of recurrent seasonal celebrations, perhaps resonating in the wider secular world as a minor variant of the mythologies of dying and rising, of decay and renewal. For those, however, who participate in thanksgiving, praise, faith, and hope in the great liturgical mysteries, the reality is otherwise. It is more like moving in a great outward spiral of grace, opening out to include all times and eras of history in an irrevocable gift, the dimensions of which only the fullness of time will disclose.

The ascension of Jesus leaves not a void but a Spirit-charged field of limitless expansion opening to the fullness of the mystery of Christ. Jesus will return from the bright cloud of God's glory, which had rendered him invisible to human eyes (Acts 2:9-11). Even as they look up to the heaven from which he will come again, the early disciples could recall the experience of grief and dread out of which their hope was born. They look forward, too, to the final effects of the great transformation that has already taken effect.

PASCHAL SENSE OF TIME

The life of hope finds its primary symbolism and structure in the paschal mystery of Christ's death and resurrection.[1] The many parables of the Kingdom of God that came from the lips of Jesus made his hearers see their ordinary world turned upside-down. His way of imagining the world and its God was different. He called into question the hitherto unquestioned system

---

1. G. Martelet, *L'au-delà retrouvé: Christologie des fins dernières* (Paris: Desclée, 1975) provides an elegant theological model.

of worldly power and status. For he summoned that world and the ages that succeeded it out of the calculations of violence and despair, into a universe of grace. Yet he is in person the supreme parable of the way God is acting in the world. His whole existence is the parable behind all the parables he uttered. Consequently, the Gospel narratives, with all their elements of fear and failure, judgment and promise, wonder and joy, continue as an invitation to hope. Believers no longer live in a world closed to the full extent of God's grace and mercy. They live now under "opened heavens" (Jn 1:51) of divine communication. Their lives are hidden with Christ in God (Col 3:3).

This time "after the resurrection" is a new experience of time. It is now the time of a new creation. Eternal life has already begun. The momentous change in the meaning of time that resulted can easily be taken for granted. Time is no longer simply the measure of change that takes place in the round of seasons. It is going somewhere. The promise it holds overflows from the transforming events that have already taken place. We hardly notice, perhaps, how that day of condemnation, shame, torture, and death came to be called "Good Friday." It is easy to forget why that following day—that longest day of defeat when Jesus is dead and buried—is named "Holy Saturday." Something occurred that changed time. The resurrection shocks time into another shape.

Before this world-changing event, what people most valued was always at the mercy of what they most feared. The dreadful power of evil and the finality of death held sway over the course of world history. For many who share with us this time under the sun still think that history runs on, forever inconclusive and undecided. Eras of progress or decline come and go. There is no final goal. They may revere the Jesus of Nazareth who died tragically two thousand years ago, but basically he is one of the many who despite a noble vision were eventually found out by the real world. He is left behind, a figure in the past, increasingly lost in the stumbling progress of history and what we can make of it. They know that his early followers reported that he rose from the dead. For them, at most, that could be a poetic way of saying that goodness will out in the long run. But that is merely a noble assumption. History is far more ambiguous and inconclusive. For the real world knows that the dead stay dead, and rising from the dead is not a common solution to the world's ills.

Christian hope has a different sense of time, for the passage of time holds within it the promise of eternal life. Christians live in time in another mode. Time is not being wasted by its apparent inconclusiveness and tragedy. It is not destined to repeat the vengeful cycles of violence and reprisal. A gift has been given. It enables hope to "make the most of the times" with the energies of an unbounded expectation. For hope looks to the reconciliation of all things in Christ, the final emergence of creation transformed (Eph 5:16; Col 4:5).[2]

Since the paschal mystery structures the content and dynamics of this hope, we pause to consider the significance of the "three holy days," the *sacrum triduum*. But to keep this consideration in focus, it is wisest to start with Easter Sunday, for reasons that will become clear.

EASTER SUNDAY

Without this third day, as we said above, the first day would never have been known as *Good* Friday, nor the second day as *Holy* Saturday. Jesus would have been one more good man, swallowed up in defeat and death. But because of what we have come to call "the resurrection," the Friday of the death of Jesus is seen as the astonishing revelation of an all-merciful love touching the world at its darkest point.[3] Likewise, the long day of that Saturday becomes holy, as hope waits on that love to penetrate the depths of human defeat, guilt, and isolation.

The Significance of the Resurrection

Paul underscores the crucial character of the resurrection of Jesus. To deny the resurrection would be to misrepresent God. It would mean having no hope for the dead and the sinful. It would preclude any assurance that faith was concerned with God's truth and that preaching the gospel was worthwhile (1 Cor 15:12-19). Putting such negative possibilities behind him, Paul asserts the positive truth. He speaks with all the force of a life that has known the deepest conversion: "in fact, Christ has been raised, the firstfruits of those who have fallen asleep" (1 Cor 15:20). The irresistible objectivity of the resurrection of Jesus places all the events of the past and future in a universe of transforming grace.[4] In the radiance of Easter, Christian hope rereads "the law of Moses, the prophets and psalms" in which the hopes of

---

2. See James Alison, *The Joy of Being Wrong: Original Sin through Easter Eyes* (New York: Crossroad, 1998), 213-19.

3. F. X. Durrwell, *The Resurrection: A Biblical Study*, trans. Rosemary Sheed (London/New York: Sheed & Ward, 1960) remains a valuable resource.

4. N. T. Wright, *The Resurrection of the Son of God* (Minneapolis: Fortress Press, 2003). See the useful summary and conclusion to this book entitled "Belief, Event and Meaning" (pp. 683-739).

Israel had been expressed (Lk 24:44). It provokes a new understanding of "all the Scriptures" and of the sufferings of Jesus (Lk 24:25-26; see also Jn 2:22; 12:16; 14:26). The resurrection of Jesus had a decisive impact on the consciousness of the disciples.[5] It inspired in them the conviction that God had acted in an ultimately decisive manner (Gal 1:1; Acts 2:23, 32). It brings into being a community of witnesses who are to proclaim salvation in the name of Jesus to all nations (Lk 24:47ff.; Jn 20:21f.).

The risen Jesus appears to the disciples precisely at the time when they are suffering the disgrace of his shameful death and their own failure. He comes as the light shining into darkness of apparent defeat, radiant with the glory of a new life. The New Testament gives lists of witnesses (1 Cor 15:3-11) and a variety of accounts of how they came to see and recognize the Lord.[6] Significantly, too, each of the Gospels relates this recognition to the discovery of the empty tomb.

These early witnesses recognize the risen One as the crucified Jesus, yet none of them ever pretends to describe the resurrection nor claims to have seen it. Nor do they show any inclination to prove the resurrection merely from the fact that the tomb was found by the women to be empty. But the evidence that these reports of the appearances of Jesus do provide points to the inarticulate groping of the early community of faith to express some massive and transforming reality. The crucified One lives, and he has revealed himself in ways unconstrained by the time and space and expectations of this world. He comes to the earliest witnesses from beyond anything they may have imagined. He breaks into their deadly world of shattered hopes. Yet they acknowledge him as the living One and are constrained to commit themselves to him as the source and way of true life.

There is an imposing objectivity in these different reports of the appearance of Jesus.[7] For all the expressions of dismay, doubt, and later confusion, they are marked by a sense of overwhelming factuality (1 Cor 15:12ff.; 2 Tim

---

5. Alison notes,

> simultaneous presence in the Gospels of two sorts of understanding: the incomprehension or miscomprehension of the disciples, and at the same time, the clear comprehension of Jesus of what was to come to pass. This presence of two understandings in the same texts was made possible by the texts themselves having been written *after* the resurrection, when the apostolic group was able to understand, for the first time, what Jesus had really been about and at the same time to understand that, unlike themselves, *he* had understood what was going on all along. (*Joy of Being Wrong*, 78).

6. See Wright, *Resurrection*, 322-29.

7. Raymund Schwager, *Jesus in the Drama of Salvation: Toward a Biblical Doctrine of Redemption*, trans. James G. Williams and Paul Haddon (New York: Crossroad, 1999), especially 119-35, treating the credibility of the Easter message.

2:17f.). The first witnesses are absolutely certain about the new thing that had happened and to whom it had happened. Because these reports derive from a uniquely experienced event, they are not, nor were ever intended to be, dispassionate scientific records. Nonetheless, the judgments they express have their own critical realism as they witness to the occurrence of a singular event and the number of different ways it was disclosed. The language used to describe how the risen Jesus revealed himself differs from reports of visions (Acts 16:9; 18:9; 23:11; 27:23), dreams (Mt 1:20; 2:12f., 19-22), and ecstasies (Acts 10:9ff.; 2 Cor 12:2-4; Rev 1:10ff.). It is in contrast to various accounts of miraculous resuscitations of the dead (Lk 8:49-56; Jn 11:1-53; Acts 9:36-42). For in the resurrection of the Crucified, something quite different has taken place. These early witnesses were not meeting a ghost or inventing a myth (cf. Lk 24:36-40; 2 Pet 1:16). A unique event, belonging to a new order of reality, had irrupted into the world. What was revealed was of crucial importance. It supplied the evidence needed for the chosen witnesses. It equipped them for the special burden of testifying to what they had seen and heard. The objectivity of Jesus' appearances to the disciples did not enclose them in a sense of exclusive privilege. There was room for the humble reception of a special gift, given in God's time and for God's purposes. Though Jesus had appeared to them, his communication looked beyond the especially privileged few to the wider world of faith. They had "seen the Lord," but more blessed were those who, without seeing, simply believed in him, even while profiting from the testimony of those who had the experience of "seeing" (Jn 20:29; 1 Pet 1:8).

Let us emphasize a point already made. This series of self-disclosures of the risen Jesus cut across any preconceptions or expectations on the part of the disciples and the world in which they lived. The cause of Jesus had collapsed with his condemnation and execution. His disciples were scattered and demoralized. The theology or philosophy of the day provided no hope or expectation that such a resurrection could happen. The Sadducees did not believe in the resurrection of the dead in any sense.[8] The Pharisees, only a small percentage of the population, believed in a resurrection of the just on the last day. The prevalent Greek worldview found any concept of a new physical embodiment after death repugnant (see Acts 17:18, 32). There were simply no clear terms and categories by which to express what happened. The transformation of the crucified Jesus and his new, living presence to the disciples were something "out of this world" and the scope of its experience. For the risen One was not resuscitated, brought back to this life, as was Lazarus, for instance (Jn 11:1-44). He came to the disciples in the form and vigor of

---

8. Wright, *Resurrection*, 131-40, 415-29.

the life beyond the power of death. He was given back to them by the will
of an all-forgiving love. Still, the evangelists certainly take care to stress that
the risen One really is Jesus of Nazareth—even to the extent of his bearing
the wounds of the Cross.

Christ's rising from the dead can indeed be set within one of the traditions
of Israel's hope (e.g., see especially the martyrdom of the seven brothers in
4 Macc 8-13 and Wis 3:1-9). It looked forward to a resurrection of the just
on the last day. But no one was expecting the resurrection of this executed
criminal on this particular Easter day. Something thought of as happening
only at the end of time had been disconcertingly anticipated in what had
happened in him. A shared eschatological hope focused on the end of time
now came up against a new barrier—the "too-good-to-be-true" quality of
what had actually happened (Lk 24:41).

There are, then, three essential features written into the Gospel accounts
of the resurrection. First, the risen One is identified as the crucified Jesus.
Even in the risen life, he is still marked with the stigmata of his passion and
death. The wounds continue to be identified not as signs of defeat but as
emblems of his victory over the powers of death and violence that had made
him their target.

Second, he discloses himself to chosen disciples with what can only be
called "divine discretion." His appearances do not overwhelm their freedom,
but bring it to a new intensity and breadth. They are drawn from doubt and
hesitation to the moment of recognition from which they never look back.
Their witness to him is expressed in the language of worship and unqualified
commitment (Jn 20:16ff.; Mt 28:9, 17).[9]

Third, the resurrection of Jesus occurs in a way that has time for the whole
of human history. This is a further measure of the divine discretion. Jesus' resurrection occurs as the all-deciding "mutation" that has taken place in human
history. It is the irruption of an incalculable grace into the world. It does not,
however, interrupt the history of human freedom. The course of history is not
arrested in a premature fulfillment. Rather, the opening of heaven (Jn 1:51)
that occurs in him is the horizon for the whole unfolding of history. The eternal life of communion with him, unaffected by the reign of death, has begun.
Yet it remains still hidden in what would appear the natural and ambiguous
course of things. Here G. Martelet makes an important point:

> If, then, the Risen Christ wishes to show himself and so confirm his
> faithful in their faith, in a world whose continued existence he has at

9. Larry W. Hurtado (*Lord Jesus Christ: Devotion to Jesus in Earliest Christianity* [Grand Rapids:
Eerdmans, 2003]) provides strong documentation for this in every writing of the New Testament.

heart . . . then he will appear only within the limits this world can tolerate; and that means keeping very close to what *he was*, with no more than a discreet hint or adumbration of what *he is*. It will be something between the two, quite unambiguous in itself, and yet necessarily impermanent . . . he conforms to the "rules of the household" (the economy), which is still the world of entropy and death.[10]

The patient compassion of the God of life allows for "the world of entropy and death." For it is the condition of our present existence. This has been partially disrupted by the appearances of the risen One. Yet the will of God works through a delicate economy. Its tact allows for continuity and discontinuity, routine and surprise, permanence and disruption. It is designed to ensure that the hope it inspires does not lose itself in entropy and death. From that Spirit of hope, there arises the imagination to see the world "otherwise." A recognition of this otherness is necessary. A world undisturbed by the resurrection of Jesus would easily continue to legitimate the forces that brought about his condemnation and execution. His rising from the dead punctures the balloons of all the desperate certitudes of a world enclosed in itself. Yet, by allowing for free decision, it allows hope to expand and express itself in a universe in which the gift of God does not suppress freedom but liberates it from the thrall of fear and evil.

The breath of the risen Lord is the Spirit of new corporate coexistence. It draws believers into the field of a God-given vitality. It is registered in human consciousness through the gifts of faith, hope, and love—the gifts that remain (1 Cor 13:13). In the light of Christ, his followers have new truths to explore and new values to live, and ever larger hopes to express.

The Empty Tomb

We mentioned above an imposing objectivity associated with the appearances of the risen Jesus. It is in the order of what we might term "salvific realism." God has acted. Jesus, bearing the marks of the cross, reveals himself. He does this in such a way as to engage the commitment of the early disciples. They are transformed, becoming witnesses to this new order of being and life. Allied to this saving objectivity is a more ambiguous indicator, namely, the fact of the empty tomb. The discovery of the empty tomb is connected to

---

10. G. Martelet, *The Risen Christ and the Eucharistic World*, trans. René Hague (New York: Seabury Press, 1976), 93.

a temporal reference to "the third day." And there is a personal reference—it was "some women of our company'" who discovered it (Lk 24:23).

How Christian hope is related to this tradition remains a complex question. On the one hand, it never was, nor could it ever be, that Christian hope could be founded on the mere emptiness of the tomb. A vanished corpse is not the same as the risen Lord. Nor does an unoccupied grave mean a transformed creation. On the other hand, a decaying corpse is not a very convincing sign of Christ's victory over death or of the beginning of a new creation. It remains, nonetheless, that the discovery of the empty tomb initially gave rise only to further perplexity and fear (cf. Mk 16:8; Lk 24:5, 11). Its discovery led to a new form of questioning, "Why do you seek the living among the dead?" (Lk 24:57). For the resurrection is a divinely wrought event; it is not explicable in terms of the emptiness and silence of the tomb. The only explanation is the transformative action of a love stronger than death. That would bring its own kind of silence. It would be the silence of wonder and joy, astonished at the victory of love for which there are no words. When it speaks, it will not be about the mere emptiness of the tomb. It would try to express the fullness of life into which the Christ is gone: "It is to your advantage that I go away" (Jn 16:7).

Hope, therefore, does not haunt a grave or linger among the dead. Rather, it confidently embraces its full-bodied connection with the risen Jesus, the form and agent of eternal life. Living contact with the risen Jesus can never be reduced to the mere fact of his empty grave. In this, the disciples' unambiguous assurance of Jesus' victory over death appears in stark contrast to the ambiguous status of his empty tomb.

That being said, the empty tomb does have its place in the salvific realism of the Gospel narrative. It is an indicator of the radical reality of the resurrection. The otherwise blank fact of the empty tomb is lifted out of its original ambiguity. Its inclusion in the Gospel accounts prevents Christian hope from remaining on an idealistic or mystical plane. There would be consequences if theology dismissed the significance of the empty tomb. The reality of the resurrection would be left at the mercy of another kind of realism. It would tend quickly to become a nice thought in a world in which the resurrection could not *really* happen. Eschatology would veer very quickly into an ideology. It would entice hope to trust in an exalted ideal to the detriment of founding itself on a transforming divine event. Moreover, it would mean dismissing the special role of women in communicating the gospel of new life. Unless it were utterly sure of what it was reporting, the Gospel would hardly base its case on the testimony of women in a culture that scarcely accepted their credibility.

In short, the empty tomb serves as a historical marker for a transcendent mystery. Right there, set within the history of human defeat and failure, is a demand for Christian hope to be defiantly eschatological in its realism. It underscores the objective basis of that hope, namely, the transcendent power of the Spirit. In the consciousness of hope, then, the empty tomb functions as a negative sign. It is an absence pointing to a new vitalizing presence. Its emptiness indicates the limitless extent of divine creativity and compassion. The light of the risen One shines more brightly from the empty darkness of the grave. By reflecting in that darkness and emptiness, hope finds a new and authentic realism. It arises as an energy of world-shattering proportions. Admittedly, the empty tomb can never substitute for Jesus' living presence. Nonetheless, it inspires a keener awareness of the divinely transforming event that has occurred. The resurrection has left its mark in time and space.

Christian hope, therefore, returns to the tomb, but not to stay there. It breaks forth into a new sense of the wholeness of life. It celebrates the real victory of the love. Death loses its sting (Acts 2:31; 1 Cor 15:54ff.). If the tomb is empty, there are far more surprises in store for the cosmos than scientifically predictable events can allow. A seed of wonder and questioning has been sown in the ground of the material cosmos. Some may reject such evidence. The world must remain for them a closed system in which God is not present or active in any real way. In that case, any affirmation of the empty tomb is deeply unsettling. A whole worldview is called into question. In contrast, there is no evidence of defensive embarrassment in the Gospel accounts. Nor, for that matter, does either friend or foe pretend that the tomb contained the remains of Jesus. One Gospel writer at least was quite aware of the allegation that the corpse had been stolen—a quite predictable reaction on the part of those for whom, for whatever reason, Jesus had to stay dead and buried (Mt 28:1-15).

The empty tomb, so soberly recorded in each of the four Gospels, does not draw attention to itself. It is first discovered as a puzzling fact. The movement of hope leaves the tomb behind in the joy of Christ's return from death. Because the Lord had so appeared, hope finds its way eventually back to the tomb where his tortured body had lain. It finds in that emptiness an indication of the cosmic realism of God's transforming action. It reaches into bodily existence itself. From there, the Christian response moves out into the limitless horizon of the Spirit's creativity embracing all creation. Hope awakens to divine dimensions: "for God all things are possible" (Mt 19:26).

The full-bodied reality of the resurrection of Jesus Christ transvalues death's dark symbols: mortality is not only transcended, for death is radically transformed. Human life is not only fulfilled, but death loses its immemorial sting. Jesus is risen not only beyond this world of death; he has risen within it. Hope is not based on nice ideas, but lives with a passionate sense of reality. The focus of that reality is the risen Christ himself. In him, the deathward gravity of our experience is reversed. Darkness is transformed into light. Yet he still bears the wounds of the cross that killed him. Thomas Aquinas quotes the Venerable Bede here, "He keeps the wounds, not because they cannot be healed, but that he may carry around the triumph of his victory forever" (*STh* 3, q. 54, a. 4). In the resurrection of the crucified One, the divine glory and victory are shown forth.[11]

Every aspect of the resurrection deeply affects human consciousness. In the case of the early disciples, we have already remarked on the journey from desolation and emptiness to a sense of joyous vindication and fulfillment. The crucifixion and burial of Jesus scooped out of the religious mind and imagination every vestige of either worldly hope or simple optimism.[12] God could not be manipulated to conform to pious expectations, nor could any notion of God as a mundane power meting out worldly justice be justified. The experience of defeat and emptiness readied the early group of disciples to be witnesses to something utterly new. Love had acted on its own terms to form witnesses responsive to it.

A Theological Note

The risen life of the members of Christ will be a participation in his resurrection: "If the Spirit of him who raised Jesus from the dead dwells in you, he who raised Jesus from the dead will give life to your mortal bodies also through his Spirit that dwells in you" (Rom 8:11). He died, and so do we. He has been raised; and so shall we be. But, though his tomb is empty, ours will not be. His resurrection is materially complete; ours must wait, at least for its full eschatological realization. Why is his case special?

Even if Jesus' mortal remains were there in the tomb, theology could still think of him as embodied in the cosmic totality as the source and exemplar of ultimate life. What is the point, then, of this singular material transformation of the dead body of Jesus in a way that left his tomb empty? The empty tomb could become a distraction from the real mystery of the resurrection.

But here it is especially important to appreciate that we are dealing with a

---

11. Anne Hunt, *The Trinity and the Paschal Mystery: A Development in Recent Catholic Theology* (Collegeville, Minn.: Liturgical Press, 1997), especially the chapter on von Balthasar, "Love Alone Is Credible" (pp. 57-89).

12. On the disciples' experience, see Sebastian Moore, *The Fire and the Rose Are One* (London: Darton, Longman & Todd, 1980), 80-87.

divine economy of action. It is designed to display the extent of God's saving love. The incarnation of the Word exists within the totality of God's transforming activity. It includes the whole of creation, matter as well as spirit. The raising of the dead-and-buried Jesus from the tomb is designed to show the glory of God in action.[13] For hope it is of cosmic significance. Jesus is transformed in the totality of what he was when laid in the tomb. The matter that made up his crucified body is transformed. It is not so much the "raw material" for his risen existence. In fact, it is the least promising material for the glory of God to be revealed. His corpse is the remains of a man who had been executed in defeat, humiliation, and apparent abandonment by the God in whose name he had claimed to act. What, then, is its significance?

Aquinas remarks that Jesus' risen body is not an imagined reality (*corpus phantasticum*) but the God-wrought embodiment of the saving Word (*STh* 3, q. 54, a. 1). His death is not the result of the entropic forces of nature, which lead to decay. It figures within the divine intention "to show forth the power of God" (*ad ostensionem virtutis divinae*) (*STh* 3, q. 51, a. 3). The resurrection and the empty tomb are related in the actual divine economy of salvation. As the agent of the Kingdom, Jesus has been defeated, condemned, and crucified; he died and was buried. For this reason, there is a certain appropriateness—or *convenientia*, as the scholastics would say, in the transformation of his crucified body. This transformation occurs to display, in an anticipatory manner, the power of God at work. The Holy Spirit is in no way constrained by the defeats, condemnations, violence, and burials that mark the human history that is summed up in this man.

The imagination of hope is earthed in a singular realism. As it contemplates Jesus rising from the tomb, it looks on him who was pierced (Jn 19:37; cf. Zech 12:10). The Lamb who was slain retains the marks of the cross even in his risen body. In his total physicality he is the medium through which the true creation of the Spirit is revealed. "I was dead, but now I live forever and ever" (Rev 1:18). Our ordinary ways of speaking of the deceased naturally use personal terms in reference the corpse—at least before burial. "He" or "she" is lying in the coffin, not an impersonal "it." But the dead body of Jesus had a further significance. This flesh, this body, was given for the life of the world. This blood was poured out for the new covenant. These overlays of significance deriving from his presence to the disciples cause his dead body to be identified as not only "it," but "his," or even "he," in a striking way. Note the announcement of the angel at the tomb, "I know that you were looking for Jesus who was crucified. He is not here, for he has been raised. . . . Come,

---

13. Alan E. Lewis, *Between Cross and Resurrection: A Theology of Holy Saturday* (Grand Rapids: Eerdmans, 2001), especially 133-63.

see the place where he lay" (Mt 28:5-6//Mk 16:1-6). Likewise the words of
Mary Magdalene, "They have taken the Lord out of the tomb; and we do not
know where they have laid him (Jn 20:2, 13, 15). There seems to be some
implication that his dead body still represents him in an unusual way. It is
Jesus-in-his-death. It points to a singular instance in the divine economy.
God raises him up in his total physical reality. The scope of his victory over
the powers of death must include his physical resurrection. In this way, his
tomb is an empty space in the fabric of this world. It is the material anticipation of the universal transformation that is in store.

Theological tradition contains a deeper explanation. For instance, Aquinas sees the dead body of Jesus as still in relation to the divine Word. The
Word was made flesh (Jn 1:14), right to the point of becoming a corpse. But
in the context of the hypostatic union, it could be said that the crucified Jesus
does not immediately become a corpse in the usual sense. For the divine person that he was and is continues to be related to this dead body. It is still the
body of the Word. The corpse of the crucified Jesus must be seen in the light
of the radical theological and metaphysical considerations flowing from the
full realism of God's self-communication to the world.

Aquinas, accordingly, places this consideration in a strongly incarnational
context. The Word was made flesh and dwelled among us. And the Word
continues to be spoken among us in the dead body of Jesus. Though the soul
and body of Jesus are separated in death, *this* dead body is still personally
possessed by the divine Word for the divine purposes. As Thomas writes,
"the body of Christ, living and dead, is the same by reason of its divine subject, because, in life and in death, it possesses no other hypostasis (personal
subject) than that of the Word of God" (*STh* 3, q. 50, a. 5). Though the
divine Word is not the soul of the body, the hypostatic union remains even
in regard to the dead body in the tomb. It is the dead body of the Word of
God who became flesh, in life and in death. Its fundamental significance is
to be sought in the manifestation of divine freedom: "God is not constrained
by necessity but acts out of freedom" (*quia Deus non ex necessitate agit, sed ex
voluntate*) (*STh* 3, q. 50, a. 2 and 3).

From beginning to end, it is all about the revelation of the unique realism
of God's saving action. For the sake of history, God has acted in history, not
by communicating a new idea but by doing a provocatively divine thing. By
transforming the physical remains of Jesus, God's intention for the whole
of creation is anticipated and distilled in this unique instance. The world is
no longer a total system of entropy and decay. It does not live a doomed life
under the sign of the graveyard. Death is still our common fate. But a transformation has been wrought to be blessing on all the tombs of the world.

Hence it is important to put the problem in the right place. It is not helped when theology leaves the dead body of Jesus in the tomb with the presumption that the resurrection has no physical effect in the world of matter. The problem is to understand how matter can be transformed. How is the risen body of Jesus a transformed materiality? How will it be for each of us in the end? How will the entire universe be transformed in him? The problem with transformations is that we cannot imagine what transformation means before it happens. In this case, it would be easier to imagine how the twenty-six letters of the alphabet could become a poem than to imagine how the body of the dead Jesus becomes the reality of the risen One. If theology glosses over the biblical evidence of the empty tomb, it cannot but look on the world as a vast graveyard, despite ultimate hopes of some kind of resurrection. But in terms of what the Spirit actually wrought in Christ, the world has ceased to be a graveyard. It is more a garden in which the seeds of eternal life are sprouting. New life has sprung up within it. The dead body of Jesus has been transformed.

THE CROSS OF GOOD FRIDAY

The often puzzled, questioning confusion of the disciples was freely recorded in the Gospels. In the light of the resurrection, their doubts and hesitations were changed into an unconditional certainty. They came to see the shocking scandal of Jesus' shameful death as revelation of divine glory.[14] The first generations of Christians sought for words to express what had happened. They recalled the immediate past of Jesus' earthly life with them, and the larger past of Israel itself. This was related to a special and embarrassing memory. The Gospels depict Jesus as clearly understanding, and the disciples just as clearly misunderstanding, that his mission would end in condemnation and death: "The Son of Man *must* suffer many things . . . and be rejected . . . and be killed . . ." (Mk 8:31; Mt 16:21; Lk 17:25). There is no suggestion of his being the victim of a blind fate or of a capricious divine will. What was clear was that God, in sending his Son, was not intent on entering the world as one more earthly power. There is no implication of divine vengefulness or putting down all opposition. The God whom Jesus represented was otherwise. He refuses any identity other than that of being the Son of *this* Father. Who *this* God was, what serving *this* God meant, how *this* God valued human

---

14. Hans Urs von Balthasar, *Mysterium Paschale: The Mystery of Easter*, trans. Aidan Nichols (Edinburgh: T&T Clark, 1990), 89-147, "Going to the Cross."

beings—especially those considered worthless in the social and religious system—were questions inherent in the Reign of God that Jesus announced. It
was the central symbol of his imagination. It enabled him to present himself
as the key agent and embodiment of the incalculable grace of God at work
in human history.

How the cross figured in God's design was an unsettling question. It
seemed to contradict everything religion stood for. Certainly there was no
immediate vocabulary available in the harsh political world in which the
early disciples lived. After all, execution by crucifixion was employed by the
Roman authorities precisely because of its obscene impact. The system would
not tolerate anyone who dared to question it. For God to allow the crucifixion of Jesus was a scandal to all Jews, including the first disciples. The God
they served had promised mighty works of vindication and liberation. It was
inevitably a folly to the Greeks. Their philosophy could never imagine such
pitiable vulnerability on the part of the divine Logos, who ordered the whole
of the cosmos. Needless to say, the imperial authorities found any suggestion that God could be identified with a criminal they had executed to be
deeply subversive of the authority of Rome. Yet Paul defiantly insists that
the "foolishness of God," acting in this shameful death, inspired hope in the
transcendent power at work: "for the foolishness of God is wiser than men,
and the weakness of God is stronger than men" (1 Cor 1:25).

The resurrection gave the early disciples a new perspective on everything.
They recalled the dramatic intensity of this climactic hour of revelation.
Evoking the covenant history of God with the chosen people, Jesus gives
himself to be food and drink for his followers in that last meal: "This is my
body given up for you . . . the new covenant in my blood which is poured out
for many for the forgiveness of sins" (Mt 26:27). The full significance of this
gesture, to be repeatedly performed in his memory, would dawn afterwards.
In the light of the resurrection these early witnesses began to penetrate the
meaning of the death he died. Their future was changed. The early Corinthian Christians will be reminded by Paul, twenty or so years after the event,
"As often as you eat the bread and drink the cup, you proclaim the death of
the Lord until he comes" (1 Cor 11:26). In what was taking place, the future
was coming to meet them.

Although there is nothing morbid or voyeuristic as the early Christians
"proclaimed the death of the Lord," there is striking and dramatic realism in
the accounts of what had taken place. The Gospels give various presentations
of the "agony in the garden." With their different emphases, the evangelists
depict Jesus' agonizing awareness of the eschatological dénouement. Mark

depicts the agony of Jesus as intense isolation. He is offered the cup of complete earthly failure. The world bears down on him as utterly opaque to the light of God. It has become pure resistance to the Kingdom. As the Son and the proclaimer of the God's Reign, Jesus has been left at the mercy of the world closed against its only future. There is no sign of the Father's presence: "His soul began to be greatly distressed and troubled" (Mk 14:33). He falls to the ground, praying that the hour might pass. So much does he feel the pressure of the infinite weight of the world's fate that Luke will add the graphic detail of the bloody sweat (Lk 22:44).

In this state of utter collapse, with his disciples asleep and the triumph of his enemies impending, he is stripped of everything except his character as Son. Nothing else remains. Even the disciples flee. This terminal moment wrings from him an act of intimate surrender to the One who is beyond everything in this world: "Abba, Father, for you all things are possible, remove this cup from me; but not what I want, but what you want" (Mk 14:36). What the God of unlimited possibilities wants is to show forth, through his Son's "obedient" solidarity with all who suffer what the world most dreads, that the world has been made open to a love and mercy beyond anything it can imagine: "In the days of his flesh, Jesus offered up prayers and supplications with loud cries and tears, to the one who was able to save him from death . . . although he was Son, he learned obedience through what he suffered" (Heb 5:7-9). Jesus is left with nothing except what the Father can be. In the Father, for whom all things are possible, now lies hope's only hope. The Kingdom must come on its own terms and in its own evidence. It demands to be represented in the full humanity of the Son, sharing the vulnerability of those who reject the way of violence: "Put your sword back into its place. For all who take the sword will perish by the sword" (Mt 25:52).

The new consciousness of faith looks back on all that had taken place. Jesus is recognized as the victim of a world in which God has no worldly power. In it, violence is the ultimate decider. Hope is left with nothing but what God can be and do. In such a world, and for the salvation of such a world, God has to be revealed as God in a way God has never been known before.

But in the recollection of that time, when the Father seemed to be answering no prayers, those who become privileged witnesses recall a sorry cycle of betrayal and desertion. One of Jesus' disciples, Judas, betrays him to the parties plotting to destroy him. They hand him over to the Jewish leaders. From the Sanhedrin he is taken to the Roman governor. Pilate passes him along to the local puppet king. Herod sends him back to Pilate. The governor offers him to the mercy of the mob. Betrayed by one of his own, denied by the leader of those he had chosen to walk with him, left for lost by the rest of

them, despised now by his own people, libeled by false witnesses, he is condemned in the courts of the secular and religious authorities alike.

Then, after being tortured by the police and soldiers guarding him, he is
taken to be executed in the hideous manner of crucifixion. In the tortuous
unfolding of these events, the eerily intractable power of evil is disclosed. No
one is exclusively to blame; but, in the dark conspiracies of self-justification,
no one is innocent.

By condemning the innocent one, the ambiguous system of the world's
justice asserts itself as just. It is the Son of God who is condemned as a criminal. He is "counted among the wicked" (Mk 15:28), "made sin" (2 Cor 5:21).
He "has become a curse for us, for it is written 'Cursed is everyone who hangs
on a tree'" (Gal 3:13). John's Gospel invites readers through Pilate's words to
"behold the man" (Jn 19:6). This man is presented as a judgment on all other
versions of humanity. The humanity of God thus confronts the projections
of human pride.

It is as though the power of evil is defying the mystery of God to reveal
itself. God would not be God if the Kingdom Jesus proclaimed ended in
futility. And it would be worse than failure if God's original intention to save
and forgive were changed into vengeance and worldly display. To answer evil
with evil, as though the law of "an eye for an eye and a tooth for a tooth"
guided God's own behavior, would be the flat contradiction of all that Jesus
stood for. Yet there is no divine vengeance. Love does not turn to hatred and
revenge. God is no self-serving worldly power. The Father sends no legion
of angels. For the God of Jesus has refused to have any presence in the world
save that of the crucified Son. As this Son prays for the forgiveness of those
who have crucified him, he rejects any worldly identity, any worldly justification or protection, save what the Father can be for him.

The cross is indeed the *crux* of the meaning of Jesus' mission and identity.
In his suffering and death the character of ultimate reality is tested: will his
Spirit be revealed as truly Holy? Will he be confirmed in his identity as Son
of the Father? Will the Kingdom come? Will God, can God, still be the
true God in the real world of this terminal encounter with the power of evil?
As hope looks back to its beginnings, it finds an affirmative answer to these
questions. For it must be a defiantly post-Easter hope, even as it recalls the
grief and failure from which it was born.

Even though it is born of the resurrection, hope continues under the sign
of the cross. It is earthed in the time and space and conflicts of history. Like
Paul, it is "always carrying in the body the death of Jesus . . . for while we live,
we are always being given up to death for Jesus' sake, so that the life of Jesus
will be manifest in our mortal flesh" (2 Cor 4:11; cf. Rom 6:3).

HOLY SATURDAY

This middle day of the paschal mystery was often passed over by theology without comment. Today, however, there is a large literature on Holy Saturday, especially in light of Hans Urs von Balthasar's profound ruminations on this theme.[15] The Gospels obviously recognize this middle day of grief and despair, but with few details. Liturgically, it is a long day leading to the Easter Vigil, ideally celebrated to greet the Sunday dawn. The altars are stripped, the tabernacle empty, the statues and pictures are veiled, and no Alleluia is sung. Hope is being invited to take its time. It must patiently wait out this day on which Jesus is truly dead among the dead—dead and buried, cut off from the land of the living. He has gone down to where hope is left with nothing except to wait on God to act. The tomb contained not only the mortal remains of Jesus but also everything he had lived for. The Father in whose name he acted, the Spirit which moved and empowered him, the very cause of the Kingdom and its promise for the poor and excluded—all were brought to nothing. Hope cannot hide from the brutal reality of this death, as the tortured corpse of Jesus lay in the tomb. He has "dwelled among us" not only on the surface of life, not only in the experience of life's mortal agonies, but now as dead and buried, dead among the dead.

Post-Easter hope reaches back to feel the hopelessness, the isolation, and the grief following the shocking death of Jesus. When people of hope contemplate his brutalized corpse, they will inevitably recall the graves of the dead they have known and come close to the meaning of this second day. Originally, this "holy," middle liturgical day of the *sacrum triduum* was experienced neither as holy nor as the middle of anything; it was only a dreadful ending. It was the day of God's obvious defeat and removal from the world of our experience. On this day, the Word of God was reduced to silence. Grief numbed the hearts of the disciples in a universe now turned grotesque. Jesus, on whom they had pinned all their hopes for something radically new—the coming of God's Reign—has been violently eliminated, and his corpse lies buried in a stranger's tomb.

To retrace the path to Holy Saturday requires a special effort of Christian imagination. The fourth-century article of the creed continues to be puzzling—as in the words, ". . . crucified, died and was buried. *He descended into hell.*"[16]

---

15. Ibid., 148-88, "Going to the Dead."

16. Nonetheless, in the judgment of serious scholars, there was no more well known and popular belief among early Christians, from the second century on. See Hurtado, *Lord Jesus Christ*, 628-33.

The Latin of the creed, *inferna, inferos*,[17] seems to mean simply "the lowest places" that human imagination can depict. It connotes that limit of God-forsakenness at which no human hope is possible. The Lord has known "the pangs of death" (Acts 2:24). There are many (over fifty) references in the New Testament to Jesus being raised "from the dead," *ek nekrōn*. In surrender to the Father's will, he has descended, dead among the dead, into the most dreaded depths of human hopelessness. The Father has "sent" the beloved Son into the underworld of the world. At that depth of darkness the problem of evil is felt as most intense. The scandal of innocent suffering is a black hole swallowing all light. The Word has become flesh right to the end. He has gone down into the world of wordless silence.

The instinct of hope recognizes that ultimate love must first of all survive the deadliness of death before it can promise a new creation. In his self-abandonment, Jesus refuses to be anything but the Son. He gives himself for the life of the world into its most hopeless depth. At this extremity, he reveals the all-embracing love of the Father and embodies the creativity of the Holy Spirit moving with inexhaustible vitality even at this depth of darkness and defeat.

The unfathomable solidarity of Jesus with the lost and the dead is a manifestation of limitless mercy. The Son dies for sinners and is dead with them. The farthest realm of ultimate estrangement now knows another presence. It is the only presence that could reach and penetrate it. It can be named only in terms of a love so absolute that it reaches out into what is most distant from itself. The Father so loves the world—and its underworld—as to give his only Son. The sinner lives apart from God in self-imposed isolation. But even that limit of estrangement is enfolded in mercy. In sending the Son to this point, "God in the absolute weakness of love . . . in [this] period of non-time, enters into solidarity with those damning themselves."[18] The cross and the death of Jesus are the way of love into the depths of all human despair, whether they be called *Hades, Sheol, Gehenna*, or *inferna*. Jesus' "descent into hell" shows the reach of salvation in Christ. It goes "deeper than the lowest place," *inferno profundior* (Gregory the Great). No dimension of human existence is outside the reach of divine compassion: "God was in Christ reconciling the world to himself, not counting their trespasses against them" (2 Cor 5:19).

And so hope finds its proper depth. Both the philosopher and the theologian may usefully speculate on the transcendent causality of God in relation

---

17. Martin F. Connell, "*Descensus Christi ad Inferos*: Christ's Descent to the Dead," *Theological Studies* 62 (2001): 262-82.

18. Hans Urs von Balthasar, in *The von Balthasar Reader*, ed. Medard Kehl and Werner Löser, trans. R. J. Daly and F. Lawrence (Edinburgh: T&T Clark, 1985), 153.

to human freedom. But here hope is given an image to feel its way toward the inexpressible creativity of love working in the depths of the heart. Human freedom is obviously capable of ultimate perversion. It can set itself up in opposition to the will and claims of the infinite Other. It can project its own violence and pride onto God. Thus, this "other," this "god," appears only as the most threatening and absolute rival. However, in Christ's descent into the realm of the lost, this hitherto menacing "other" is revealed as searching out those who have damned themselves with the offer of infinite mercy. Christ's decent into hell, his "being buried" and going down to "the lowest places," is a doctrine of double significance. It underscores both the realism of the incarnation and the inclusiveness of redemption. Because he has gone down into this lowest place, there is a way out. There, too, "nothing in all creation, nothing in life or death . . . can separate us from the love of God in Christ Jesus" (Rom 8:38).

Love's outreach, then, includes the impenetrable realm of the dead. At this point hope is supported by the perfect love which casts out even this final fear (1 Jn 4:18). Admittedly, we can speak of Jesus' experience of death and his solidarity with the dead only in symbols and metaphors. Despite such limitations, there is no limit to exploring the ever deeper sense of the love that reaches into all the dimensions of human existence. The radically indescribable state of the dead, the defeated and the terminally estranged cannot be excluded from the universe of grace. Through his death, Jesus is "the atoning sacrifice for our sins, and not for ours only, but also for the sins of the whole world" (1 Jn 2:2).

There is an ancient homily that appears in the Office of Readings for Holy Saturday.[19] Composed by an unknown author of the third century, it beautifully evokes the saving significance of Jesus' descent into hell:

> What is happening? Today there is a great silence over the earth, a great silence and stillness, a great silence because the King sleeps; the earth was in terror and was still, because God slept in the flesh and raised up those who were sleeping from the ages. God has died in the flesh, and the underworld has trembled.

The author leads hearers to question the significance of the "silence and stillness" of Christ in the tomb. But it is not the stillness of inactivity. Because of Christ's solidarity with those who have died in ages past, a great transformation is occurring. The underworld that had held the dead in its grasp

---

19. See the second reading of "The Office of Readings for Holy Saturday," in *The Divine Office: Liturgy of the Hours according to the Roman Rite* (London: Collins, 1974), 2:321-22.

now trembles in the presence of "the King." His death is an act of universal significance. It touches the very origins of human history:

> Truly, he goes to seek out our first parent like a lost sheep; he wishes to visit those who sit in darkness and in the shadow of death. He goes to free the prisoner Adam, from his pains, and his fellow-prisoner, Eve—he who is God and Adam's Son.

Christ greets Adam, bearing his cross. He addresses the father of the human race, whose son he also is. He grasps Adam's hand with the words, "Awake, O sleeper and arise from the dead, and Christ shall give you light!"

The homily continues. It imagines Jesus addressing the realm of the dead in tones of command:

> I am your God who for your sake became your son, who for you and your descendants now speak, and command with authority those in prison: Come forth; and those in darkness, Have light; and those who sleep, Rise.
>
> I command you, "Awake, sleeper. I have not made you to be held a prisoner in the underworld. Arise from the dead."

He is reclaiming what is his all along. For Christ is united to each individual person in life and in death:

> I am the life of the dead. Arise, O man, work of my hands, arise, you who were fashioned in my image. Rise, let us go hence. For you in me, and I in you, together we are one undivided person.

Christ then speaks and recounts the sufferings freely borne for the salvation of all. He has become the son of Adam and taken the form of a slave. He has come "on earth, and under the earth." Adam had left the garden of paradise. But Jesus has suffered in a garden. The blows and humiliation he suffered are designed to refashion the divine image in those who were lost. After recalling further dimensions of his passion, he addresses his hearers: "Arise, let us go hence." His reaching out to the dead not only reverses the fate the dead have suffered, but promises more:

> The enemy brought you out of the land of paradise; I will reinstate you, no longer in paradise, but on the throne of heaven. I denied you the tree of life . . . but now I myself am united to you, I who am life.

I posted the cherubim to guard you as they would slaves; now I make the cherubim worship you as they would God.

With a marvelous interplay of symbols, this ancient homily of hope comes to a triumphant conclusion:

The cherubim throne has been prepared, the bearers are ready and waiting, the bridal chamber is in order, the food is provided, the everlasting houses and rooms are in readiness, the treasures of good things have been opened; the kingdom of heaven has been prepared before the ages.

CONCLUSION

Easter Sunday looks back to Friday and Saturday that went before. It changes forever the meaning of those days of grief and defeat. But it also looks forward. In the time of hope, life is to be lived "after Easter." When the crucified and risen One is taken up into heaven, the time of "seeing" is over. The Word made flesh dwelling among us is no longer visible to human eyes. The ascension symbolically depicts the completion of the way of Jesus in his ascent to the Father. He is now to be found in the realm of the infinite so that, in the power and activity of the Spirit, "he might fill all things" (Eph 4:10). All time and space are so filled with his presence. Hope must meet the challenge of acknowledging the universal dimensions of what has taken place. Paul's words to the Colossians are a powerful summons to awaken hope to its full proportions:

So if you have been raised with Christ, seek the things that are above, where Christ is seated at the right hand of God. Set your minds on the things that are above, not on things that are on the earth, for you have died, and your life is hidden with Christ in God. When Christ who is your life is revealed, then you also will be revealed with him in glory. (Col 3:1-4)

This "seeking" and "hidden" life of hope has ethical and spiritual consequences. Its form must be clothed with "compassion, kindness, humility, meekness and patience" (Col 3:12), and with a "love the binds everything together" (Col 3:14). Its demands a life of union with Christ manifest in continual thanksgiving to the Father (Col 3:17).

When the economy of "seeing" is over, only by believing and hoping can the eschaton be possessed. Pentecost occurs as the outpouring of the Spirit. The divine Gift is given to make this paschal parable the vital form of the church's life in every generation of its existence. In the vitality of the Spirit, Christ and his followers are one in a life of communion. They are united around him who is the beginning of the new creation. He forever embodies the power of love triumphing over the crucifying power of evil and the burying power of death. The threefold character of this love enfolds our existence in its every dimension. The ultimate life source is the Father. The ultimate life form is the Son. The ultimate life force is the Spirit. As trinitarian love opens the tomb of the self-enclosed world, the crucified Jesus emerges to breathe the Spirit of life into the despairing and the dead. Hope inhales this "breath of life" to move toward a fulfillment of what has already begun.[20]

The three holy days, the *sacrum triduum*, are the fundamental parable of Christian hope. Any statement on a particular theme, heaven or hell, purgatory or the end of the world, is nothing more than a retelling of this parable at a particular point.

---

20. See Denis Edwards, *The Breath of Life: A Theology of the Creator Spirit* (Maryknoll, N.Y.: Orbis Books, 2004), 171-79.

5

Death

Threat or Gift?

I F THIS ACCOUNT OF HOPE is to be realistic, we cannot defer considering the subject that tends most to concentrate the mind on matters eschatological: death. Hope would be a fantasy of wish fulfillment, and eschatology would be a paper-thin theory if it tried to hurry past the fact that we will die. We must give death its due and feel its ability to weave through every thread in the fabric of our existence. Individually, we will die. Collectively, civilizations flourish, wane, and die. Believers and nonbelievers alike are united in the ecumenicity of death, and all philosophies have at least one reality to think about. Pure objectivity on the subject of death is impossible, for there is no deathless vantage point. Eschatology may be about "the last things," but death, in a rather obvious sense, has the last word. In its terminal silence, it swallows up our theories. Increasing longevity may defer the issue, but death remains a constant.

DEATH AND NATURE

Death figures in the perceptions of our cultures in all kinds of ambiguous ways. There is a cooler view. Death is a matter-of-fact biological reality. Indeed, it is a necessary feature inscribed into the dynamics of evolution. There can be no progress in the evolutionary scheme of things unless death ensures the succession of generations. It is the price to be paid for the evolution of life on this planet. It makes possible the emergence of differentiated, complex living beings in a world of wonderful biodiversity. Unless they were part of a world of mortality, human beings would never have come into existence.[1]

---

1. Denis Edwards, *Breath of Life: A Theology of the Creator Spirit* (Maryknoll, N.Y.: Orbis Books, 2004), 137-38, 174.

Moreover, there is a sober, scientific backdrop to individual death. It is the eventual collapse of the solar system, even if only billions of years from now. It will mean the extinction of all life on this planet. Of more dramatic menace is the most probable recurrence of cosmic events that have been lethal to planetary life in the past. William R. Stoeger in his scientific account of catastrophes in this life-bearing universe, considers matters within a time frame of fifty million years—enough time for the appearance and disappearance of a species. He writes,

> The prime reason for discussing [such possibilities] . . . is though they are remote and of long-time-scale occurrence, they are certain to happen. They also represent the ultimate demise of life on this planet, and, in the case of the universe, of the cosmic life-bearing womb itself. As such, they represent a very formidable challenge to our religious understanding of what ultimate destiny, eternal life, the resurrection of the body, and the new heavens and the new earth might mean.[2]

In other words, "the mystery of life and death are written into the very heart and essence of material creation."[3] The law of entropy is built into the cosmos itself. All systems break down, and the fundamental chaos that they order and control finally takes over. So much for the "cooler" scientific account.

DEATH AND CULTURE

There is a "hot" version of death as well. It is no apocalyptic fantasy to observe that the globe has lived under the threat of megadeath for decades. The possibilities of collective death are a factor in contemporary consciousness. Though human history has always known its catalogue of natural disasters, famines, earthquakes, plagues—"acts of God"—we now live with the eerie possibility of "human acts" leading to planetary suicide. Biological warfare, thermonuclear incineration, and ecological destruction still menace all life on this planet. Compared to the threat of violent death on a global scale, individual death might appear to be almost insignificant.

On the other hand, when a culture lacks any public language to express the reality of death, its imagination takes an oddly morbid turn. Its social

---

2. William R. Stoeger, SJ, "Scientific Accounts of Ultimate Catastrophes in Our Life-Bearing Universe" in *The End of the World and the Ends of God*, ed. J. C. Polkinghorne and M. Welker (Harrisburg, Pa.: Trinity Press International, 2000), 19-28, here 21.

3. Ibid., 28.

communication is marked by a pervasive dread. The daily news of death is a catalogue of tragedy: murders, terrorist attacks, natural disasters, newsworthy accidents, epidemics, famines, wars, and so on. Moreover, the depiction of death-dealing violence features prominently in various forms of entertainment—the thrillers of pulp literature and blockbuster catastrophe movies, TV crime series, and so on. The imagination is persuaded that death happens dramatically and tragically to others. Through the safe distance of the media, we become death-watchers, voyeurs of what has become culturally obscene. The cult of death-as-catastrophe buries our sense of common mortality. If that proves too much, the TV commercial break will return us to a world in which no one ever dies, where all would live happily ever after—if only they possessed the desired product!

The voyeuristic world lives in close alliance with a culture of consumerism. Before death consumes us, we must in a way "consume" death, not only for our entertainment but for our use. Death becomes an instrument for regulating a finally meaningless and hopeless system to one's advantage. Suicide becomes a social option in order to secure a "death with dignity." Euthanasia becomes a socially acceptable way to release others from suffering, after those responsible for their care have assessed what is lacking in their "quality of life." Abortion sacrifices at least 15 percent of the next generation, thus saving them from the fate of being unwanted. These are unwelcome thoughts for many. But whatever the present divergences in moral conscience, they point to the way death has become an instrument in a radically violent way of life.

But these instances are only a tiny indication of the death-dealing systems that shape the ecological, social, political, and economic world. The individual use of death as an instrument reflects public attitudes and cultural habits, even if not explicit policies. Huge new resources are demanded to keep fueling a consumerist economy. This gives rise to new forms of exploitation. If persuasion is not effective, then violence and expropriation have their use. The enormous military arsenals at the disposal of dozens of governments openly include weapons of mass destruction designed for biological or thermonuclear warfare. This range of lethal capacities is the material expression of a readiness to wipe out whole populations if the necessity arises.

There is no point in denying the impact of this dismal outlook. As both cause and effect, it is related to the cultural atheism of modern consciousness. The great "masters of suspicion" have done their work well. Nietzsche, Marx, and Freud have banished from the modern mind the "god" they identified with the forces of oppression and repression. If life has been liberated from such a "god," so too has death. A "god-less" culture necessarily intensifies the impact of death. There is nothing and no one to receive one's last breath. The culture has nowhere to go; death is unrelated to any natural or spiritual fulfillment. Funeral rites are marked by a banal, perfunctory finality. There is no drama of final judgment for either the dead or those who caused their deaths. With death reduced to a brute terminal event for the biological individual, there is no passing on, no passing over, no possibility of an entry into life in some other dimension. Some may be enshrined in human memory—but that too is death-bound and includes those once hailed as celebrities.

One reaction is to so emphasize the natural phenomenon of death that it comes to lack all personal significance. In death the human being, always an ambiguous reality, returns to the engendering nature from which it came. This view can take the modern form of "nature spirituality," in which the fate of the individual is consigned to an amorphous wholeness. The universal totality of nature swallows up personal existence irrespective of the history of its freedom. The great nurturing womb of the world is all. Only the cosmos, nature, the race, the nation, the family, or the cause endures. These encompassing totalities hold within themselves whatever there is in reality of the individual.

DIFFERING APPROACHES

Clearly, the topic of death is a peculiarly complex matter.[4] Its complexity is indicated in the titles of two remarkable books, each a classic in its own genre. The first is Ernest Becker's *The Denial of Death*, the second is Ladislaus Boros's *The Moment of Truth: Mysterium Mortis*.[5] In what follows, I shall refer to both these works, the better to position Christian hope in the face of death.

From Denial to Acceptance

Becker diagnoses modern cultural consciousness as suffering from a fundamental denial of death. He expresses his main thesis in these words:

> The idea of death, the fear of it, haunts the human animal like nothing else; it is the mainspring of human activity—activity designed largely

---

4. See the review symposium in *Horizons* (2001): 363-79 on the recent book of Lucy Bregman, *Beyond Silence and Denial: Death and Dying Reconsidered* (Louisville: Westminster John Knox Press, 1999).

5. Ernest Becker, *The Denial of Death* (New York: Free Press, 1973); Ladislaus Boros, *The Moment of Truth: Mysterium Mortis*, trans. G. Bainbridge (London: Burns & Oates, 1962).

to avoid the fatality of death, to overcome it by denying in some way that it is the final destiny for man.[6]

Becker generously accepts the enormous influence of Freud in the understanding of psychopathology. But he is critical, too. Relying on the insights of Søren Kierkegaard and Otto Rank, he lays bare a certain inconclusiveness in Freud's approach when it touches on the matter of death and the deep terror that it strikes into every human being. Becker argues that the fundamental repression or denial in human life is not sex, as Freud had taught, but death. Whatever therapy might be brought to bear on human problems, it is most effective if it frees us to live with the most radical fear of all, namely, death, as it arises from the perception of our mortality. The courageous acceptance of one's creatureliness is the only authentic stance: "By being or doing we fashion something, an object or ourselves, and drop it into the confusion, make an offering of it, so to speak, to the life-force."[7]

Becker refers to Frederick Perls's analysis of the four protective layers that structure neurosis. The first two layers are the mundane, everyday layers of social cliché and role. But there are two further layers where the challenge most arises. This is the point of resistance, for in various layers structuring human identity, "the third is the stiff one to penetrate: it is the impasse that covers our feelings of being empty and lost, the very feeling we try to banish in building up our character defenses."[8] Hidden beneath this character defense is a radical fear of death. It is identified as

> the layer of our true and basic animal anxieties, the terror that we carry around in our secret heart. Only when we explode this fourth layer . . . do we get to the layer of what might call our "authentic self": what we really are without shame, without disguise, without defenses against fear.[9]

Having evoked the primordial terror experienced in the human psyche in the face of death, Becker points to the need to accept our finitude and creaturehood. Only in a proper practice of humility and self-surrender can human authenticity be realized. Though Becker is not conventionally religious, he positively appreciates the value of religious experience of a certain kind. It is, for him, a "creature feeling" in the face of the massive transcendence of

6. Becker, *Denial of Death*, ix.
7. Ibid., 285.
8. Ibid., 57.
9. Ibid.

creation and the crushing and negating miracle of Being. He understands this experience to tie in with some of the basic concerns of modern psychology. For religion and psychology meet "right at the point of the problem of courage."[10] Faced with the immensity of the universe and its impassivity in regard to individual fate,

> man had to invent and create out of himself the limitations of perception and equanimity to live on this planet. And so the core of psychodynamics, the formation of the human character, is a study in human self-limitation and in the terrifying costs of that limitation. The hostility to psychoanalysis . . . will always be a hostility against admitting that man lives by lying to himself about himself and about his world, and that character . . . is a vital lie.[11]

Quite simply, to deny our mortality is to live a lie. This denial and flight from truth are deeply intertwined in the identity or character we have formed for ourselves to defend ourselves against the uncanny mystery of life and the fact of our own mortality. Science might strip away illusion, but religion, however unsettlingly, poses larger questions. In this regard, science improperly absorbs all truth into itself. Religion stands for truths that cannot be scientifically absorbed or controlled. Opening up these larger dimensions of meaning, religion enables human beings to

> wait in a condition of openness toward miracle and mystery, in the lived truth of creation, which would make it easier to survive and be redeemed because men would be less driven to undo themselves and would be more like the image which pleases their creator: awe-filled creatures trying to live in harmony with the rest of creation. Today we would add . . . they would be less likely to poison the rest of creation.[12]

A religious sense of the mysteries of creation and the Creator tends to counteract the violent and illusory self-assertion that infects both culture and the biosphere. A genuinely creaturely consciousness enables us to live in a condition of "relative unrepression." The acceptance of our puniness in the face of the overwhelming majesty of the universe leads to an awareness of the

---

10. Ibid., 50.
11. Ibid., 51.
12. Ibid., 282.

unspeakable miracle of even a single living being. Even though this brings with it a sense of "panic" within the immense, inconclusive drama of creation, it is in fact a point of healing.

If there is a healing at such a depth, it is because we begin to live in humility—a sense of radical finiteness, our creatureliness.[13] We suggest that the great value of Becker's work consists in his revaluation of humility, in the most original sense of the word.[14] It evokes the basic mode of any authentic human consciousness. As a word, "humility" derives from the Latin *humus*, meaning "earth," "soil," "dirt." It expresses the character of human existence as earthed and grounded, and so bound up with nature, in whose processes we are each and all immersed. The liturgy of Ash Wednesday at the beginning of Lent suggests as much. The ashes are traced on our foreheads with the biblically inspired formula, "Remember that you are but dust, and unto dust you shall return" (cf. Gen 3:19). Humility is a *virtus* in the ethical sense, a quality informing conscience and personal responsibility. It equips human consciousness to respond positively to the dread of death. It allows death to emerge from its subterranean place of influence. Named and accepted (in "relative unrepression"), death is no longer able to sap our energies or drive us to the frenzy of illusory projects of immortality designed for our self-perpetuation—even to the detriment of others.

The trembling, courageous acceptance of mortality is the path to true wisdom. Life remains a question. It is lived within an overwhelmingly questionable universe, but this openly questioning experience of existence brings home to each consciousness a fundamental fact. None of us is the center of that universe. Every human being has emerged out of a vast cosmic process and is dying back into it. To reflect on the real center, is to move closer to the true life force of this overwhelming universe. At that point, a healing acceptance of self as mortal and finite begins. Even if this does not immediately inspire an act of religious adoration and praise, it is at least an attitude of surrender to the unnamed, incomprehensible, generative Other. Only a decentered self, beholden to the infinite Other, can live meaningfully. It is the task of religious faith and theology to articulate the relationship between accepting ourselves as creatures and experiencing the presence of the Creator.

---

13. Ibid., 58.

14. On this point, S. Bulgakov calls for a revaluation of humility as the active expression of faith in divine providence. The humble Christian "sees history and every individual human life as the realization of a divine plan. While the plan is incomprehensible to him in its details, he humbles himself before it through an act of faith. In consequence he is free from the spell of heroic pretensions and ready for the day at hand" (cited in Paul Valliere, *Modern Russian Theology: Bukharev, Soloviev, Bulkakov; Orthodox Theology in a New Key* (Grand Rapids: Eerdmans, 2000), 247.

This is some indication of how Becker confronts the denial of death that gives rise to the frenzied violence of self-assertion infecting human culture. His analysis bears on what most undermines a life of authentic hope and provokes despair. Though apparently agnostic about specific religious claims, he opens the way to a deeper appreciation of Christian hope. His work enriches eschatology with a psychoanalytic vocabulary with which to denounce the desperate absurdities of the consumer society and to announce the Gospel of him who is "the resurrection and the life" (Jn 11:25).

Death as Fulfillment

There are alternative voices. One would be the Death Awareness Movement. As Lucy Bregman has recently described it, this many-faceted movement approaches the phenomenon of death as a meaningful experience outside the specifically medical context.[15] At first glance, this movement can appear to be purely secular. In fact, it tends to draw on the spirituality latent in classic and popular expressions of Judaism, Christianity, and Buddhism—and more besides. This movement is really the social and professional rediscovery of quite traditional philosophical and theological understandings of death. Many traditions converge in speaking of death as a fulfillment. They recognize in each individual a spiritual reality and a personal destiny. They represent resistance to the annulling flux of nature and the depersonalizing influences latent in society and culture. With Plato, the true and lasting self is achieved in the contemplation of the Good and in union with it. Authentic human consciousness must move to the mouth of the dark cave of nature, to turn from the flickering world of shadows to the light of day. To die is to be released from the play of shadows, to awake from the dream; and only by keeping vigil before such a death is true wisdom gained and the city of true culture possible. This remark brings us to a brief consideration of Boros's *Moment of Truth*.

Located in the classical philosophical and spiritual tradition, Boros's approach takes up where Becker's ends. Boros concedes that, empirically speaking, death implies dissolution and destruction. But he is intent on asking,

> whether the complete removal from self which we undergo in death does not conceal a much more fundamental process which could be

---

15. Lucy Bregman, *Death, Dying, Spirituality and Religions: A Study of the Death Awareness Movement* (New York: Peter Lang, 2003).

described . . . in terms of the progressive achievement of selfhood, of actively initiating the self to life.[16]

Like Becker, Boros purports to be exploring human consciousness. But instead of highlighting the strategies involved in the denial of death, Boros seeks to illumine the dynamics of self-transcendence occurring in our actual living. The thrust of human life is toward fulfillment—in, and even through, death. In dying, an individual existence moves to the bounds of its being. It awakes to a kind of full knowledge and liberty. The dynamics of personal existence that moved and motivated life in its normal course have lain hidden. But at the moment of death they surface into full awareness. Our deepest being is revealed as "of unimaginable splendour." It comes rushing toward us as the full dimensions of our being unfold.[17]

We die out of our limited individuality into a more deeply relational form of being. We become aware of ourselves as part of the universal whole, so that there appears,

> all at once and all together the universe that [the human person] has always borne hidden within himself, the universe with which he is already most intimately united, and which, one way or another, was always being produced from within him.[18]

The horizon in which this totality is experienced at the limits of our existence is now bounded only by the infinite mystery of God: "Being flows toward [the person in death] like a boundless stream of things, meanings, persons and happenings, ready to convey him right into the Godhead."[19]

Death, therefore, is meeting with God. This limitless Other has been present in every stirring of our existence. It has been within us as our "deepest mystery." It has worked within all the elements and causes that have formed us, moving us toward an eternal destiny.[20] In the light of God, we are brought to a moment of final decision:

> There now man stands, free to accept or reject this splendour. In a last final decision, he either allows this flood of realities to flow past him, while he stands there eternally turned to stone, like a rock past which

---

16. Boros, *Moment of Truth*, viii; see further pp. 1-23.
17. Ibid., viii, 73-81.
18. Ibid., viii.
19. Ibid.
20. Ibid., ix.

the life-giving stream flows on, noble enough in himself no doubt, but abandoned and eternally alone; or he allows himself to be carried along by this flood, becomes part of it and flows on to eternal fulfilment.[21]

Thus Boros dramatically evokes the moment of decision. The previous isolation and individualistic limits of our self-regarding projects are called into question. We come to a moment of truth. We can stand stonelike against the flow of life or become part of it. Death is the final opportunity to crystallize one's life in a completely personal act. Paradoxically, it is our most fully conscious and free moment. It faces us with the decision—to choose life and the God of life for whom we were made.

Where Becker takes us back to the psyche's primordial terror in the face of mortality, Boros bids us yield to the movement of the human spirit anticipating its final homecoming. In his analysis, he draws on a wide range of experiences. For instance, all our willing and desiring, all our love for the truly good, lives from the attractiveness of an absolute good that in this life we could never attain. Similarly, our search for truth and meaning is always looking beyond this or that object to the ultimate meaning of everything. Each experience of insight, each true judgment, anticipates what can never be grasped in this life. Such acts are a presentiment of Light eternal in its fullness. All in all, art, mysticism, love, and intelligence are promises that are yet to be kept. Admittedly, life demands its sacrifices and dispossessions. Yet it is also moving us beyond egocentric limits, summoning us to live up to our responsibilities, to follow the ways of love and wisdom. At death, this self-transcending movement will find its ultimate point of rest and its final vindication.[22]

Both of these approaches appeal to reasonably accessible levels of human experience. One points to the repressed depths of consciousness; the other to its heights. The one uncovers a primitive terror resulting in the face of death; the other presents the thrust of life as somehow positing death as the door to a final self-realization in the light of the infinite. Psychologically speaking, Becker's approach is more archaeological. It searches into the psychic terror that causes a culture to be a "denial of death." The other is more teleological, goal-directed. It points to the movement in our existence that can be described as the affirmation or vindication of life.

We must always remind ourselves that, though we can reflect on death, it

21. Ibid., ix, and elaborated in 73-84.
22. See Karl Rahner, *On the Theology of Death*, trans. C. H. Henkey (New York: Herder & Herder, 1962), 30-31. See also Peter C. Phan, *Eternity in Time: A Study of Karl Rahner's Eschatology* (Selinsgrove, Pa.: Susquehanna University Press, 1988), 75-115.

is from a distance. It is not yet our experience. We experience ourselves only as alive. Whether we are caught in a "denial of death" or drawn to an affirmation of life, we are to some extent caught between the two. Hope in the face of death must realistically acknowledge the complex and often cacophonous consciousness of our present existence.

"THE WAGES OF SIN"

We must now try to appreciate this complexity more deeply. As Becker has already suggested, there is an illusory sense of life. It can be reduced to a personal "project." I can pretend to exist to the extent of my planning and control. This kind of self-making is at root self-regarding, exhibiting an individualism that gives scant attention to any other—unless, and to the extent that, they figure in one's plans. It evokes a sense of the individual as an ego somehow circling the planet in search of some form of deathless incarnation in a self-expressive project. From that illusory center, the individual constructs an egocentric sense of meaning and worth, designed, one way or another, to earn the respect of others. But any life project, constructed in this way, is vulnerable. The larger world constitutes a threat. The individual must consequently develop techniques of "damage control." As the threatened ego endeavors to "cope," it invokes the whole repertoire of the sophisticated "coping mechanisms" that the culture affords—medical, technological, scientific. But the illusion remains. Each of us exists not by virtue of a self-creating "project" but as having been uncannily "pro-jected"—or, as Martin Heidegger would say, "thrown"—into a universe immeasurably more awesome and inviting than the tiny measure of an ego-centered project.

There is in fact no way of coping with fundamental finitude and mortality. The utter "otherness" of reality disrupts any egocentric system. No controlling mechanism can be "put in place," when the self-regarding ego is the center of significance. There is the limitless Other which is alone the source of all meaning and worth. Its judgment whispers at the heart of all being and unsettles conscience. Clamorous others confront us, each inviting us to responsibilities not of our choosing. These others resist being merely raw material, let alone victims, in relation to one's individual project. In the presence of death, the fabricated system of projects and coping mechanisms breaks down. The "vital lie" of character formed through the fear of death begins to hear the voice of a vital truth. It speaks of my being more than my self-making. It calls on every finite, mortal being to let go of illusion. The path to reality is through surrender in hope to what is unimaginably "Other." Without this self-yielding, this self-surrender of hope, the only valid position is nihilism.[23] The nihilistic view of reality is fixated in autistic materialist objectivism that refuses to allow the reality of the personal subject in one-self or in others. Any intimation of the infinite, any responsibility to what is other and outside my autistic purpose and control, is illusory. Soskice cites both Rahner and Paul Ricoeur on the spiritual necessity of letting go into the depths of mystery. Here she wittily describes the intrinsic autism of the nihilistic position as, "If I can't be God, I don't want to play."[24]

Through such reflection we come nearer to the biblical position, which connects death to sin. It helps explain why death is experienced as so "unnat-ural" and alien. Death is shrouded in a darkness deeper than the inevitable termination of biological life. The biblical tradition is summed up by Paul when he identifies death as the "wages of sin" (Rom 6:23). In some way, death is the consequence and manifestation of sin. Sin is basically alienation from God. It is the refusal of communion with the Creator—and creation. It is the choice for one's self against all others. In this context, the seemingly natural fact of death becomes the carrier of a profound sense of rupture and guilt. It looms through life as "the last enemy" (1 Cor 15:26).[25]

It helps to imagine an alternative. What if human history had in fact unfolded as progressive communion with God? What if life were experi-enced as a growing conformity to the love and wisdom of the Creator, lead-ing to a final communion with the source of all life? If that were the case, it is hard to see how death would have been experienced as alien or as a dreadful threat to our whole being. In a God-centered universe, what would have been unintelligible, and most alien to the true meaning of life, would be to live a life without direction or fulfillment in God. Life separated from the source and goal of life would have been a living death. Conversely, the way of wis-dom would accept dying as a dimension of life's ripening into the fullness of freedom, and as self-surrender to the further purposes of the Creator. Death would be experienced as peaceful passing over into a fulfillment that further life in this world could not offer.

Our historical situation is of course different. Human culture is infected with the bias of "original sin."[26] We are born into a world skewed away from its center and closed to the communion that God intends. To the degree that our existence is self-absorbed, in the measure that such self-absorption

23. See Janet Martin Soskice, "The Ends of Man and the Future of God," in Polkinghorne and Welker, *The End of the Word and the Ends of God*, 78-87, here 79.

24. Ibid., 86.

25. James Alison, *The Joy of Being Wrong: Original Sin through Easter Eyes* (New York: Crossroad, 1998), is illuminating in this whole area.

26. Alison, *Joy of Being Wrong*, is once more a basic reference.

makes life simply a self-contained personal project, death is experienced as menacing and meaningless. Life and death are locked in an absurd conflict, with death assured of victory. In such a dislocated pattern of experience, history is the sum total of egocentric projects. To a world premised on that kind of self-enclosure, the transcendent Otherness of God and the created otherness of our neighbor (and the neighborhood of nature) cannot but appear to be a threat. Everything is subjected to the self-serving demands of a skewed human freedom. As a consequence, the more human existence is turned in on itself, the more it occupies a shrinking universe. Identity is formed in competitive self-assertion against the Other. If the self-assertive ego works tirelessly to occupy center stage, it must interpret its role as dominating all else. Here death is the deepest threat: "The wages of sin is death." Death holds no promise of life; it is the carrier of all that is meaningless and threatening to the life we have chosen and made.[27]

Religion of one kind or another might be admitted as part of the picture. It is of some value if it cultivates the right kind of "god." The divinity in question would be the guarantor of the life we have chosen. It would be made in our image, and the projection of our own self-glorifying projects. Religion in this sense would be intent on invoking an idolatrous projection of the diseased and violent self. In that case, the glory of "god" would be intrinsically bound up with the life of self-promotion and domination of all others. To risk death for the sake of any other would be absurd. If God were anything more than a bounteous and helpful collaborator in hallowing my name, in bringing about my kingdom and implementing my will, that would be a most unsettling possibility; and my death would mean facing what my life in no way anticipated. If "god" were to appear in any other guise, it would be as the great rival waiting in the wings. Divine judgment would appear as a violent irruption into the system of self-worth.

All forms of idolatry and cultural atheism must cash their checks in the foreign currency of death. There are, of course, instances of heroic acceptance of absurdity and mortality. In a gesture of defiance, some may rage against the dying of the light. But in regard to the death such people die or even the deaths they may have caused, the universe is empty and silent. Still, unavoidable questions stir: Is death the meaningless outcome of the promising worlds of meaning in which lovers and artists, scientists and mystics, philosophers and scholars, parents and caregivers have lived? Is all the brave creativity of human freedom nothing but a futile posture in a world in which everything is destined to fail, and in which conscience informed with the highest values receives no vindication?

---

27. Rahner, *On the Theology of Death*, 32-51; Phan, *Eternity in Time*, 103-8.

The illusion cannot be total. Sooner or later, however much repressed, death faces each human being with his or her utter powerlessness to reduce life to a personal project. In the heart of this darkness and dispossession, there is also the possibility of a decisive choice. Will our death be in the end a final renunciation of illusion and our egomaniac projects, and become a final act of self-surrender to the will and purposes of the Other?[28] Or will it be the opposite: a final act of clinging to one's own project in pride and defiance in a meaningless universe?

Christian faith sees things differently. God is not made in our image; rather, we are made in the divine image. And the image of God is that of a Creator whose gifts of being and life culminate in the most radical form of self-giving. God so loved the world as to send his Son for its healing and salvation. The divine Other is the God of limitless love and mercy. To live to the full is to share in divine life, in union with the Son and breathing his Spirit. Those who have entered this other realm of existence, the Kingdom of God, pray that the reign of God will be fully realized among us, that God's will for our salvation will be accomplished, and that the name of the God of such self-giving goodness will be hallowed throughout all creation. In Christ, crucified and risen, his followers pass from a self-serving existence into a realm of eternal life. It is already begun in faith, hope, and love, gifts that will last (1 Cor 13:13), for those who have been open to the divine Gift. In this context of communion with God, the source of all life, death remains as the limit of this form of earthly life, but is transformed. It is an act of ultimate surrender to the Father in union with Christ. It is yielding to the ultimate creativity of the Spirit who makes all things new. Though death is experienced as a limit, it imposes no limits on the life-giving mercy of God.[29]

THE GIFT OF DEATH

Death and the Other

In moving to an explicitly Christian focus on the death and resurrection of Jesus, another kind of question can be asked. When considering the positive and negative aspects of death, have we been attempting to include it in some

---

28. Phan, *Eternity in Time*, 110-13.
29. Karl Rahner, "On Christian Dying," in *Theological Investigations*, vol. 7, trans. David Bourke (New York: Seabury, 1971), 285-93.

kind of larger synthesis? Have we been appealing to a kind of universal and somewhat abstract principle? Take the more positive approach of Boros, for example. As humbly as we can, we may ask whether what began as a correlation between the creativity of the human spirit and its fulfillment in death tames the reality of death in some way. It tends to homogenize the otherness of death into more of the same—that is, into the present experience of self. The ego is represented, theoretically at least, as repelling the lethal power of death and remaining essentially unaffected by it. Could it be that this mode of thinking, however profound and justified, ends in protecting the self from the utterly "new"? Is the self in question really welcoming the ultimately Other?

There is another important perspective to be considered. Becker has powerfully expressed what the German philosopher Martin Heidegger would call our "being-toward-death."[30] The humility and honesty that enter human existence through the recognition of our mortality progressively bring to awareness the uncanny "otherness" that is continually breaking into the system of expectations and controls. Through education, the startling otherness of human culture and science summons the child out of undifferentiated selfhood—beyond the experiential immediacy of infancy, beyond the pressures of the peer group, into a world of fact and truth and individual responsibility. More fundamental still, the face of the suffering other strikes home far more strongly than any ethical theory. The look on the face of the sufferer is a kind of moral accusative.[31] The self we experience is a self always claimed by the other. Authentic humanity is the quality of those who feel the weight and tug of responsibility in a world of many others.

The implication is that human consciousness is not a pure, open-ended, undecided subjective awareness seamlessly enfolding everything into itself. It is the experience of the self, in its deepest constitution, as bound and beholden to the other in its disconcerting strangeness and claim. This is not the cognitive grasp proper to an idealized, independently rational ego. A theoretical system of its nature can never quite handle the "otherness" of the Other. The rationally knowing self tries to keep this disconcerting Other at a safe distance by reducing it to the same and the familiar. But as life singles us out in a unique responsibility in regard to the other, the prospect of our own deaths (and the experience of the deaths of others) takes consciousness to an

---

30. Martin Heidegger, *Being and Time*, trans. John Macquarrie and Edward Robinson (Oxford: Blackwell, 1995).

31. Points powerfully made by Emmanuel Levinas in his many works. See especially *Otherwise Than Being or Beyond Essence*, trans. Alphonso Lingis (Pittsburgh: Duquesne University Press, 1999), 84-94.

inexpressible limit. It marks the outer limit of self-contained independence, while evoking the near edge of the Other that has called us into being.[32]

The experience of our moral and answerable existence affects the way we feel about death. It makes death appear as the moment of finally facing that original and final Other. Hitherto this Other had been only partially disclosed in all the others who have had a claim on our lives. But death is a final summons. It demands an unreserved self-surrender to this Other, and, implicitly at least, for the sake of others. In this way of looking at things, death is the moment when the reality of the Other breaks in on all self-defensive systems.[33] It breaks down our freedom to the point of pure self-abandon. The self can cling to nothing of its own. Hell, as "the second death" (Rev 20:14) would result from refusing this surrender, and being deliberately fixated on what offers no support. Was it Dostoevsky who said, "Hell is the place for those who refuse to die"? But it also leads to some intimation of heaven and to some notion of judgment and purgatory. The grain of wheat falling on the ground does not remain alone (Jn 12:24). From what has been said, it appears that death is of social and relational significance. Individual existence dies into a pure relationship of responsibility to the Other, for others, and even for the whole world.

At the heart of that history, death is the abyss that allows no theoretical solution. The dizzying extent of current scientific knowledge and control conceals the lack of any livable answer to the question posed by death. That answer has to be given, right into the black hole of death itself. It is up to human responsibility to wait on (at least the possibility of) such a gift. It can be received only in hope. It is shaped by the readiness to venture, beyond any knowledge or security, into the total risk of all that it can cling to. It must rely on what is totally Other. It must wait on the gift that only this Other can give.[34]

Death as Gift

Has it been given? Christians respond in terms of the gift of Christ's self-giving unto death for the sake of the world's salvation. This gift occurs so

---

32. See Jacques Derrida, *The Gift of Death*, trans. David Wills (Chicago: University of Chicago Press, 1995).

33. See Alison, *Joy of Being Wrong*, 74-78.

34. S. Bulkgakov asks, "Is this criterion of self-evaluation to be supplied by the image of the perfect divine personality incarnate in Christ or by the self-deifying human being in one or other of his limited earthly guises (humanity, the people, the proletariat, the superman), i.e., in the last analysis by his own ego standing before him in an heroic pose?" (cited in Valliere, *Modern Russian Theology*, 248-49).

that "by the grace of God, he might taste death for everyone" (Heb 2:9). Even more specifically, Christ is sent "so that he might . . . free those who all their lives were held in slavery by the fear of death" (Heb 2:14-15). In the gift of Christ, a multidimensional giving is at work. Christ gives himself in death for the salvation of the world. This looks back to the Father giving the Son into such a death. In the power of the Spirit, this death becomes a gift given into the dark abyss of the death of each Christian: "Those who believe in me, even though they die, they will live" (Jn 11:25). The realm of death is not annihilation or ultimate isolation. It is included in the way of the Son reaching into the darkest of human depths. The point most distant from life and from God is reached by self-giving love. The dark abyss of death is not outside the reach of the divine giver.[35] Nature is not the all-encompassing totality, but the gift of God that heals and transforms all that nature is. Nor is this gift simply identified with the dynamics of spiritual desire and aspiration. The eros of the human spirit, even when it looks beyond this world, does not hold within its grasp what can only be divinely given.

Christian hope opens itself to receive the gift of the One who "loved his own unto the end" (Jn 13:1). Jesus' self-offering in death is given as the form and energy of true life: "We know love by this, that he laid down his life for us—and we ought to lay down our lives for one another" (1 Jn 3:16). Paul, with his vivid awareness of this new order of grace, asks, "He who did not withhold his own Son, but gave him up for all of us, will he not with him also give us everything else?" (Rom 8:32). He goes on to proclaim that "neither death nor life . . . nor things present nor things to come . . . nor height not depth, nor anything else in all creation, will be able to separate us from the love of God in Christ Jesus, our Lord" (Rom 8:37-39).

When hope awakens to the universe of grace, all existence is laid open to the transforming power of the gift disclosed in the cross of Jesus. The more hope moves toward it, the more the lower and upper limits of the mystery of death are intensified. The crucifixion of Jesus was experienced by his first followers as the defeat of all he was and stood for. He was condemned, tortured, executed; he died and was buried. But now, in the light of his resurrection, Christian hope is sustained by the witness of these same early disciples. He appeared to them in the radiance of another life, as the conqueror of sin and death. Both the lower and upper limits of hope are extended. Theology, focused on the revelatory event of the death of Christ, holds together two seemingly conflicting vectors of experience. The saving mystery of this death

---

35. See Anthony J. Kelly and Francis J. Moloney, *Experiencing God in the Gospel of John* (New York: Paulist Press, 2003), especially chapter 11, "The God of Life in the World of Death" (pp. 238-50).

reaches deeper than any death we know. Jesus, in "tasting death for everyone," tastes the extent of evil, isolation, and rejection, the full weight of the sins of the world. His death reaches higher than anything life might naturally aspire to, namely, sharing in the deathless life of God. The crucified and living One embodies the ultimate life-form: "I am the first and the last, and the living One. I was dead, and see, I am alive forever and ever; and I have the keys of Death and Hades" (Rev 1:18).

Though hope relies on the God whose love is stronger than death, it has the realism to admit that "in the days of his flesh, Jesus offered up prayers and supplications, with loud cries and tears to him who was able to save him from death" (Heb 5:7). The God of life has acted. But the Father did not save Jesus from death, but vindicated and glorified him in his death, by raising him to a new order of life. As the form and source of new life, he is the firstborn from the dead (Col 1:18). The same realism contemplates his risen body marked forever by wounds of the cross. He bears forever the marks of his solidarity in suffering what most terrifies and defeats mortal beings: "by his wounds you have been healed" (1 Pet 2:25).

In the light of the gift of this death, hope looks through death and beyond it. But it does so first of all by being a way into it—in union with Christ in his death: "Since therefore the children share in flesh and blood, he himself like-wise partook of the same nature, that, through death, he might destroy him who has the power of death" (Heb 2:14-18). To be united with him in his death is to share his victory over all the demonic forces that work in human culture through the threat of death. By sharing in his death, hope is already sharing in his resurrection (cf. Rom 6:3-5). Still, hope remains hope. It is never immune to the darkness of life. It must show its own patience. It means waiting for the whole mystery of love to prove itself stronger than death and all the demonic powers that use the threat of death for their purposes. The New Testament expresses a sober realism:

> As it is, we do not yet see everything in subjection to them. But we see Jesus who for a little while was made lower than the angels, crowned with glory and honour because of the suffering of death so that by the grace of God he might taste death for everyone. (Heb 2:8-9)

There is a further edge at which theology trembles: the mystery of God. The holy and immortal God does not die (*hagios athanatos*). Yet there is some-thing about the way God is God, about the way the Trinity is these three self-giving divine persons, which leads death into the deepest darkness of all. This deeper darkness is not a threat, but an intimation of life in its trinitarian and most vital dimensions. Union with Christ in his death is most radically self-abandonment to the Father. It yields to the incalculable creativity of the life-giving Spirit. It means incorporation into the body of Christ. In this trinitarian frame of reference, a self-surrender is inevitably asked of each mortal one of us. But that is to share in the unreserved self-emptying of the divine three in relation to each other and to the world that they have created and drawn into their communal life.

Our dying demands a final letting go of all that we have and are in this life. In this, it is the last, and perhaps the only truly genuine act of adoration of the God whose life is self-giving love. Only by dying out of the cultural and biological systems and projects structuring this present existence are human beings remade in conformity with the self-giving and communal trinitarian life of God. Death is a revelatory entry into the divine vitality: "What we will be has not yet been revealed . . . when he is revealed we shall be like him" (1 Jn 3:2). With Paul we have pondered why it is that "the wages of sin is death," but the rest of the sentence points to a more hopeful conclusion: "but the free gift of God is eternal life in Christ Jesus our Lord" (Rom 6:23).

Only when the believer finds no support save in God's gift can hope come into its own. As Ghislain Lafont points out, dying in Christ means a recentering of our existence along truly personal lines.[36] Autonomous existence within the world yields to an unbroken life of communion with God, and with all in God. To hope is to live the conviction, "whether we live or whether we die, we are the Lord's" (Rom 14:8). In the dark radiance of this gift, "living is Christ, and dying is gain" (Phil 1:21).

---

36. Ghislain Lafont, *Peut-on connaitre Dieu en Jésus-Christ?* (Paris: Cerf, 1969), 237-58. For the broader context, see Anne Hunt, *The Trinity and the Paschal Mystery: A Development in Recent Catholic Theology* (Collegeville, Minn.: Liturgical Press, 1997), chapter 2, "Death and Being, Human and Divine" (pp. 37-56). In regard to eschatology, see Anne Hunt, *Trinity: Nexus of the Mysteries of Christian Faith* (Maryknoll, N.Y.: Orbis Books, 2005), chapter 11, "Trinity and Eschatology" (pp. 200-215).

6

Purgatory

The Realism of Hope

THE DOCTRINE OF PURGATORY is a realistic dimension of hope. Hope does not need to pretend. No human one of us is without imperfections, blind spots, and ambiguities. All of us have been affected by the violence of history. If such distortions are not evident to oneself, there are plenty of others to remind us that we have not reached a state of pure perfection. There is room, then, for a final stage or state of growth, and this will mean some form of purification from the residue of sin and selfishness.

The Christian doctrine of purgatory has a family resemblance to the immemorial spiritual traditions of Southeast Asia regarding reincarnation (*metempsychosis*, or "transmigration of souls"). In general, reincarnation envisages that the human soul assumes another body after death. As long as a state of true purity of being is not reached, terrestrial life will go on in some other appropriate form. By a strange mutation, this typically Eastern doctrine of purification has entered into the popular religiosity of the West as a kind of hope. It is estimated that some 25 percent of Europeans believe in some form of reincarnation. It displays both similarities to and differences from the way Christian hope speaks of purgatory. Some comparison and contrast, then, is both desirable and inevitable.

THE CHRISTIAN DOCTRINE OF PURGATORY

But first let us clarify the theological meaning of purgatory. A variety of historical investigations have thrown considerable light on the historical emergence of this doctrine. For example, it appears that Augustine was the first to consider 1 Corinthians 3:10-15 in a purgatorial light. There was, however, always a larger context. For Augustine and other early theologians, purification was a divine, redemptive activity at work in the trials of life and anticipating the final judgment.[1] Historians such as Jacques Le Goff have

---

1. Jaroslav Pelikan, *The Emergence of the Catholic Tradition (100–600)* (Chicago: University

deftly placed many of the stages and turns in the development of the Catholic doctrine of purgatory in their historical and cultural settings.[2] Moreover, the ecumenical context of theology today has expanded the mystery of God's purifying and transforming love beyond the bounds of its distinctively Catholic formulation. As a result, purgatory has been set in a larger, more nuanced, and generous context.

Church Teaching

The formal church teaching on purgatory is quite modest. For the most part, it arose out of the tradition of praying for the departed. Some sense of purification in, or after, death has been present in both Western and Eastern Christianity at least from the third century. As a doctrine, it was defined only in the West—at the Second Council of Lyons (1274), the Council of Florence (1439), and the Council of Trent (1563). The first two instances arose out of discussion with the Eastern Churches. The third was a response to the Protestant Reformers.

These definitions are in fact quite minimal. They add up to three points:

1. There is a state of purification after death.
2. In this state of purification, any guilt is expiated and punishment is remitted as a prelude to admission to the beatific vision.
3. Those in purgatory can be helped by the prayers and good works of the faithful in this life.

The Council of Trent, while affirming the existence of purgatory and the church's solidarity with the fate of the dead through prayer and the eucharist,[3] warns against excessive theorizing about what is necessarily beyond our experience:

> The difficult and subtle questions which do not make for edification and for the most part are not conducive to piety must be excluded from popular sermons . . . likewise anything belonging to the realm of superstition or smacking of dishonourable gain.[4]

---

of Chicago Press, 1971), 355-57; idem, *The Spirit of Eastern Christendom (600–1700)* (Chicago: University of Chicago Press, 1974), 279.

2. Jacques Le Goff, *The Birth of Purgatory*, trans. A. Goldhammer (Chicago: University of Chicago Press, 1984).

3. Peter Beer, "Purgatory, Trent and Today," *Australasian Catholic Record* 61, no. 4 (October 1984): 369-84.

4. J. Neuner and J. Dupuis, *The Christian Faith in the Doctrinal Documents of the Catholic Church* (London: Collins, 1982), # 2310.

Vatican II introduces purgatory in referring to the pilgrim nature of the church. The communion of believers spreads over time and reaches beyond the barrier of death:

> Some of [Christ's] disciples are pilgrims on earth, while others have died and are being purified, and still others are glorified . . . we all in various ways . . . share in the same love of God and neighbour, and we all sing the same hymn to the glory of God. (*Lumen Gentium* 49-50)

Scriptural Witness

Today's biblical scholarship does not permit any direct proof of Catholic teaching on the existence or nature of purgatory. Its biblical foundation has to be sought more in the abundant scriptural reference to the holiness, justice, and love of God purifying the individual and the community. Biblical references to the whole scope of God's purifying and liberating action cannot be compressed into the particular Catholic theme of purgatory as it emerged within the tradition. Still, there are some key biblical texts:

- 2 Maccabees 12:39-46: the exhortation to pray for the dead who have fallen in battle and are found to be wearing pagan amulets
- 1 Corinthians 15:29: the mysterious practice of being baptized for the dead
- Luke 12:59: the necessity of making full reparation
- 1 Corinthians 3:9-15 (this most frequently used text): the "fire" that tests the sort of work each one has done

Clearly, the focus of the New Testament is on the salvation that God has wrought in Christ. What that salvation means in particular contexts, such as the post-mortem fate of the Christian believer, was left to later generations to ponder.[5]

Some Historical Witnesses

The church has always included the dead in her prayers. A beautiful example of intercession for the dead is to be found in the *Acts of the Martyrdom of St. Perpetua*. As she awaits her execution in Carthage, in early March 203, Per-

---

5. Joseph Ratzinger, *Eschatology: Death and Eternal Life*, trans. M. Walstein (Washington, D.C.: Catholic University of America Press, 1988), 218-28.

petua is inspired to pray for her young brother Dinocrates, who had probably died without being baptized. Her vision ends ". . . when I awoke and understood that he had been translated from his pains."[6] Another familiar example is St. Augustine's prayer on the death of his mother, Monica. Though he knows her to be a holy woman, he can acknowledge that she, too, was subject to human frailty and so could profit from prayers for the dead. He wrote in his grieving,

> At last, that wound of my heart was healed which might have seemed blameworthy for the earthliness of its affection, and I pour out unto thee, our God, on behalf of thy handmaid, a far different kind of tears, flowing from a spirit stricken by the remembrance of the dangers of every soul that "dies in Adam." Therefore, my praise and my life, God of my heart, as I lay aside her good deeds for which I rejoice and give thanks to thee, I now entreat thee for the sins of my mother.[7]

Augustine's prayer exemplifies the deep human need to deal with grief and the loss of dear ones, the desire to be reunited with them, and the recollection of the ambiguity inherent in every human life.

The original prayerful mood out of which this doctrine arose is classically expressed in the great intercession from the liturgy of St. John Chrysostom:

> Let us pray also for the repose of the souls of the departed servants of God, and for the forgiveness of their every transgression, deliberate and indeliberate . . . give rest, O Lord, to the souls of your departed servants in a place of light, in a place of refreshment, in a place of repose from which pain, sorrow, and sighing have fled. Because you are so good and love mankind, forgive their every offence, whether in word or deed or thought; for there is no one living and never will be, who does not sin: but you alone are without sin.[8]

"For there is no one living and never will be who does not sin." Here we are close to the fundamental meaning that the symbol of purgatory conveys. It suggests a sober estimate of the human condition coupled with surrender to the transforming power of grace. There is no optimistic repression of our flawed humanity, nor any pretending to a perfection that would take us out

---

6. See *The Passion of SS. Perpetua and Felicity*, trans. and ed. W. H. Shewring (London: Sheed & Ward, 1931).

7. *The Confessions of St Augustine* (New York: Airmont, 1969), 168-69.

8. Quoted from George Maloney, *The Everlasting Now* (Notre Dame, Ind.: Ave Maria Press, 1980), 64.

of our pilgrim state. The realities of human frailty in even the best of us invite hope to a further limit. We offer them, and ourselves, to the purifying love of the Crucified.

In this context, St. Catherine of Genoa's pre-Reformation *Treatise on Purgatory* (1510) is of special value. Unfortunately it did not appear until 1551, forty years after her death, at a time when Protestant reactions to the Catholic tradition in this matter were most intense.[9] What is remarkable in this saint's writings is the way she removed the purificatory suffering from any implication of divine punishment inflicted on the sinner from the outside, as it were. For her, the process of purification is freely and even joyously embraced for the sake of union with God:

> I believe no happiness can be found worthy to be compared to the soul in Purgatory except that of the saints in paradise. And, day by day, this happiness grows as God flows into these souls more and more, as the hindrance to his entrance is consumed. Sin's rust is the hindrance, and the fire burns the rust away, so that more and more the soul opens itself up to the divine inflowing. As the rust lessens and the soul is opened up to the divine ray, happiness grows, until the time be accomplished, the one wanes and the other waxes . . . As for the will, never can the soul say these pains are pains, so contented are they with what God ordains with which, in pure charity, their will is united.[10]

We can keep St. Catherine's words in mind when we come to the topic of purgatorial suffering. But first, a larger context.

The Communion of Saints

A theology of purgatory develops from the point where the mysteries of our unity in Christ and our communion in the Holy Spirit intersect and find expression in the practice of praying for the dead. The symbol of purgatory is part of the corporate imagination of hope. The church prays for the departed and expresses its hope for each one: "Remember those who have died in the peace of Christ, and all the dead whose faith is known to you alone."[11]

---

9. Herbert Thurston, *The Memory of Our Dead* (London: Burns & Oates, 1918), 195-200.

10. St. Catherine of Genoa, *On Purgatory*, trans. Charlotte Balfour and Helen Irvine (New York: Sheed & Ward, 1946), 18-19.

11. The Roman Missal, Eucharistic Prayer IV.

When Christians pray for the dead, it is as a consequence of their solidarity in the communion of saints.[12] Any suggestion that the prayers of the living are an attempt to interfere, however benignly, in the personal destiny of the other arises out of a comparatively recent, highly individualized notion of personhood. It is possible to think of oneself as an enclosed monad, unrelated to anyone or anything else. But this is more a symptom of the self-assertive individualism of late capitalism. It certainly has no place in a truly philosophical or Christian understanding of the intrinsic relationality of the human self. On the other hand, when an aggressively individualistic attitude dominates social life, it becomes the engine of consumerist obsessions. When this self-absorbed, all-consuming sense of personhood appears as its most desirable or "natural" expression, we have further reason for hoping that some form of purgatory will exist.

What bears stressing today is that our actual individuation in the worlds of both nature and grace is a far more corporate matter than the individualist bias of modern culture suggests. To exist as a person is to be in relation to others. Born into a family, each person lives from others. Living in a society, each one lives with others. Sharing and breathing a common culture, each one lives through others and the multiple ways in which they have made the world intelligible and hospitable to life. When each one lives in a community, he or she cannot escape the responsibility of living for others in the promotion of the common good. In other words, as individual persons we coexist in communities and societies. In our responsible relationships with others, we not only coexist, but "pro-exist," that is, exist "for the other" in our freedom and generativity. Every human person carries the grace and burden of the whole human community. But Christian hope sees all this subsumed in an even higher level of shared life, namely, our corporate unity in Christ and the Spirit.

The more the collective and social dimensions of human existence are acknowledged, the more the value of praying for others can be appreciated. But we must note, first of all, that all prayer is a gift. Whether we pray for ourselves or others, we pray through the grace of the Holy Spirit. Our asking and seeking and knocking on the door (Lk 11:9-13) are not a matter of changing the will of God. On the contrary, they signify that the gracious will of God is being actualized within us. For the desire expressed in prayer is from God. It is a grace. God works to make us receptive to that fullness of

---

12. Elizabeth Johnson (*Friends of God and Prophets: A Feminist Theological Reading of the Communion of Saints* [New York: Continuum, 1998]) contributes a distinctive perspective to this traditional theme.

life that God wills for each and all. In this perspective, intercessory prayer, as a hope-filled desire for the good of the other, is the gift of God. It inspires a more intense unity in the Spirit and a more compassionate solidarity in Christ. Praying for others is a relational conduct proper to the members of the body of Christ. The Spirit of Christ, acting within the interpersonal reality of human freedom, makes it an expanding field of love, compassion, and communion.

Understood in this way, intercession is a sharing in the self-giving love of God. The Spirit of love inspires the members of Christ to be agents of grace for one another, and "for everyone" (1 Tim 2:1). The life of the whole body is involved in each of its members, just as the progress of each individual member affects the life of the whole. Praying for the dead is a specific form of intercession. It acts out of the fundamental solidarity of all in Christ. Paul assures us that neither "death . . . nor heights nor depths, nor things present nor things to come, can separate us from the love of God in Christ Jesus" (Rom 8:38f.). Neither do such cosmic realities separate us from one another in the communion of life and love that the Spirit gives.

Understood in this way, it is immaterial whether our prayers are strictly contemporaneous with the death of the departed. What matters is not the space-time extension of our present existence but the eternal dimension of God's love in which we are members of one body and commune in the one Spirit. All the intercessions that have been made, or will be made, for anyone are of the Spirit's inspiration. All our prayers for others share in the prayer of Christ "since he always lives to make intercession" for us (see Heb 7:25). In the universe of grace, such prayers are all part of God's gift to each one in life and in death. In the eternity of love, therefore, it is not as though prayer works to make God's love more merciful. The opposite is the case. An indicator of God's predestining grace for each one is the Spirit's continuing inspiration of intercessions on their behalf. In the eternity of love, each one comes to salvation through the prayer of all. In the communion of saints, all participate in the salvation of each one.

Admittedly, in the history of the West, the practice of praying for the dead was often infected by a rather legal or even penal form of imagination.[13] This was notably instanced in abuses associated with the sale of indulgences. But that unfortunate caricature should not be allowed to obscure the reality of the intercessory bond, in life and in death, joining all in the communion of saints.

---

13. Wolfhart Pannenberg, *Systematic Theology*, vol. 3, trans. G. W. Bromiley (Grand Rapids: Eerdmans, 1998), 308-11, in relation to the "sacrifice of the Mass."

THE SUFFERING OF PURGATORY

It is important to keep in mind that eschatology offers no guided tour of the afterlife. The only way anything about "the other side" can be expressed is by way of analogies drawn from human experience and by cultivating a certain holographic sense of how all the mysteries of faith interconnect in the consideration of any particular question of hope. We have already drawn attention to the reverent negativity characteristic of all New Testament expression of hope (chapter 3). Only in terms of *here* can a tentative language of the *hereafter* be possible. By extrapolating from the present we can come to some dim approximation of what is to come. With this qualification, purgatory is a symbol of a possible future purification.

When considering the suffering involved in post-mortem purification, it is important to keep the imagination focused on the central mysteries of faith and hope. Otherwise, the sense of proportion so tellingly expressed in the previously cited words of St. Catherine of Genoa is distorted. When the sufferings of the holy souls are imagined as penalties inflicted or imposed by God on the sinner, hope must protest. The divine realm of grace and mercy is being subverted by petty, penal calculations arising out of thoroughly unredeemed systems of justice. The Father of mercies does not "go by the book" in the administration of an economy of scarce grace. Little wonder Protestant theologians of the past and the present protest against any such implication. If the doctrine of purgatory should ever compromise the all-sufficiency of the grace of Christ, it can hardly figure in Christian orthodoxy. Moreover, there is the problem of "dolorism," as though the final stage of salvation was reached by sheer suffering. This is the burden of Paul Tillich's complaint: "In Catholic doctrine, mere suffering does the purging . . . it is a theological mistake to derive transformation from pain alone instead of from grace which gives blessedness within pain."[14] Jürgen Moltmann, pondering the question, Is there life after death?, considers that the reformers were not criticizing the idea of God's history with human beings continuing after death.[15] Nor, he states, were they questioning the community of the living and the dead in Christ.[16] It is clearly time for a more ecumenical grasp of the

---

14. Paul Tillich, *Systematic Theology III* (Chicago: University of Chicago Press, 1951), 417.

15. Jürgen Moltmann, "Is There Life After Death?" in *The End of the World and the Ends of God*, ed. J. C. Polkinghorne and M. Welker (Harrisburg, Pa.: Trinity Press International, 2000), 238-255. The more traditional Protestant view is expressed in Stanley J. Grenz, *Theology for the Community of God* (Grand Rapids: Eerdmans, 1994), 589-92.

16. Moltmann, "Is There Life After Death?" 248.

issues.[17] The Reformation tradition has rightly insisted that any interpretation of God's love as either merited or appeased by suffering would be a distortion. The Christian psyche would be sent reeling in hopeless contradictions. The God of such a purgatory would be hopelessly less than a human lover. If suffering established our worth in God's eyes, then an eternity with such an exacting God would be a fearful prospect.

Yet hope must be realistic. It does not paper over the human situation nor ignore the desirability of further purification for the unfinished beings we are and know, in order that all arrive at the full integrity of their being in Christ. Still, purification does involve some kind of suffering. But it is a suffering born out of love. As this love grows to its fullest realization in unreserved surrender, it works to purge the soul of all attachments to anything less than the infinite mystery of God.

The first and last thing, in this context as in all eschatological questions, is God's saving grace. Consequently, purgatory must be interpreted in terms of the divine compassion for the human condition. God's love reaches the limited human beings that we are. Far from pretending that evil is good, that imperfection is fulfillment, or that our fragmented being is already our best selves, redemptive love works for our complete transformation. But transformation looks to conversion. Human freedom throughout life is distracted and stratified. It prays to be integrated into the pure love of God, with whole heart and soul, mind and strength. We are commanded to love our neighbor as ourselves, not as selves destined to be left unfinished and ambiguous, but as selves fully conformed to Christ (Mk 12:30-31).

The symbol of purgatory refers, then, to our unfinished existence exposed to the living flame of the Holy Spirit. Our existence becomes fully attentive to the living and active Word of God at the deepest level of our being. At that point, there can be no evasion: all are "naked and laid bare to the eyes of the one to whom we must render an account" (Heb 4:12-13). The suffering involved is not so much imposed or inflicted by God. It is rather suffering *from* God, or, more simply, suffering *God*. For the divine mystery is encountered in the utter otherness of its reality. It is also the love for whom we were made, and in whom alone we find our real identity or "glory." The Holy Spirit is the fire that burns away the wood, hay, and straw of all egoism to expose the foundations of what we truly are and most desire to be (1 Cor 3:12-15). The demons that have driven us are finally exorcised. The idols we have cultivated are exposed for what they are, projections of a self fearful of the infinite otherness of God, even if that Other is believed to be love.

---

17. Note Pannenberg's historical analysis of the situation in *Systematic Theology*, 3:573-80.

But love purifies as "the fire that burns away our dross and reforms us to be vessels of eternal joy."[18]

A THEOLOGY OF PURGATORY

Purgatory has, then, its place in the theology of hope. In a theology of purgatory, the following eight perspectives converge.

A Purifying Self-Realization

Purgatory supposes a purification appropriate to the realization of the self that God intends us to be. The Spirit of holiness is acting in the moment of death or in the "process" of dying. Under the action of the Spirit, the self moves out of the "concupiscence"[19] of our complicity in the dynamics of violence and exclusion that are so inextricably bound up with the history of the world. The last vestiges of presumption now yield to the unconditional surrender of hope. The inevitable self-centeredness that has structured each life is now confronted with that infinite Otherness that was, at every moment, the eternal depth and source of our being. The restless fragmentation and compromise of our being-in-the-world now comes to a decisive moment of integration. It is a moment of yielding without reserve to the Reign of God. It is no longer a matter of backing defensively into this other Kingdom. The wariness born of being too vulnerable to a world dismissive of the power of love and forgiveness is dissolved. The self is now called to turn forward and to embrace, in full freedom, the mystery of love in all its dimensions.

As the Other draws near, "what we shall be" (1 Jn 3:2) begins to appear. We begin to breathe the pure air of another place, which we recognize as our true home. The self that was in the making, that stirred beneath the egotistic stratagems and projections of a lifetime, now awakens to its full proportions. Our true identity is found only in God. The self that we thought was our exclusive possession is revealed to be a self-in-God and a self-for-God. It is as though we arrive at our first pure act of adoration—of the infinitely Other who all along was our loving creator and our final goal. This true self had always been there. But it was often enough concealed beneath the masks of an ego shaped by the pressures, distractions, defenses, compromises, and projections inherent in our divided existence (i.e., "concupiscence") in the world. It was

---

18. Ratzinger, *Eschatology*, 231.

19. James Alison, *The Joy of Being Wrong: Original Sin through Easter Eyes* (New York: Crossroad, 1998), 222.

there, likewise *incognito*, in the intimations and anticipations of hope and prayer, in egoless moments of love, joy, wonder, gratitude, and forgiveness. In this purgatorial self-realization, the fragmentation and meandering of life in time come to an end. The true self comes into its own, in the utter simplicity of its God-ward-ness. Before this integrating moment, the tumbling torrent of life had just swept us along. We had either been ahead of our true selves, impatient with the ambiguities of our life in time. Or we had been behind our selves, clinging to false versions of who we really were. But now an eternal love gathers all the scattered fragments of our selves in time into the form and features of our true being. We catch up with the person, the self that God has been creating all along.[20] We begin to know who we are for the first time, and so to confront all that is false and unfinished in our being. If this can be called suffering, it is the pain of being born into the inexpressibly other world in which God is the light.

Purgatory as "Particular Judgment"

To awaken to one's real identity in its deepest God-ward-ness is a moment of truth. It takes place inevitably as what has been traditionally called "particular judgment." But this is not a judgment passed on us by God. One's spiritual performance is not being assessed by an external authority. The judgment concerned takes place as the disclosure of the reality that one's entire history has distilled. What we truly are, what we have decided to be, what we stand for, now appears in its full evidence. As if waking from the semiconsciousness of a coma, we "come to" in that Light (1 Jn 1:5) in whom there is no darkness.[21] There is no place to hide. To change the metaphor, the torrent of our episodic freedom and flickering loves finally settles into a space that can fully contain it. Freedom now knows its final shape. Whatever appears, cannot be denied. With the dawning of eternity, the time of evasion, pretense, and partly living vanishes forever.

Meeting Christ

This particular judgment is necessarily a moment of decisive encounter with Christ. In him, we are confronted with the ultimate form of human exis-

---

20. See Ladislaus Boros, *The Moment of Truth: Mysterium Mortis*, trans. G. Bainbridge (London: Burns & Oates, 1962), 86-98.
21. Compare John Polkinghorne, *The God of Hope and the End of the World* (London: Yale University Press, 2002), 125-31.

tence. He is met as the "truth" fundamental to each one's unique identity. We become aware of ourselves as being made through him, for him, in him (Col 1:15-18). In that piercing encounter, the distortions of our existence are made evident. With that meeting comes the realization that we are not yet in every aspect of our being wholly in Christ and fully subject to him. To accommodate the graphic phrase of Paul, the "rubbish" of false alliances and justifications must now be renounced and left behind. It is a matter of suffering "the loss of all things in order to gain Christ and be found in him" (Phil 3:9). We are left with no other identity, no other power of action, save through what we have in him. It is as though every believer comes in the end to what Paul describes about himself in his desire to know Christ and to be conformed to him in his cross and resurrection: "Not that I have attained this or have already reached the goal; but I press on to make it my own, because Christ Jesus has made me his own; but this one thing I do: forgetting what lies behind and straining forward to what lies ahead, I press on toward the goal for the prize of the heavenly call of God in Christ" (Phil 3:12-14).

The terminal tension between Christ as the goal and form of our existence and what, in fact, we are, suggests in some way in what the purifying suffering of purgatory consists. In short, Christ is the particular judgment passed on our existence, the incendiary light in which all is made clear. Ladislaus Boros summarizes this point with special eloquence:

Christ looks with utter love and complete graciousness on the one who comes to him. At the same time his gaze burns right into the innermost parts of that human existence. To encounter God in Christ's eyes of fire is the highest fulfilment of our capacity for love and also the most fearful suffering our nature ever has to bear . . . the encounter with Christ would be our Purgatory.[22]

Conformity to the Crucified

Implicit in the encounter with Christ is conformity to his self-surrender to God for the life of the world. If this moment of truth reveals the anti-Christ or the counter-Christ within us, it is also a final entry into his dying. We are summoned to die as he died. We must now fully participate in his self-offering to the Father in the love of the Spirit. It is dying to all that resists God's Kingdom. In the depths of the resistant self, Christ now appears as

22. Boros, *Moment of Truth*, 138-39.

"the way." He has descended into the hell of every aspect of our separation from God. From there, he now summons us to follow him in his death and to share in his dying, to become pure self-surrender to the Father. Purgatory is the process of participating fully in his self-emptying for the world's salvation. He who died *for* us now dies *in* us in order that each individual existence will be a passion for God. The Crucified comes to release us from all clinging to life in any other form. To meet him leads to the moment of unqualified self-surrender—the loving but dreaded letting go of anything less than being totally from and for God. As Paul writes, "I want to know Christ and the power of his resurrection and the sharing of his sufferings by becoming like him in his death, if somehow I may attain the resurrection from the dead" (Phil 3:10-11).

The eminent Anglican theologian John Macquarrie nicely sums up this point:

> The kind of suffering envisaged in Purgatory is not an external penalty that has to be paid, but it is our suffering with Christ, our being crucified with him as we are conformed to him, the painful surrender of the ego-centred self that the God-centred self of love may take its place.[23]

The Suffering of Love

The suffering of purgatory is the suffering born of love. Any experience of love, be it in marriage, family, friendship, or community, is experienced as uncanny gift: to be loved and to love in return. With love, something new occurs in the foundations of our being. It touches the depths of who we are. It calls forth wondrous other-directed energies. At the same time, we are given back to ourselves in a greater intensity of life. But precisely because love is such a gift, it brings its own kind of suffering. To the degree that any great love possesses us, it makes us aware of ourselves in a new humility. For love unmasks our selfishness. It threatens our independence by demanding too much, not unlike the way the birth of a child subverts the settled organization of its parents' lives.

Though love may be a bracing liberation of what had too long lain hidden, it also becomes in some sense a burden and a demand. This kind of suffering is not inflicted on us by the beloved other. It is, rather, the pain inherent in

---

23. John Macquarrie, *Principles of Christian Theology* (London: SCM, 1970), 329.

unsettling claims of love itself. As love inspires and summons forth our best selves, it also brings into awareness our tendencies to possessiveness, self-absorption, and envy. There is even a certain dread of losing what is most valued. In this sense, love is a painful gift. Augustine's appeal, "Show me a lover and he will understand," is applicable here. Only the lover understands the pain of not being fully accessible to the other, of not having enough freedom to be completely for the beloved.

In this regard, there is a further curious aspect of human experience that suggests some analogy of purgatorial suffering. It is the fear of being loved. We are tempted to cling defensively to the security of an isolated self. Hidden deep in the joy of new loves and old, there is an intimation of a special kind of death: the need to die out of a self-centered pattern of life into a new world of relationships. The new self that love summons forth can only be realized through a continual struggle of self-giving and yielding to the other. The cost of entering this new, more real world can appear too high.

There are many examples of the suffering that love can cause. The searching intimacy and open-ended responsibilities of marriage and family, the continuing negotiations of true friendship, the ongoing discipline of communication for any community, the taxing agenda of all the meetings required in the promotion of a worthwhile cause—all are examples of what is usually taken for granted. These familiar experiences tell us something about the suffering of purgatory. The lucid but burning awareness of an ultimate love exposes all our residual unworthiness and unwillingness in its regard. Purgatory, from this point of view, is the moment when the fundamental love of one's lifetime finally comes to terms with itself.

Attaining Compassionate Existence

Through the suffering inherent in love, purgatory represents the expansion of our being to a truly compassionate existence. We awaken to the demands of ultimate Christlike love and to all the relationships that this implies: "Amen, amen, I say to you, unless a grain of wheat falls into the ground and dies, it remains just a single grain; but if it dies, it bears much fruit" (Jn 12:24). The individuality of one's existence must become open to the many, in the solidarity of suffering that compassion implies. Each member of the body of Christ begins to feel something of the totality of suffering of the whole Christ—to which each has undoubtedly contributed. Sinfulness has in fact held us back from a fully creative immersion in human history. Our lack of love has left others unloved, unforgiven, ignored, and rejected. In moving out of any self-regarding exclusion of others, the vitality of true life stirs within us: "those who hate their life in this world will keep it for eternal life" (Jn 12:25).

Our purgatory is, then, the process of our becoming a truly compassionate presence in the heart of human history. Suffering of this kind is not the kind of pain that isolates us from the rest of the world. On the contrary, it causes us to belong more deeply to crises and struggles that had previously left us indifferent and unconcerned.

In some larger sense, purgatory can be conceived of as leading to a universal reconciliation, as Miroslav Volf has suggested.[24] There must be a time of forgiving and asking forgiveness, in ways that were not possible within the course of history. All have profited from the exploitation of others, as one race drives out the weaker and empires are built on any number of oppressed peoples. Heaven can be populated only by those who have forgiven the sins of the past and asked forgiveness for the harm they have caused. It is not fanciful to imagine that this process of reconciliation is the purification implied in any theologically valid notion of purgatory.

This may be the point that Christians have most to learn from the myths of reincarnation. Though theology is reluctant to put too much credence in reports of souls being sent back to earth to undo the harm they have done, and so forth, there is a deep truth hidden in such necessarily naive expressions. The world we have left behind has suffered from the distortion of our own particular history. Each human life has, at least to some degree, left a polluting vapor trail in the atmosphere of life. We may have loved humanity, but the actual human beings who formed the community of our lives were the problem. We easily rationalized our indifference to the sufferings of others. They were not our responsibility. Our failures to forgive were often paraded as tough intolerance of human stupidity or wickedness. On the other hand, we could easily be very tolerant of what was most destructive of the community and society, hardly aware of our complicity in patterns of exploitation and oppression. Perhaps everyone has to admit that in so many ways we simply did not connect with the reality of the actual people who made up our lives: parent, child or relative; friend and neighbor; stranger and enemy. These were all *there* in the drama of our life's history, but we never had enough love to give.

Purgatory, then, must be considered a deeper immersion in the Spirit of unity and compassion, as each becomes more fully a member of the body of Christ. We die out of the violently patterned individuality into the real-

---

24. See Miroslav Volf, "The Final Reconciliation: Reflections on the Social Dimension of the Eschatological Transition," *Modern Theology* 16, no. 1 (2000): 91-113.

ity of true personhood. The hard core of the individuality we so carefully defended is now melted. True life beckons as a loving embrace of the other. It flows in a tide of relationality. Like the trinitarian persons themselves, each one of us is called to become a pure relationship to the other and to all. We must suppose that this expansion of our being will be humbling and painful. Yet there must be joy too: we are on the way to becoming pure grace for others. We begin to affirm and value the other, where before, in any number of ways, we may have ignored or denied it. Love burns the resistant selfishness out of us and transforms us into agents of healing and redemption, especially for those who have been given into our care. This phase of purification brings about within us that "greatest love" of laying down life itself for others. We begin to share in the compassion of Christ himself (Jn 15:13; 1 Jn 3:16). It will mean knowing for the first time, completely and unambiguously, that "we have passed from death to life because we love one another" (1 Jn 3:14).

The Flame of the Holy Spirit

The purifying fires of purgatory are most radically exposure to the "living flame of the Holy Spirit" (cf. Lk 3:16; 12:49; Acts 2:3; 1 Thes 5:19). It possesses and transforms. As the Spirit of God reaches into the deepest core of our being, it transforms and purifies. This purgatorial action must be set in the larger context of the Christian vocation.[25] The Spirit of love gives life, redeems, reconciles, liberates, and purifies,[26] to open every stage of existence to a further fulfillment. The Holy Spirit indwells the human spirit as the ecstasy toward the otherness of the ever-greater God. It is the Spirit of rebirth, of awakening to a new order of life. In this present life, the Spirit works to detach us from any clinging to the past or to lesser versions of ourselves, to lead us on to what was still to be realized, to the eschatologically new. The Spirit of unity turns the bias of individualistic self-enclosure out of itself toward a larger belonging to the community of others, in love and service. The Spirit works to conform us to the crucified Christ that we might die and rise with him. As the Spirit of the creative love, it cannot rest content with anything less than our whole, free selves in a transformed universe.

But each transformation implies a death. It is the suffering of dying out of lesser egocentric versions of the self, and of dying into the ultimate dimen-

---

25. On the fire of purgatory, see Pannenberg, *Systematic Theology*, 3:617-20.

26. For the tradition of the cleansing fire, see R. B. Eno, "The Fathers and the Cleansing Fire," *Irish Theological Quarterly* 53, no. 3 (1987): 184-202.

sions of life. The great mystics speak of the "dark night" of suffering as all the glaring objects of secure little worlds become dark in the radiance of ultimate light.[27] As Yves Congar observes, "in Purgatory, we will all be mystics."[28] John of the Cross begins his *Living Flame of Love* with the following stanzas:

> O living flame of love
> That tenderly wounds my soul
> At is deepest centre! Since
> Now you are not oppressive,
> Now consummate! If it be your will
> Tear through the veil of this sweet encounter!
>
> O sweet cautery, O delightful wound!
> O gentle hand, O delicate touch
> That tastes of eternal life
> And pays every debt!
> In killing you changed death to life.[29]

The great Spanish mystic gives a clue to the final purification as the flame of the Holy Spirit penetrates, possesses, and finally transforms all that we are.

The "Time" of Purgatory

When speaking of the duration of purgatory, there are two possible types of language. Admittedly, we cannot escape from imagining such duration within the space-time structure of our present existence. Insofar as purgatory is an encounter with the risen Lord, inasmuch as it is a definitive entry into the death of Jesus, the language of a *moment* of purification and perfect contrition seems appropriate. From such a point of view, temporal duration makes little sense.

On the other hand, if we conceive of purgatory as a new, compassionate relationship with the history of the world adversely affected by our failures in love, then we can speak of it in terms of *historical duration*. We cannot be completely in heaven as long as our sin-affected history continues.

---

27. See John of the Cross, *The Dark Night* in *The Collected Works of John of the Cross*, trans. Kieran Kavanaugh, OCD, and Otilio Rodriguez, OCD (Washington, D.C.: Institute of Carmelite Studies, 1991), 358-457.

28. Quoted in G. L. Mueller, "Purgatory," *Theology Digest* 34, no. 1 (Spring 1987): 31-36.

29. John of the Cross, *The Living Flame of Love*, stanzas 1-2, in *Collected Works*, 639-40.

Leaving the matter there confronts us with a number of paradoxes. Perhaps these can be resolved only by yielding to a larger mystery still—the manner in which Christ himself suffers the incompletion and imperfection of his body. The great third-century Alexandrian theologian Origen wrote as follows:

> You will have joy when you depart from this life if you are a saint. But your joy will be complete only when no member of your body is lacking to you. For you too will wait, just as you are awaited. But if you who are a member do not have perfect joy as long as a member is missing, how much more must our Lord and savior who is the head and origin of this body consider it an incomplete joy if he is still lacking certain of his members? . . . Thus he does not want to receive his perfect glory without you: that is not without his people which is "his body" and "his members." (*In Leviticum homiliae* 7.1-2)[30]

This passage is not, of course, speaking about purgatory, and certainly not about Christ's sufferings in any purgatorial sense. On the other hand, it might suggest an understanding of purgatory both as a moment of purification and as an ongoing relationship with history. The way the head of the body awaits his "complete joy," the way the members of the body who are in glory await their complete joy, must have some parallel in the way those "in purgatory" await their complete joy. Suffering the incompleteness and distortions of our history occurs in different ways. But these are all aspects of how the eternal mystery of love has time for our full growth to humanity. Purgatory as we have been presenting it is not an ominous imposition but a deeply hopeful aspect of the gift of God. God has time, makes room, for our full purification, in a "time" and "space" proportioned to God's inexhaustible love. From this point of view, "time" is the divine gift. It is the time of purification, a time related to the course of history, yet also beyond it. Its true character can be sought only in the infinite dimensions of eternal love as these embrace all time and space and history. It can be measured not so much in Einsteinian relativity as in a divinely ordered relativity appropriate to our full growth in Christ.

We can think about purgatory only through analogies with present experience, and within the holographic field of all the interconnected mysteries of faith. Hope here works in the dark. But there is a luminous focus: the creative extent of God's love penetrating all the resistant dimensions of our

---

30. See Ratzinger, *Eschatology*, 185, for full text.

being, to conform us to itself, and to lead to the "perfect love [which] casts out all fear" (1 Jn 4:17). In the end, purgatory is not a state of dread, isolated torment, but of love's overcoming our basic fears: the fear of God as a threat; the fear of the other as a rival; the fear of dying as extinction; the fear of self-surrender as a loss; the fear of loving as a demand too great to bear.

REINCARNATION

As a general symbol of post-mortem purification, we noted above that purgatory appears to bear a family resemblance to the Eastern traditions of reincarnation.[31] More broadly, it can be related to more philosophical notions of the true self dying to the pretensions and entanglements of the ego. All hopes share a realistic concern for the healing or liberation of the true self. On this point, Herbert Fingarette's *The Self in Transformation* remains a valuable reference.[32] Calling on wide psychological, philosophical, and religious resources, he describes how, within the psychic realm, we are condemned to an endless cycle of repetition—unless we do eventually break out of self-destructive compulsions and obsessions. The release of genuine self-transcending freedom comes at a cost. It often involves what is experienced as terrifying suffering. A good example is those who heroically struggle against drug addiction. The "vital lie" (Ernest Becker) of human character, with its fear-driven compromises and self-absorption, does not easily give up its defenses.[33] There are clearly whole ranges of questions here that Christian theology has barely begun to ponder. In past centuries limbo provided a convenient solution. It left "on hold" as it were all questions relating to the fate of those human individuals who seemingly never had a chance to live a history of freedom.

A Dialogical Impasse?

In the decades to come as interfaith/hope dialogue proceeds and the exploration of the human psyche goes on, a lot of the questions that have been pending for centuries will certainly be discussed in a new context.

---

31. Perry Schmidt-Leukel, ed., *Die Idee der Reinkarnation in Ost und West* (Munich: Eugen Diederichs Verlag, 1996). See Pannenberg, *Systematic Theology*, 3:549-51, 564-68, 572-73.

32. Herbert Fingarette, *The Self in Transformation: Psychoanalysis, Philosophy and the Life of the Spirit* (New York: Harper Torchbooks, 1963), 216-37.

33. See the treatment of Becker's *Denial of Death* in chapter 4 above.

We will make a brief remark on reincarnation as it appears in the classic Eastern religions/philosophies. It has a certain similarity to Christian purgatory.[34] It too seeks to speak of a state or a phase resulting from not yet having attained the fullness of enlightenment or freedom. In this regard, it has four general features:

- Our present existence is just one among many, in the past and into the future. Hence, it precludes the idea of this present life being the definitive sphere of final decision.
- The successive embodiments are progressive; they are determined by a cosmic law that will eventually bring everyone to perfect self-realization. Hence there is no possibility of eternal damnation as a state either chosen or imposed.
- Progress is determined by the merits of the person involved. There is no divine grace or mercy involved, but merely a processive self-realization brought about by one's own merits. All in all, it is a process of self-redemption.
- The progress implied is one of gradual dematerialization or release from bodily existence. It is a path of advance to pure spirituality and independence from matter.

The Christian hope of sharing in the resurrection of Christ seemingly contradicts each of these points.

- For good or ill, the present life of the individual is decisive in coming to any ultimate state of fulfillment. It is not one life among many. Now is the acceptable time in which salvation is offered—or refused.
- This present life, lived within the offer of grace, leads to an ultimate self-determination. This present life brings with it the possibility of turning terminably against God and one's true self.
- The Christian journey is dependent neither on amassing personal merit nor on some universal, impersonal law of karma. From beginning to end, and at every moment, it presupposes the gift of God's grace and mercy. God's initiative, the divine gift, precedes all personal merit.
- Far from envisaging a progressive disembodiment, Christian hope is focused on the resurrection of Christ. It looks to a future (and possible progressive) embodiment in the body of Christ. The person brought to fulfillment is incarnate in a universe transformed in the Spirit.

---

34. A. Couture, "Réincarnation ou résurrection? Revue d'un débat et amorce d'une recherche," *Science et Esprit* 36, no. 3 (1984): 351-74; 37, no. 3 (1985): 75-96.

It is most likely that the ancient teachings on reincarnation, and even its more recent "New Age" versions, are in fact a reaction to materialism that so affects the human condition. Disproportionate attachments to material objects, taken in whatever sense, through possession or obsession, clearly demean the value of human existence. *Having* is given preference over *being*. From another perspective, the sense of worthlessness and futility concerning one's present form of life can be so keen as to demand some other form of meaningful existence in another time or state of being. Further, guilt over the harm one has caused might lay claim to the opportunity to perform some form of expiation in order to undo the evil influences that have emanated from one's actions.

As far as the modern forms of reincarnation are concerned, they have appeared at a time when a deeply secularized culture has been deprived of any language of saving grace. It has lost the ability to speak of the need for conversion. Confessing one's sins in their destructive reality is a foreign language. The ability to talk of "the last things" as the ultimate dimensions of human life is comically irrelevant. But this gaping hole in modern secular culture is a vacuum waiting to be filled. On a practical pastoral level, then, this apparently exotic topic of reincarnation deserves close attention.

An approach to purgatory in the manner sketched above quite easily moves into the area of interfaith dialogue on post-mortem purification. In fact, the doctrines of reincarnation/transmigration of souls have never been explicitly condemned by the church. It was never a realistic alternative to a Christ-centered hope: Christ has died for our sins once and for all (1 Pet 3:18). He has risen from the dead, no more to die; and death has no more power over him (Rom 6:9). Christians are called to be ever with the Lord after their resurrection (1 Thes 4:17). Everything occurs in one single, Christ-centered history, formed and energized by the incarnation, death, and resurrection of Jesus himself.[35] There is, however, a strongly negative dimension of Christian hope, as we have already emphasized. The more we come to appreciate the extent of human history and the variety of cultures that have formed it—especially given the comparatively small scope of explicit Christianity, the more we can anticipate a vigorous engagement within interfaith dialogue on the need and significance of post-mortem purification.

True, there are problems. If, for instance, reincarnation is taken to mean the denial of the grace of redemption and resurrection of the body, as well as the possibility of hell, then it is simply incompatible with Christian faith. Moreover, in its East Asian setting, the doctrine of reincarnation is often

---

35. C. Schönborn, *From Death to Life: The Christian Journey,* trans. B. McNeil (San Francisco: Ignatius, 1995), 125-70.

connected to attitudes that are intrinsically repugnant to a Christian sense of life: for example, the Hindu caste system in India, or, according to some Buddhist teachings, re-embodiment in forms of life lower than the human.

Then, there are further questions. Would not the prospect of an endless series of rebirths in accordance with some cosmic law mean not so much a hoped-for purification but a state of perdition, a kind of infernal system? And then, if the soul is basically independent of matter, but successively immersed in various material forms, does this not result in a complete dualism? As a result, the human person is not naturally incarnate in matter, but is essentially a detached spirit, haunting the world rather than inhabiting it. As was said previously, *duality*, that is, understanding the human person in terms of the complementarity of interrelated partial principles of spirit and matter, does not mean *dualism*, with its implication of two antagonistic principles.

Problems aside, it is clear that, just as the Christian doctrine of purgatory is an outgrowth of the realism of hope, the classic East Asian doctrine of reincarnation is something similar. Stripped to essentials, it is an answer to the philosophical and religious question of justice in a world in which the lot of human beings is so evidently characterized by inequality and injustice. The doctrine of reincarnation suggests an answer to deep human questions about the nature, origin, and future of the true self. While *karma* is an impersonal cosmic law, it may well mediate a sense of salvific providence at work in all human lives. However such large issues may be explored in the future, the doctrine of reincarnation expresses for billions of people the mythic wholeness of life and human destiny, from its origin to its end. In this regard, it is a system of moral pedagogy. It inspires both ethical responsibility and compassionate behavior.

Possible Meeting Points

A possible meeting point between these two approaches is the experience of death itself and its connection with freedom. There is a piercing question here. What happens when death occurs before a person has really had a chance, by any human imagination, to awaken to any kind of freedom? How can such an issue ever be decided? Theology in the past referred vaguely to the region of "limbo." Today, from the perspective of a more Christ-centered eschatology in which "the last thing" is God's merciful love, it is presumed that the Holy Spirit, loving the unborn or handicapped more than is humanly possible, would lead those who lacked liberty in this life to the maturity of making a choice for eternal life. Admittedly, this may seem to indicate a very modest possibility of dialogue. But any point of contact with world religions that have traditionally expressed their hopes in "reincarnationalist" terms is of great significance.

Second, the doctrine of reincarnation is related to a hope for liberation and self-realization. As mentioned above, there are similarities here with the psychoanalytical experience in which the patient has to confront repressed aspects of consciousness, disowned memories, and so forth, in order to arrive at a new integrity and freedom. In this regard, psychotherapy deals with a subjective experience and seeks to find a language for it. The symbolic and mythological expressions that therapy might employ belong to a different realm of discourse compared to the objective language of Christian faith—which is not to say that a Christian believer may indeed profit from professional psychotherapeutic counseling. We may speculate, therefore, that "reincarnation" is as real and unreal as the language of psychoanalysis. For example, a man in psychoanalysis might talk of his relationship to his father in terms of an "Oedipus complex" or the like, without thereby implying that he is trying to kill his father in the real world. Is the language of reincarnation a similar kind of language, at least from some points of view?

It seems unwise, without appreciating the psychic-spiritual tone of reincarnation language, to compare it without qualification to the doctrinal realism of Christian faith. Fingarette, in his illuminating study of these issues, notes that the great discovery of the major civilizations is the many dimensions of consciousness. The human person is a "plurality in unity."[36] He goes on to say,

> In the Western tradition, this differentiation has been expressed in terms of body and soul, mind and psyche, subjective and objective, individual and social, natural and personal, and so on. In Eastern traditions, the language is less differentiated and more holistically symbolic. While the language and symbolism of "reincarnation" is employed, it is noteworthy that there is a widespread indifference to dating previous incarnations in terms of actual history and a precisely measured time-span. It is not a matter of delving back into the past, but of examining the present in which the past is alive and present. On this point alone, the classical Eastern tradition is notably different from the popular reincarnationalism professed by contemporary Westerners.[37]

---

36. Fingarette, *Self in Transformation*, 277.
37. Ibid., 230.

Fingarette gives a healthy bit of advice against eclecticism, since both Christian hope and that of classic reincarnationalism demand their own integrity:

> What each conception, each vision, demands is that it be the genuine organising and generative seed, that its integrity be respected and enhanced, that it receive the utter commitment which guarantees the dominance of its spirit and excludes that which is alien to its spirit. We cannot toy with the idea of reincarnation as an intellectual and cultural curiosity having a certain piquant and quaint validity and still discover its power and worth. Nor can we along Christian lines, only half suppose that on this moment everything rests and still discover the life of which such a conception is the seed.[38]

While there are different worlds of language, religious experience, and anthropology, Christian eschatology demands a dialogue with all people of hope. If Christ is the savior of the world, he saves the world in its hopes. It will be no small advantage if, from the perspective of Christian hope, we can gain some understanding of the ancient tradition which expresses itself in terms of reincarnation. While serious dialogue on this point is only beginning, possibilities are opening up. The main points of contact remain first of all, the paschal mystery itself, as a "passover" into the fullness of life. Second, there is the theology of purgatory itself; and, third, the language and praxis of psychoanalysis and its links to the Christian experience of conversion. "Inter-hope" dialogue on eternal life can only enlarge the dimensions of hope itself.

---

38. Ibid., 235-36.

7

Hell

The Defeat of Hope?

M OST OF WHAT CAN BE SAID ABOUT HELL as a possible terminal point in human destiny has been implied in the previous chapters.[1] But the problem remains: If God is love, how can there be an eternal hell? If there is no hell, how does God truly respect human freedom? By the oddest of paradoxes, thinking about hell is occasioned by hope in the resurrection. The realm of hell is what hope has left behind—the state of being enclosed in oneself, with its sorry fruits of envy, greed and violence. To turn away from the "resurrection and the life" (Jn 11:25) and turn back to a hopeless world is to risk a permanent state of self-enclosure. Human freedom is confronted not only with death but with dying into a deeper death, the "second death" (Rev 20:14) of hell.

How much can or should theology say? There is a place for reserve; and surely it is here. Uncertainty seems to be part of our human condition.[2] Jesus himself admitted that the final hour was known only to the Father—not even to the Son (Mk 13:32). Theology participates in this Christlike unknowing, as it defers all certainties to the divine freedom. Still, David Hume's words express, in fact, a deep conviction at the heart of Christian tradition: "The damnation of one man is an infinitely greater evil in the universe than the subversion of a thousand millions of kingdoms."[3]

THE CONSEQUENCES OF EVADING THE ISSUE

Misplaced reserve can be a mask for evasiveness. As a result, the realism of hope suffers. It is shown in the lack of courage to face what is most dreaded,

---

1. For historical background, see Alan E. Bernstein, *The Formation of Hell: Death and Retribution in the Ancient and Early Christian Worlds* (Ithaca: Cornell University Press, 1993), especially 203-65.

2. Bernard Sesboüé, "L'enfer est-il éternel?" *Recherches de Science Religieuse* 87, no. 2 (1999): 201.

3. Quoted by John Orme Mills, OP, "Preface," *New Blackfriars* 69 (November 1988): 469.

as a possibility for oneself and others. In fact, silence on hell solves nothing. What cannot be spoken of can continue as a subterranean fantasy affecting our deepest feelings and impeding moral responsibility. When what is most dreadful in human imagination is repressed, it can surface in nameless fears, in attitudes of aggression and vengefulness. When the topic of hell cannot be mentioned, the destructive force of evil is unacknowledged. Talking only of the goodness of God becomes nauseatingly unreal and so fuels an angry despair over the evils of the world. Repression of either death or "the second death" (Rev 20:14) is not a sign of living hope.

Still, one must tread here a thin line.[4] A pastoral approach based on fear has had a long history.[5] Discretion and discernment are called for on the subject of hell. This is especially the case when culture and society are all too familiar with evil. The human imagination is still traumatized by the horrors of the past terrible century. For the millions who suffered through two world wars and the genocidal horrors of, say, the Holocaust, the Killing Fields, or Rwanda, hell had become an appalling reality. To a world aware of the infamies and destructiveness marking its recent history, hope must offer promise, but not by intensifying the sense of pervasive guilt and despair. And so, to urge the threat of eternal damnation when the mood of the times is bereft of any intimations of salvation can be tragically misplaced. And yet, when hell ceases to be a theological topic, there are unfortunate results.

Hannah Arendt makes a point in judging that "the most significant consequence of the secularisation of the modern age may well be the elimination from public life, along with religion, of the only political element in traditional religion, the fear of hell."[6] One immediate result of the modern elimination of the religious symbol of hell is its reemergence in a secular guise. As the symbols of God, immortality, salvation, and heaven are displaced into secular substitutes, and so too is hell. Floating free from its original religious significance, hell begins to occupy a place in the secularized world of self-enclosed human experience. There are consequences. James Schall makes a good point:

> Whenever hell is neglected, it returns under another form. The tradition of Aquinas is that all evil will be punished ultimately, that all human evil is precisely chosen. But it need not be the function of

---

4. In what follows, I am especially indebted to Sesboüé, "L'enfer est-il éternel?"; Henry Novello, "Death as Privilege," *Gregorianum* 84, no. 4 (2003): 779-827; and J. R. Sachs, "Current Eschatology: Universal Salvation and the Problem of Hell," *Theological Studies* 52 (1991): 227-54.

5. For example, the French historian Jean Delumeau speaks of "la pastorale de la peur" (*Le péché et la peur: La culpabilisation en Occident: XIIIe-XVIIIe siecles* [Paris: Fayard, 1983]).

6. Hannah Arendt, *Between Past and Future* (New York: Viking, 1968), 133.

politics to punish all evils or to correct all evil choices . . . the effort
to create a perfect, self-conceived society on earth invariably seems to
result in a kind of incarnate hell.[7]

When the symbol of hell loses its transcendent significance, it returns as some
form of historically identified "evil empire" deserving of utter reprobation. Its
rulers, its servants, its members, are judged to be among the collective of the
damned. The blocs of the historically saved, of the ideologically justified, can
make no peace with these damned and the demonstrably evil forces: "In the
modern era, evil and hell have become objects and movements to be overcome rather than mysteries lying deeply at the heart of human choice."[8] The
result of reducing the religious symbol of hell to an empirical historical form
of reprobation has a double consequence. First, theologically speaking, hell
ceases to be understood as an objective eschatological possibility for all. Second, hell is now attached to the dreadful "other" (people, country, party, etc.)
within the world and its history. The damned and dreaded "other" becomes
the focus of historical hatred and reprobation. Forgiveness and reconciliation
are not only impossible but also undesirable. Human freedom is frozen into
the hopeless divisions of the good and bad. Possibilities of growth or change
cannot be entertained. Satan reigns in the realm of the evil "other."

Shorn of its theological significance, hell becomes a boundary marker in
the history of violence. The imagination of hope is stultified. History is no
longer the ever-inconclusive play of the human drama. It is burdened with
the weight of ultimate judgments. Those "on the side of the angels" have to
keep up the pretense of being inhabitants of a heavenly city. Their judgments
on anything or anyone on the other side cannot allow for any ambiguity.
There can be no compromise with the realm of the evil "other." There Satan
reigns. The ferocity of this kind of merciless moralism permits of no response
save that of eliminating the enemy.

In contrast to a socially or politically determined hell, the theological
doctrine of hell frees social and political interactions from being terminally
overloaded. Schall makes an anthropologically astute point. A theologically
understood hell "frees politics from an impossible worldly burden inasmuch
as it enforces a contingent, imperfect civil order in such a way that the same
civil order is not required to exercise absolute justice and punishment."[9] In any
theological understanding, ultimate judgment is not pronounced and executed

7. James V. Schall, "Displacing Damnation: The Neglect of Hell in Political Theory," *The Thomist* 44, no. 1 (January 1983): 43.

8. Ibid., 44.

9. Ibid., 33.

by some group of the enlightened. It is not the function of politics to punish all evils and correct all abuses. If any political group attempts to implement an ideologically pure society in the world, the last state is worse than the first. The unfortunate result can be too often described as "hell on earth."

THE HELL OF CHRISTIAN ESCHATOLOGY

There is something to be said, then, for a sober theological approach that keeps hell where it belongs. It is a possibility residing in those depths of human freedom that can be known only to God. Hell is a theological symbol of the sinner's self-chosen ultimate fate. It allows for the possibility for any individual to be terminally frozen in the choice of evil. Such perverse personal freedom not only excludes all good will. It also has the power to frustrate the patience and mercy of the God who does not want "any to perish, but all to come to repentance" (2 Pet 3:9).

Whether or not such an ultimate fixation on evil occurs, we simply do not know. What we do know, with all the force of Gospel, is that such a judgment is reserved only to God. Any creaturely rush to judgment is halted by the biblical injunction, "Judge not and you shall not be judged" (Lk 6:37-38). Cursing those whose conduct we may rightly deplore by consigning them to hell, if meant or taken seriously, cannot figure in Christian communication. Indeed, when Christian faith necessarily speaks of sin and the sinner, it always stops short of anything approaching ultimate reprobation. Saints are solemnly declared to be in heaven. No one is declared to be in hell. Some might be tempted to go beyond this limit and indulge in exercises of eschatological judgment. One way of recalling them to a more genuine Christian attitude would be this: the surest way of going to hell is to arrogate to oneself God's final judgment on the personal worth of others. That would amount to replacing the inexhaustible possibilities of ultimate mercy with a narrow, vindictive "last judgment" of one's own. The mercy of God reaches out to each mortal one of us. It seeks out the lost whatever ways of guilt and darkness we may have followed. The "last thing" is always the mercy of God. It forbids any human judgment to pursue any evildoer to the end.

THE DATA

What, then, of the Christian doctrine of hell? The biblical data on hell have been frequently, though never neatly, summarized.[10] As Israel's sages and

---

10. Zachary Hayes, "Hell," in *The New Dictionary of Theology*, ed. Joseph A. Komonchak, Mary Collins, and Dermot A. Lane (Wilmington, Del.: Michael Glazier, 1987), 457-59.

prophets contemplated the scope of God's action, gradually a more differentiated notion of hell, *Sheol, Gehenna*, emerged. From being a rather neutral, shadowy existence, hell becomes the place of darkness and wrath. Divine judgment on both the good and the bad is not exhausted merely in terms of this life. For the irremediably wicked, there is a final dimension of exclusion from the God of life. The apocalyptic imagination began to fill it with fire, worms, chains, and so forth. These lurid descriptions passed over into received language of the New Testament writers themselves (Mt 3:12; 5:22, 29ff.; 10:28; 13:42, 50; 18:9; 2 Pet 2:17; Jude 1:6-8; Rev 21:8).[11]

There is a clear urgency in the New Testament's presentation of the ministry of Jesus. It would be scarcely intelligible without a sense of some ultimate possibility of loss on the part of his hearers. His mission to open the way to life necessarily implies the possibility of an ultimate form of death. The dark possibilities from which we need deliverance are expressed in the various creeds and councils through the ages.[12] The church teaches that anyone terminally fixed in evil suffers the reality of hell immediately after death (*Benedictus Deus, DS*[13] 1000f.). Hell is essentially the loss of God. To this, certain other punishments due to particular forms of sinfulness were joined (*DS* 780). Further, hell is everlasting (*DS* 801, 856-58, 1306, 1539, 1575). In that dark eternity, no final reconciliation of sinners is possible, even if the great Origen considered other possibilities (see below).[14] Though no individual human person is declared to be in hell, though no limit is placed on Christian hope, the doctrine is sober, definite, and clear. As such it has been reiterated in recent times.[15]

The biblical texts of division and judgment must be placed in a larger context. Peter, preaching outside the temple after Pentecost, allowed that his Jewish brethren "had acted in ignorance, as did your rulers" (Acts 3:17; cf. Lk 23:34). Yet he calls all to repentance in the light of Christ's sufferings, who now must "remain in heaven until the time of universal restoration (*apokatastasis*) that God announced long ago through his holy prophets" (Acts 3:21).

---

11. To the New Testament texts referring to judgment and separation (Mt 13:24-30, 36-43, 47-50; 18:23-25; 22:1-4; 25:1-13, 31-46; Lk 16:19-31; Rom 2:2-11; 1 Cor 3:11-15; 2 Cor 5:10; 1 Thes 1:5-10) can be added references to Gehenna (Mt 3:12; 5:22; 18:9), eternal fire (Mt 13:42, 50; 18:8), and outer darkness (Mt 8:12; 22:13).

12. Hayes, "Hell," 457-58.

13. Henricus Denzinger and Adolfus Schönmetzer, eds., *Enchiridion Symbolorum Definitionum de Rebus Fidei et Morum* (Freiburg: Herder, 1965), n. 3019. Hereafter referred to as *DS* and followed by the article number of the citation referred to.

14. See the Synod of Constantinople (543) (*DS* 411). Origen's teaching on a final restoration was condemned as a matter of doctrine, not as an object of humble hope, as we will later suggest.

15. See the document of the Sacred Congregation for the Doctrine of the Faith, *A Letter on Certain Questions concerning Eschatology*, May 17, 1979, par. 7. See also *Catechism of the Catholic Church* (Sydney: St Pauls, 1994), ##1033-37.

For his part, Paul contrasts the reign of death with the superabundance of grace (Rom 5:12-21). He declares that nothing "in all creation will be able to separate us from the love of God in Christ Jesus, our Lord" (Rom 8:39). Even evils inherent in human liberty figure in the divine design so that God "may be merciful to all" (Rom 11:32). The Captivity Epistles speak of "a plan for the fullness of time, to gather up all things in him [Christ]" (Eph 1:10), so that the whole of creation may acknowledge Jesus as Lord to the glory of God the Father (Phil 2:10), as God reconciles "all things" to himself through the blood of the cross (Col 1:20). The Pastoral Epistles recommend that the intercession of the community be extended to all since "God our Savior . . . desires everyone to be saved and to come to the knowledge of the truth" (1 Tim 2:4). Our hope is "set on the living God, who is the savior of all people (1 Tim 4:10), for "the grace of God has appeared, bringing salvation to all" (Tit 2:11). The Second Letter of Peter praises the loving patience of God "not wanting any to perish, but all to come to repentance" (2 Pet 3:9). In the Gospel of John, Jesus promises, "I, when I am lifted up from the earth, will draw all people to myself" (12:32). In his victory over the world (Jn 16:33), Jesus addresses the Father, who has given him authority over all people, so that he can give eternal life to all (Jn 17:2). Jesus is revealed as the embodiment of God's eternally merciful intention, the Lamb slain "before the foundation of the world" (Rev 13:8; 1 Pet 1:19-20).

HOPE AND HELL

There are four ways in which the theme of hell fittingly appears in an account of Christian hope. We present them under the headings of salutary fear, the transcendent character of divine justice, the desire for God's judgment of evil, and the reality of human freedom.

Healthy Fear

First, we must candidly admit that hell figures in Christian discourse as the language of fear and threat. We have already noted how such language can be abused, but that need not always be the case. If Christian preaching speaks of the possibility of suffering the loss of God, it need not be emotionally manipulative. The feeling of fear has its part to play in motivating genuine human freedom, even if such motivation is not the most mature. Still, the fear of failure, self-destruction, and disgrace can powerfully energize a choice for the good. This fundamental human psychology is exploited, say, in techniques of therapeutic conditioning in treating addiction, just as it is assumed in all legal systems with their variety of penalties prescribed for offenses committed. It is worth noting, too, that the fear of hell is a dominant feature of any genuinely popular religion. When each one is faced, whatever their social position, with the dreadful possibility of losing God, a certain leveling of human pretensions occurs. Human society is most truly a democracy when it has a spiritual recognition of a transcendent and universal judgment by which evil and evildoers will be contained and unmasked.

To the degree that the symbol of hell is a carrier of wholesome fear, it objectifies the opposite of self-transcendence, namely, the possibility of self-destruction and an ultimate form of self-enclosure. It is designed to shock conscience into taking stock of the direction one's freedom has taken. It summons each of us to the confession of sins, to hope for mercy and healing, and to the work of reconciliation and forgiveness. It leads to the rejection of destructive choices and to a free decision for the truly good. It negatively represents a fundamentally hopeful attitude. The fulfillment of any one of us cannot envisage a heaven based on the exclusion, let alone the destruction, of others. The threat of hell is the voice of the community, especially heard in its most vulnerable and "hopeless" members, those who have been disowned, neglected, or exploited as mere material for the aggrandizement of others. The Christian doctrine of hell presumes that it is a possibility for everyone. It is an explosive charge set at the foundations of the arrogant individualism that would see the world only as a field of exploitation and domination. The fear of hell, then, must be placed where it belongs. It does not legitimate any kind of reprobation of others. Rather, it is one aspect of our common experience of the enigma of human liberty.

This can be no bad thing. The humble acceptance in oneself of the potential for evil and the possibility of ultimate loss is at least an initial recognition of a moral universe in which human liberty is taken seriously. Freedom means responsibility for, and to, others. Our choices will be finally revealed for what they are. This kind of "fear and trembling" (Phil 2:12) is not servile. Far from crippling the psyche with terror, it provokes an awareness of the responsibility of freedom in its individual and social forms. It candidly acknowledges the precariousness of human liberty in a universe that is not a giant automatic salvation machine. It contains the possibilities of a terminal self-destruction. Wholesome fear flows from reverence for God as the source and goal of human freedom. It is associated with the "fear of the Lord," one of the seven gifts of the Holy Spirit, connected by Aquinas to the virtue of hope (*STh* 2-2, q. 19, a. 1-12). Holy fear manifests itself as sensitivity to threat of evil—in oneself and in the world at large. The doctrine of hell arises from the humble acknowledgment that we human beings can choose the dreadful banality of an ultimate self-enclosure. It appears on the map of the moral universe as a black hole into which the light of love and compassion cannot enter. The state of damnation is not to be imagined as joining a defiant rebellious company. It is a choice for ultimate aloneness, in which no fellow feeling or companionship is possible. It is, in the end, being stuck with oneself, in the living death of loveless isolation.

Hope for Judgment

Then there is another paradox. Put most shockingly, Christians must hope that hell exists. But at once we must add a qualification. We are longing not for the damnation of others but for the final state in which evil will be revealed for what it is and be brought to nothing.[16] Enormous evils have left their mark on history. They have generated a murderous depersonalizing force. Such evils have a global impact. In their demonic power, they outstrip the wickedness of any one individual or group.[17] Nonetheless, a spiral of vengeance and violence is unleashed that can affect cultures and histories for centuries. The power of evil is unsleeping in its ability to weave itself into any cultural or social or scientific achievement. The new sins of civilized humanity are a fact. Everyone laments the entrenched global structures of economics that leave billions in poverty and poison the ecological well-being of the planet itself. Weapons of unimaginable destructive power lie ready in the arsenals of several governments. World peace and justice seem ethereal possibilities in the world of competing and antagonistic forces that has come into being.

The symbol of hell, for all the reserve with which we must explore it, points to a theological reality. It represents God's ultimate judgment on the evil perpetrated by historical human agents.[18] It marks the limit, in this sense, of God's patience with what most contradicts the divine will to save. It looks to the point at which there will be no more room for the hatreds and violence arising from exalting oneself, defying God, and denying Christ. Hell has its place, then, in the language of hope as the reprobation of the actual evil-

---

16. Wolfhart Pannenberg, *Systematic Theology*, vol. 3, trans. G. W. Bromiley (Grand Rapids: Eerdmans, 1998), 637-42.

17. See the outstanding trilogy: Walter Wink, *Naming the Powers* (Philadelphia: Fortress Press, 1984); *Unmasking the Powers: The Invisible Forces That Determine Human Existence* (1986); *Engaging the Powers: Discernment and Resistance in a World of Domination* (1992).

18. See Anthony J. Kelly and Francis J. Moloney, *Experiencing God in the Gospel of John* (New York: Paulist Press, 2003), 79-83, 126-30, 169-74.

doing that we experience in ourselves or others. It forbids any representation of God's love as tolerance of evil or a compromise with it. Hell is where evil is contained, rendered impotent, and made to serve the higher purposes of a good creation. It is where the Antichrist is vanquished and evil is revealed for what it was all along. It will be disclosed as a parasite living off the original good of creation. But the light of God is the radiance in which no pretense, no evasion, no compromise, no further subversion of the good will be tolerated. The mighty will be toppled from their thrones. The mass murderer will no longer triumph over innocent victims. Pride and violence will be brought to nothing, and Satan will be humbled.[19]

There is no question of positively hoping that individual evildoers will be condemned to hell. Nonetheless, it seems essential to authentic hope to pray and work for a final state in which the power of evil is negated once and for all. What conscience has found most hateful and worthy of utter reprobation will have no part in the new creation.[20] Though it is true that evil has no power unless it is the work of evildoers, today we have learned to identify social structures of evil and the social and cultural conditioning that make it morally impossible for people to act in peace, reconciliation, and forgiveness. Hell, from this point of view, must mean the inglorious collapse of these evil social conditions.

The extent of evil resists any conceptualization. On the other hand, traditional symbols expressed in terms of Satan, the devil, and Antichrist are part of the Christian inheritance and demand to be further explored: "For our struggle is not against enemies of blood and flesh, but against the rulers, against the authorities, against the cosmic powers of this present darkness, against the spiritual forces of evil in the heavenly places" (Eph 6:12). In Johannine theology, for example, the life-giving generativity of God is frequently set in contrast to the perverse generativity of evil. Believers must choose which is to be the determining factor in their lives.[21] In a terrible conflict with his adversaries, Jesus declares,

> You are of your father, the devil, and your will is to do your father's desires. He was a murderer from the beginning and has nothing to do with the truth because there is no truth in him. When he lies, he

---

19. Quoted in Hans Küng, *Eternal Life? Life after Death as a Medical, Philosophical and Theological Problem*, trans. E. Quinn (New York: Doubleday, 1984), 198.

20. Wink, *Unmasking the Powers*, 39-40.

21. Kelly and Moloney, *Experiencing God*, especially chapter 7, "Between Different Paternities: Making the Choice," 169-204.

speaks according to his own nature, because he is a liar and the father of lies. (Jn 8:44)

In this dramatic language, the diabolic power at work in human history is expressed as an intrinsically murderous and mendacious force, enlisting human beings into its dominion. John's First Letter takes up these themes: "everyone who commits sin is a child of the devil" (1 Jn 3:8). It goes on to say, "we must not be like Cain, who was from the evil one and murdered his brother. And why did he murder him? Because his own deeds were evil and his brother's righteous" (1 Jn 3:12). The destructive power of evil is further expressed as a form of murder: "all who hate a brother or sister are murderers, and you know that murderers do not have eternal life abiding in them" (v. 15).

What then is the reality of this diabolic power?[22] Satan is mentioned thirty-seven times in the New Testament, along with other references to the devil, the adversary, the evil one, the tempter, Beelzebul, the prince of this world or the "god of this world" (2 Cor 4:4; Eph 2:2), a liar, and a murderer from the beginning (Jn 8:43). It appears that this personification of evil is especially concentrated against Jesus and his mission. In the drama of salvation, Jesus breaks the power of the evil one and shares his victory with his followers.

What then, is the reality of this evil force? Two extremes are to be avoided. To suggest that the devil is a purely literary personification fails to respect the biblical data. Nor does such a literary solution recognize the demonic excesses of evil throughout history. At the other extreme, if theology dignifies the diabolic with a distinct personal existence presiding over the kingdom of the damned, that does not quite accord with the biblical data either. We note, in this regard, the New Testament expressions of the nullification of the diabolic powers. Jesus destroys the influence of the evil one: "The Son of God was revealed for this purpose, to destroy the works of the devil" (1 Jn 3:8). The Epistle to the Hebrews is even more direct in regard to the devil-destroying power of Christ: "so that through death he might destroy the one who has the power of death, that is, the devil, and free those who all their lives were held in slavery by the fear of death" (Heb 2:14-15). In this connection, Alison makes a good point:

The only role which the devil/Satan has in the New Testament is one who is in the process of being defeated. Jesus has seen him fall like

---

22. Sesboüé, "L'enfer est-il éternel?" 202-5.

lightning from heaven (Luke 10:18)—which is to say his transcendence is on the way out. In Colossians 2:15, Christ is described, in
an image taken from a Roman military triumph, as having "disarmed
the principalities and powers and made a public example of them, triumphing over them in it [i.e., the cross]. That is to say: by revealing in
the Cross the mechanism by which the devil was the princ(ipl)e of the
world—that is, the principle of collective murder as the basis of human
order—and making this knowledge available, the principal arm of the
devil has been destroyed.[23]

Jesus rises from the dead. Since his death was brought about by the powers
of evil, his rising means a radical victory over the world-forming destructive
forces that were ranged against him. God, then, is revealed as the love that
overcomes evil; and the followers of Christ are called to be participants in its
revelation. In this context, it is important to note that these quasi-personal
forces of evil make their appearance in opposition to God's saving will. What
is of key importance for Christian hope is the revelation of the triumph of
God's love in Christ. The rest is a matter of speculation. When a sense of
proportion is lost, any tendency to theorize on the reality of the diabolic is
more likely to diminish the experience of salvation than to enlarge it. Still,
one point is clear. The devil appears as the *diabolos*, literally, "one who throws
things apart." Diabolic influence is evidenced in human history as a disin-
tegrating and isolating force. It is the root of envy and of defiant alienation
from God. Note the testimony of the Book of Wisdom, as it reflects the reaction of the wicked to the witness of the good:

> Thus they reasoned, but they were led astray; for their wickedness
> blinded them, and they did not know the secret purposes of God, nor
> hoped for the wages of holiness nor discerned the prize for blameless
> souls; for God created us for incorruption, and made us in the image of
> his own eternity, but through the devil's envy, death entered the world,
> and those who belong to his company experience it. (Wis 2:21-24)

The transpersonal effects of evil are objectified in the symbol of the devil.
Human beings do not exist alone, just as they do no good alone. We exist
in ripples of coexistence. Family, community, society, culture, and the whole
of history determine the existence of each one and are in turn affected by it.

23. James Alison, *The Joy of Being Wrong: Original Sin through Easter Eyes* (New York: Crossroad, 1998), 157. He refers further to René Girard, *The Scapegoat* (London: Athlone, 1986), 184-97.

This is to say that the evils we do enter into a larger history. Human existence can be so conditioned by fear, hatred, suspicion, estrangement, and vendetta, that the moral good can appear to be an impossibility. Each bad moral choice resulting in greed, resentment, or violence enters into a network of alliances. An individual evil act, or even the pretension to provide the total human solution to all ills, is always more than an individual perversion of life. It can unleash demons of destruction, especially in the World Wide Web of communication that is both the blessing and curse of life today.

To suggest that the devil is a symbol of all this will probably sound like too weak a description. The extent of evil needs no documentation. But to explain it in terms of a global symbol of self-destruction may not appear to respect either the biblical data or the dismal dimensions of our experience. When the diabolic is interpreted in a symbolic manner, it may not appear real enough. There is another side to this, however. A deep cultural or social symbol can be more "real" to our human perception than so-called objective realities.[24] A "peace process," say, in the Middle East, might be envisaged as a series of steps to be taken. Structures need simply to be "put in place" as a cure for the violence and disruption that are occurring. On the other hand, the problems of the disease seem infinitely more than any one diagnosis or prescription. There are demonic forces at work that can be exorcised only by a kind of love, forgiveness, and hope that cannot be simply plucked out of the air. No process or structure can take such transcendent energies for granted. Not only do the limits of any given situation need to be acknowledged. For what has taken place is the poisoning of hearts and communities, infecting even worlds of culture and history.

Gaston Fessard at this point calls on the insights of the cultural anthropologist Claude Lévi-Strauss: symbols are more real than what they symbolize. They are the constitutive or inner meaning of culture. Symbols enter into the personal and communal sense of identity. They motivate social behavior. They resonate in language itself, deeply affecting the tone of interpersonal communication.[25] In other words, the symbols of a culture are more real than

---

24. In this regard, note the words of Pope John Paul II, in his *Message for the Celebration of the World Day of Peace, 2005*:

> From the beginning, humanity has known the tragedy of evil and has struggled to grasp its roots and explain its causes. Evil is not some impersonal, deterministic force at work in the world. It is the result of human freedom. Freedom, which distinguishes human beings from every other creature on earth, is ever present at the heart of the drama of evil. *Evil always has a name and a face*: the name and the face of those men and women who freely choose it. (*L'Osservatore Romano* [English version], December 22/29, 2004, 6-7, par. 2).

25. Sesboüé, "L'enfer est-il éternel?" 204.

mere "things," since they enter into the deepest meaning of human existence itself. We fail to recognize the reality of human culture if we think of symbols as less real than things objectively considered. To that degree, theology can recognize the symbolic reality of the devil as the tempter and the liar and the murderer from the beginning, without making Satan the God-defiant prince of an eternal hell.[26] In the history of salvation there is terminal conflict between good and evil, between Christ and the Antichrist. The basic symbolism of the diabolic and the Antichrist deals with the terminal and definitive nature of that conflict. It is focused on the power of evil to infect the human condition. But there are other symbols and imaginative ways of expression that stem from the basic symbolism. They range from the serpent in Genesis to the beast of the Book of Revelation (e.g., Rev 17). These are particularized depictions of the demonic power of evil, employed in biblical, theological, and religious discourse in the variety of cultures in which they occur. Christian hope, for its part, relies on the ultimate mercy working through forgiveness and healing to save all from the power of evil. It hopes that "hell exists" as the final and utter defeat of evil. It envisages the obliteration of Satan, the diabolic force that has parasitically infested human history. In a transformed humanity, Satan will be no more.

I suggested previously (in chapter 2), that the universe of God's creation, if we are open to the full witness of tradition, includes angels, the realm of pure spirits. It is one thing, then, to hope for the existence of hell as the eternal victory of God over evil. It is another thing to hope that it is eternally inhabited by angels who have fallen from grace.[27] Must hope accept that God is finally defeated in this instance? Here we are at the outer reaches of theological speculation. But once more hope need impose no limits on divine mercy, and its capacity to restore all things in Christ. In that case, hope can allow for a certain sense of the eternity of hell, in that all who will live in the eternal light of God will be conscious of the evils from which they are saved, and which they now experience as forever defeated. We can know nothing for sure of the dynamics of angelic freedom. Thomas Aquinas, in his powerfully reasoned treatise on angels, interpreted the freedom of pure spirits as far more definitive than is the case with us human beings (*STh* 1, qq. 50-64). He assumed that there was an intrinsic clarity of angelic intelligence compared to the more flickering human mode. An angelic choice of evil, because fully conscious, is therefore definitive (*STh* 1, q. 64, a. 2). Thomas does allow, however, that the blessed can love even those fallen angels so that their natural

---

26. Gaston Fessard, "Enfer eternal ou Salut universal?" in *Le mythe de la peine* (Paris: Aubier, 1967), 249.

27. Sesboüé, "L'enfer est-il éternel?" 205-6, again in reference to Fessard.

existence will contribute to the glory of God: "We can also love the nature of demons out of charity, insofar as we wish those spirits to be kept in their natural existence for the glory of God" (*STh* 2-2, q. 25, a. 11). But once more hope can keep going where even the greatest theologians must be silent. It can leave everything to the inexhaustible creativity of God's love for all that it has summoned into existence. It could be that the "glory of God" will be manifested in a way of final salvation for the "fallen angels"—even despite the theological logic of the Angelic Doctor.

A Universe of Freedom?

The mystery of creation implies that the world exists in its proper independence. Creation, indeed, is never more creation than when it is independent and free to be itself. Each person is created by God to be a free subject. Liberty is a gift. It is not merely permitted or tolerated by the Creator. It is a God-given gift of free self-determination. Our capacity for freedom is initiated, willed, sustained by God, and destined to be fulfilled in God. The theoretical and practical recognition of such freedom must allow the free person to be truly free. Therein lies the possibility of eschatological tragedy: free human agents can opt for themselves, against God; and do so definitively. We are talking not of occasional sins or moral impotence but of the self-determining choice into which evildoers have put the whole deliberate weight of their lives.

If we disallow this possibility of ultimate self-enclosure, then hope is in fact diminished. Freedom would be merely make-believe. If our capacities for self-determination were all along destined to be overwhelmed by God's more powerful action, God would appear at best as a manipulator or, at worst, as the source of illusory freedom. If salvation were automatic, the new creation would, in the end, be populated by automata.[28]

The nature of this tragedy has been unforgettably evoked in Dostoevsky's *The Brothers Karamazov*. The saintly Father Zossima asks, "What is hell? It is the suffering that comes from being unable to love."[29] C. S. Lewis adds his own memorable commentary:

To love at all is to be vulnerable. Love anything, and your heart will certainly be wrung and possibly broken. If you want to make sure of

28. Pannenberg, *Systematic Theology*, 3:642-46.
29. Fyodor Dostoevsky, *The Brothers Karamazov* (various editions), bk. 6, ch. 3.

keeping it intact, you must give your heart to no one, not even to an animal. Wrap it carefully around with hobbies and little luxuries. Avoid all entanglements: lock it up in the safe casket or coffin of your selfishness. But in that casket—safe, dark, motionless, airless—it will change. It will not be broken. It will become unbreakable, impenetrable, irredeemable. The alternative to tragedy, or at least the risk of tragedy, is damnation. The only place outside of heaven where you can be perfectly safe from the dangers and perturbations of love is hell.[30]

Hell is the human possibility of ending, with a heart "unbreakable, impenetrable, irredeemable." Thus, the terrible question arises. Is hope left speechless when it recognizes the capacities of the human heart to choose an ultimate selfishness? Does hell have the last word, as the frustration of divine creation and grace?

Human Justice and Divine Mercy

When considering the possibility of an absolute and ultimate "loss," theology must speak with great care, in language and categories appropriate to Christian hope. Theological discourse on hell has been too often infected by metaphors drawn from an unredeemed experience of the world. Too rarely has the fundamental reference point been the universe of superabundant grace. A sure sign of cultural and even religious development is recognized when, say, a society admits the inhumanity of its own past legal systems. The humanity of a culture is judged in its willingness to abolish torture and the death penalty, even if that means accepting new risks when the ultimate deterrent is not part of the system. From this attitude flow the declaration of periods of amnesty, the establishment of "truth and reconciliation" committees (Chile and South Africa), and appeals to international courts of justice to adjudicate on crimes against humanity wherever they have occurred. Moreover, criminologists now generally recognize that the penalty of incarceration must not preclude a program of rehabilitation.

The Holy Spirit working in such developments in human culture will not allow theology to lag behind. Its past treatment of hell was often too dependent on the violent terms of penal justice. With the advantage of hindsight—and, I would hope, under the guidance of the Spirit—we can see past distortions more clearly. These resulted from thinking of divine justice through analo-

---

30. C. S. Lewis, *The Four Loves* (London: Bless, 1960), 138–39.

gies drawn from the penal justice system, in which a criminal offense must be punished in accord with the principles of equity and deterrence. The punishment must fit the crime. By analogy, divine law exacts its punishments and imposes proportionate sanctions if divine justice is to be satisfied. But there is destructive distortion inherent in this kind of reasoning. It seems to have affected our most venerated masters in the Western tradition.[31] St. Augustine was deeply pessimistic concerning the fate of most human beings—the *massa damnata* depicted in the *City of God* (21.12). The theological textbook of the Middle Ages, Peter Lombard's *Sentences*, considered in book 4 that the sufferings of the damned increase the joy of the blessed. This opinion received qualified acceptance even from the young Thomas Aquinas (*In IV Sent.* d. 50, q. 2, a. 4, s. 3). Nonetheless, divine mercy and love cannot be restricted to what is least developed in the human world of penal justice. God is not bound by the laws of an unredeemed world. The gospel must not be made to conform to the world. It must challenge the world of violence to reimagine itself in the light of the gospel. When this begins to happen, theology can express its questions more clearly. Are the laws of punitive human justice binding even on God? Is the punishment of the offender, the sinner, an essential value in the realm of divine justice?

Obviously we are at a point when analogies drawn from familiar human experiences of penalty and punishment need to be theologically subjected to the way of negation. Theology must be on its guard against appealing to analogies drawn from human experience when that experience is radically distorted by egoism and vindictiveness. Human justice can be little more than the culturally embedded despair that has lost hope for any grace beyond its own system.

If a theology of hell continues to be burdened with analogies drawn even from the most enlightened systems of justice—since any "reforms" are always bitterly contested—then hope has a difficult time when it considers the theme of hell. There is all the more reason in this somber context to keep the limitless mystery of God's love in focus. Paul's rhetorical question becomes a real question for any theology of hell: "Who shall separate us from the love of Christ?" (Rom 8:35). He gives an ecstatic assurance, "I am sure that neither death nor life . . . nor things present nor things to come . . . nor anything in all creation can separate us from the love of God in Christ Jesus" (Rom 8:38-39). There is a question, then, to ponder, in hope-filled humility and adoration. If "nothing in all creation" can separate us from God's love in Christ Jesus, how is hell to be understood as the ultimate possibility of loss and

---

31. Sesboüé, "L'enfer est-il éternel?" 189-90.

separation? As we have implied above, even while admitting the possibility
of the sinner's ultimate self-separation from God, the theologically ultimate
reality is the love of God—even if this poses problems for a theology of hell.
The First Letter of John inspires eschatology to live with this problem in the
most hopeful manner, for John writes, "there is no fear in love, but perfect
love casts out fear. For fear has to do with punishment, and he who fears is
not perfected in love" (1 Jn 4:18-19). Humility would advise against anyone
of us imagining that she or he has arrived at "perfect love." Though, as mentioned above, punishment-related fear has its place in Christian discourse,
hope must look further.

HOPE AGAINST HOPE

The New Testament repeatedly draws attention to what is possible only to
God. The scope of infinite mercy and love surpasses and surprises all human
calculations (e.g., Mt 19:26; Mk 10:27; Lk 18:27).[32] Such passages can hardly
be presented as proof texts for the universality of salvation and the nonex-
istence of hell. Nonetheless, each in its own context invites hope to look
beyond the cultural and social structures of any system of human justice and
to place no human limits on the possibilities of divine grace and mercy. If
"in Christ God was reconciling the world to himself, not counting their trespasses against them" (2 Cor 5:19), heaven and hell are not simple alternatives.
Not only is there the positive will of God for the reconciliation of the world
with its Creator. There is also the excess of divine compassion, manifested in
a love and mercy that do not count offenses against the sinful creature: "But
God proves his love for us in that while we were still sinners Christ died for
us" (Rom 5:8).

Karl Rahner has famously represented a larger wisdom in this matter. He
takes as axiomatic that, despite the unknown decisions of individual freedom, God's eschatological Christ-centered intent for human history will
have a happy outcome "as a whole."[33] The fate of individuals who have seemingly defied the divine saving will of God can never be resolved by human
judgment. There is no theological justification for a theoretical declaration
that all will be saved in the end. That would mean abolishing the ambiguity
of human freedom. But neither is there any reason to prevent the Christian

---

32. Note the series of texts strongly affirming universal salvation: 1 Cor 13:7; Rom 11:32; Eph
1:10; 2:14-18; 1 Tim 2:4; 4:10; 2 Pet 3:9.
33. Karl Rahner, *Foundations of Christian Faith*, trans. W. V. Dych (New York: Seabury, 1978),
435.

from praying and hoping that no one will be damned and that all will be reconciled with God in a way that exceeds human thinking.[34]

In other words, the last thing determining the fate of the sinner is neither the balance of a system of justice nor, for that matter, the impenetrable and terminal possibility of the sinner refusing salvation and being fixed in evil. The first and last thing is the limitless saving creativity of God. Hope must take its stand on the fact that God alone is God. This God is the creative source of all being and existence. Only this God has the transcendent power of moving the human will to freedom. And this God desires all to be saved and to come to the knowledge of the truth (1 Tim 2:4).

While hope takes its stand in the saving will of God, neither adoration of God's gracious will, nor love for our neighbor, can rest there. Even theologians know in their own way what C. S. Lewis described as "the dangers and perturbations of love." Every effort to explore the ultimate things in human fate finds its clearest focus in Christ. In the paschal mystery of the suffering, death, burial, and resurrection of Jesus, God has already gone beyond the most fearful of human presentiments into dimensions of love we can scarcely imagine. On this matter, we recall our previous remarks in chapter 5 on the mystery of Holy Saturday.

The Subterfuge of Love

Here theology must bear in mind that there is no dimension of creation—even in its freedom—that is not contained, as it were, in the creative love of God. Even the most isolated self-enclosed being is not isolated from God. It is still held in existence by the divine power and goodness. In creating the world, God has already allowed for all being and its possibilities. God is more "within" every creature, more present to it, than it is to itself, no matter what its state. In his powerful reflection on the paschal mystery, especially in regard to Christ's descent into hell, Hans Urs von Balthasar represents Jesus descending in loving solidarity to be even with the "lost" in their self-enclosed hell. Christ disturbs this self-chosen isolation as the embodiment of the infinite love that has never been withdrawn. The sinner may be isolated from God, but Christ is not isolated from the sinner.[35] Admittedly, this is an extraordinary—though not unprecedented—statement of hope. On the one hand, such a theological insight respects human freedom, for there is no

---

34. Ibid.
35. *The von Balthasar Reader*, ed. Medard Kehl and Werner Löser, trans. R. J. Daly and F. Lawrence (Edinburgh: T&T Clark, 1985), 153.

divine violence involved. On the other hand, this freedom is "disturbed" at
its foundations. At its foundation and in every moment of its exercise, God is
present and acting as the giver of being and freedom. We may assume, too,
that God is lovingly aware of the residual flickerings of goodness and love
in the sinner that no amount of malice can gainsay. Hope can imagine God
healing and blessing this largely disowned dimension of self, to bring it to
its destined completion.[36] But in this extreme case, God is not intervening
as the great rival, the limitlessly threatening "Other" that the sinner defied
or feared. Rather, the divine Other is now revealed in another "otherness,"
namely that of the vulnerable and compassionate love. This love originally
summoned the alienated creature into being, created it in the divine image,
and offered it the fullness of life.[37]

Hope, then, must allow for this kind of loving "subterfuge." God refuses to
be anything but love. That love cannot allow the divine image to be defaced
in any creature. Having said that, the language of hope can probably go no
further. The rest is the silence that can speak only in prayer. When all theories or human judgments are silenced, the ultimately determining realities
are found only in depths of divine wisdom and the unbounded freedom of
God's love.

Even those who seem determined to be damned still remain the object of
the prayer of the church. They are enfolded in the compassion of the saints as
they intercede for them. These great intercessors have refused to put any limit
on God's love. Because their hopes "touch upon the infinite" (Thérèse of
Lisieux),[38] they live beyond the world's calculations of merit and punishment,
and breathe the air of pure grace. In this surrender of hope, St. Thérèse is
accompanied by many of her sisters in the past—who, in fact, left little mark
on the theological tradition until recently. From the Middle Ages on, we
mention Mechtilde of Hackeborn, Mechtild of Magdeburg, Angela of Foligno, Lady Julian of Norwich, and Catherine of Siena. It is worth noting, too,
that both the Dominican Catherine of Siena and the Carmelite Thérèse have
been recently proclaimed Doctors of the Church. Though these holy women
made little impact on the official theology of their times, there existed a more
hopeful patristic tradition, many centuries before them. It is represented by

---

36. For further apposite remarks, see Sachs, "Current Eschatology," 247–48.

37. *The von Balthasar Reader*, 153.

38. Her words: "mes espérances qui touchent à l'infini" in Lettre A, Soeur Marie du Sacré
Coeur, Manuscrit (B 2v, 28) in *Sainte Thérèse de l'Enfant-Jésus et de la Sainte-Face: Oeuvres Complètes*
(Paris: Cerf-Desclée de Brouwer, 1992), 224. See also *The Story of a Soul: An Autobiography of Saint
Thérèse of Lisieux*, trans. John Clarke, 3rd ed. (Washington, D.C.: Institute of Carmelite Studies,
1996), 192, "my desires and longings which reach even into infinity."

such figures as Clement of Alexandria and Origen, whom we have already mentioned,[39] along with Gregory Nazianzen, Gregory of Nyssa, Didymus the Blind, Evagrius Ponticus, Diodorus of Tarsus, Theodore of Mopsuestia, Maximus Confessor, and John Scotus Eriugena. To hope for the ultimate reconciliation of all with God is to find oneself in good company.[40]

The Demands of Hope

Hope—without conditions or limits—raises its own questions. Are we all too easily "abolishing hell"? Are we influenced by the facile tolerance that has compromised too much with evil and lost a sense of true goodness? That kind of tolerance expects little of human freedom. But the "abolition" of hell in the name of genuine hope is a harsh demand. The love that "hopes all things" (1 Cor 13:8) looks to a reconciliation of cosmic proportions.[41] To hope that there is no hell, or that there is no one in hell, has consequences. It means that one must be ready to share eternal life in God with those who have been most feared, most despised, most condemned, and found to be most unforgivable. For hope to "empty" hell, it must be open to the possibility of filling our heaven with those we may have found, either in the intimate or public conduct of our lives, or in the course of history, most hateful and harmful.[42] This is the point where true hope passes over completely into the compassion of God. It leaves behind all self-regarding notions of what heaven and eternal life mean for ourselves or others. Hope for the emptying of hell can only come from a heart ready to "forgive seventy-times seven times."[43]

Hoping against hope in this way can cling to no consoling doctrine or theology. It can lay no claim to any special revelation. It is still threatened by the dreadful, intimately known, and publicly evident power of evil. The

---

39. It now appears that the condemnation of Origen's views at the Synod of Constantinople (543) and the Second Council of Constantinople (553) was aimed more at philosophical views concerning the preexistence of souls than at anything else. After all, the opinions of others here mentioned were not regarded as unorthodox. See Novello, "Death as Privilege," 784-89.

40. An accessible account of this hopeful tradition is found in Hans Urs von Balthasar, *Dare We Hope 'That All Men be Saved'?* trans. D. Kipp and L. Kranth (San Francisco: Ignatius Press, 1988). He suggests that not only may we hope for all, but that we have a duty to do so.

41. Note the profound remarks of Miroslav Volf, "The Final Reconciliation: Reflections on a Social Dimension of the Eschatological Transition," *Modern Theology* 16, no. 1 (January 2000): 91-113.

42. For further astute remarks in this context, see James Alison, *Raising Abel: The Recovery of Eschatological Imagination* (New York: Crossroad, 1996), 176.

43. Ratzinger, *Eschatology*, 217-18.

only choice for those who dare express an unconditional Christian hope is to give themselves over to Christ, in order to become instruments of a mercy that will appear as folly in the world built on judgments of violence and revenge. It is essential to our Christian calling to put all living energies into the destruction of the hells that we human beings have created. It is to live in the conviction that "love never ends" (1 Cor 13:8) and that "hope does not disappoint us" (Rom 5:5).

In the Second Book of Samuel, the wise woman of Tekoa pleads for the life of Absalom. Hope can only be enlarged by such age-old wisdom:

> We must all die; we are like water spilled on the ground, which cannot be gathered up. But God will not take away a life; he will devise plans so as not to keep an outcast banished forever from his presence. (2 Sam 14:14)

8

Heaven

The Homing of Hope

T HOUGH WE ARE ALL ONLY A HEARTBEAT AWAY from the moment of truth, the theme of heaven is not often treated in recent theology. No doubt, theologians fear to trivialize the ever-abiding mystery of God. They recognize the value of reserve when it comes to speaking of eternal life in terms of human analogies. Besides, theology has taken to heart Marx's taunt that religion is the "opium of the people." On the other hand, it is now clear that the opium of the people is the rootless doomed consumerism of our day, and it may be that things will change. A lot, of course, depends on the way God is identified in eschatology. Here, as elsewhere in theology, the distinction between human projections and critical analogical thinking based in the Christian mystery is not always clear.[1]

A BIBLICAL PERSPECTIVE

An incident recorded in the three Synoptic Gospels situated immediately before the passion narrative is a good place to start (Mk 12:18-27; Mt 22:23-33; Lk 20:27-38).[2] In this confrontation with the death-bound world of the Sadducees, Jesus strikingly expresses his sense of God as the source of endless life. The life-giving power of God is in no way limited by death. The Sadducees were well aware that many of their Jewish contemporaries hoped for eternal life. For example, this is remarkably expressed in the seventh chapter of the Second Book of Maccabees. But they felt that this was a later heretical excess, without foundation in the Torah of the Pentateuch—hence their ploy

---

1. For a sense of the history of thinking about and imagining heaven, see C. McDannell and B. Lang, *Heaven: A History* (New Haven: Yale University Press, 1988); and Alister E. McGrath, *A Brief History of Heaven* (Oxford: Blackwell, 2003).

2. For a profound exegesis of this text, see James Alison, *Raising Abel: The Recovery of Eschatological Imagination* (New York: Crossroad, 1996), 34-41.

in posing the question from what they understood to be undeniably good Mosaic theology:

> Some Sadducees, those who say there is no resurrection, came to him and asked him a question, "Teacher, Moses wrote for us that 'if a man's brother dies, leaving a wife but no child, the man shall marry the widow and raise up children for his brother.' There were seven brothers; the first married, and when died, left no children; and the second married her and died, leaving no children; and the third likewise, none of the seven left children. Last of all, the woman herself died. In the resurrection, therefore, whose wife shall she be? For the seven had married her." (Lk 20:27-33)
>
> Jesus said to them, "Those who belong to this age marry and are given in marriage, but those who are considered worthy of a place in that age and in the resurrection from the dead neither marry nor are given in marriage. Indeed, they cannot die any more, because they are like angels and are children of God, being children of the resurrection. And the fact that the dead are raised Moses himself showed, in the story about the bush, when he spoke of the Lord as the God of Abraham, the God of Isaac, and the God of Jacob. Now he is God not of the dead, but of the living, for to him all of them are alive." Then some of the scribes answered, "Teacher, you have spoken well." For they no longer dared to ask him another question. (Lk 20:27-40; see also Mt 22:23-33; Mk 12:18-27)

The text is not about marriage, though it does link procreation to a world in which death reigns (Lk 20:34-36). Without children the race would die out. But the issue here is the character of God and the nature of eternal life. Whatever the inevitable process of decay in this biological form of life, for God the human person is endlessly alive. The fact that the great patriarchs of Israel, and our ancestors, are dead for us, does not mean they are dead in the sight of God. Nor, for that matter, do they need to be dead for the Christian community in any absolute sense. In the above-sited passage, Jesus is engaging the Sadducees concerning the interpretation of the key text in the Pentateuch to which they had appealed (Exod 3:6, 15, 16). In the parallel text in Mark, Jesus adds, "Is not this the reason why you are wrong, that you know neither the scriptures nor the power of God?" (Mk 12:24). He goes on to declare that his interlocutors are "quite wrong" (Mk 12:27). God is life: to be with God is to live. For those living in a death-bound world, living means not being dead; but for God, the source and goal of life, the human person is always a living reality—in life, in death, and after death. The scholarly scribes react positively to Jesus' reading of the matter.

Jesus, in effect, is dramatizing a great alternative facing every mortal being. Either we live in fear in a world of futility, bounded inexorably by death (cf. Rom 1-2) or we live in hope. For hope opens to a horizon in which the death-less vitality of God is the all-determining consideration. From a New Testament perspective, whether we live or die, we are all and always alive to God and belong to Christ (1 Cor 3:22; Phil 1:20). In a radical sense, heaven, as eternal life, has already begun. Our real lives "are hid with Christ in God." To God, the infinite ocean of life and love, no one is ever just "dead," least of all when they die. Clearly, Jesus radiated a sense of the boundless ebullience of divine life, and of the unending life that would result from surrendering to the source and goal of all the living. Heaven, from this point of view, is our full awakening to that life, in the company of all those who have lived for God.

A THEOLOGIAN'S WITNESS

But how do we begin thinking about the life-giving, deathless reality of God? A fairly long quotation from one of the great theologians of our time points us in the right direction. A few months before he died in 1984, over eighty years of age, Karl Rahner recorded his last words on the last things.[3] He expresses disappointment that the eternal life that Christians hope for is regarded as nothing special compared to this life. The way it is spoken of owes more to human projections than to a genuinely theological approach. As a result, a harmful trivialization of God's final gift occurs. Eternal life is made to look like too much a part of the system of the way things are. The inexpressible otherness of life in God is homogenized into a familiar blend of fantasy and routine experience. As Rahner writes, "What we call the direct vision of God in eternal life is downgraded to one pleasant activity among others that go to make up this life. What is not properly perceived is the unspeakable wonder of the fact that the absolute divinity, God's very self, stoops down naked and bare into our narrow creatureliness."[4]

Hence the problem for theology today, and for every day, is to express in telling terms "the unspeakable wonder" of the divine self-gift. How can

3. Karl Rahner, "Experiences of a Catholic Theologian," trans. Declan Marmion, SM, and Gesa Thiessen, *Theological Studies* 61 (2000): 3-15.
4. Ibid., 14.

eschatology most fittingly speak of such matters? Rahner invites us first of all to ponder more deeply the meaning of death. He conceives of it as a moment of pure freedom, but now shorn of all the triviality of life's distractions, self-serving projects, and uninspired projections. It leads into a vast silent abyss. But there is more: "Then, within that immense terror that is death, will come a cry of unutterable joy which will reveal that the immense and silent void we experience as death is in reality filled with the primordial mystery we call God. It is filled with God's pure light, with his all-absorbing and all-giving love."[5]

In this pure light of God, Jesus appears. He is the one in whom the Infinite Mystery has come out of itself toward us, to become *our God*—in a way that is possible only to God: "in this incomprehensible mystery we can catch a glimpse of Jesus, the blessed one who appears to us and looks at us. It is in this concrete figure of Jesus that all our legitimate assumptions about the incomprehensibility of the infinite God are *divinely surpassed*."[6]

The eighty-year-old theologian concludes with a humble testimony:

> I would not like to call what I have just said a description of what is to come. Rather I have merely offered, however falteringly and provisionally, an indication of what one might expect in what is to come, namely, by experiencing the descent that is death as already the ascent of what still awaits us. Eighty years is a long time. For each of us, however, our allotted life-span is that brief moment in time which will be what constitutes our ultimate purpose and meaning.[7]

In speaking of what is "our ultimate purpose and meaning," theology needs to be both humble and creative. It is dealing with what is beyond the scope of any human eye, ear, or imagination (1 Cor 2:9).[8] Not to appreciate the humble God-focused negativity of the New Testament leads to trivializing the mystery of Heaven.

There is more than negativity in the New Testament, however. The world's surpassing fulfillment in the Reign of God is evoked in the interplay of many rich images. These are drawn from nature as with the garden of paradise, the stream of living water, the light of God, and so forth. In interplay with such metaphors there are images of a more cultural kind, such as the city

---

5. Ibid., 15.
6. Ibid.
7. Ibid.
8. See the remarks in chapter 3 above on the "negativity" of New Testament hope.

and Reign of God, reconciliation, and new covenant. These in turn interact with images of personal union as in mutual indwelling, marriage, family, communion in the Spirit and in the body of Christ. A dominant analogy is that of conviviality, as with the great banquet and communal celebration. The image that has most deeply affected the tradition in regard to heaven is drawn from our experience of enlightenment and vision: we will see God, face to face. In this exuberant interplay of images and symbols, each evokes some aspect of eternal life.

The range of these images would be drastically reduced should heaven be presented as neatly located object or place uncritically extrapolated from the world of human experience. Hope for eternal life is narrowed if its expression congeals in one or other particular image. We must allow for the relativity, multiplicity, and interplay of the scriptural images—and the biblical reserve in which they are used. To pretend to know too much is to cause a certain distaste or repugnance regarding the subject of heaven. Heaven begins to look like a cloyingly ethereal state designed for the consolation of the devout. More grossly, it can appear as something like an unending binge for a consumer society.

THE HEAVEN OF GOD-IN-CHRIST

For each particular life, heaven is the moment in which God's self-giving purpose is fulfilled.[9] Our limited imaginations are inclined to think of God as the infinite object that we attain through the right use of our freedom. The possession of God is the reward of a good life. But it is easy to forget that God is the primary agent. God is the first and final giver. The Holy Trinity at every moment of each life is inexhaustibly and lovingly involved. God is intent from the beginning on drawing each human being into the divine life. When John declares that "God is love" (1 Jn 4:8, 16), he goes on to remind us that it is not as though we first loved God, but that God has first loved us (1 Jn 4:10). The divine initiative is always the determining factor in bringing the human person to the fullness of life. The creature's coming to be in God is the outcome of the divine self-giving through the course of a lifetime. The life of each one of us occurs in a history claimed by the divine Word and permeated by the Holy Spirit. The grace of God is at work to make the finite creature capable of an ever-greater gift. The Spirit of God transforms

---

9. See my *The Trinity of Love: A Theology of the Christian God* (Wilmington, Del.: Michael Glazier, 1989), 103-7, 165-68.

our minds and hearts. The gifts of faith, hope, and love will lead to the final gift.

In this perspective, heaven is the point when all the gifts of God in life (and death) reach their culmination. As self-giving love, the Trinity is an open circle of a divine communion into which the created person is drawn. The dynamism of this divine "drawing" or attraction reaches an irreversible moment of success in the destiny of each of the blessed. The divine self-communication fully occurs only when each of the blessed enters the joy of the Lord.

Heaven is, then, a theological mystery. It is for each one an instance of divine success. Put this way, heaven is not first of all a reward for a life well lived, nor the glorification of the moral achievements of a particular person. Nor, more philosophically, is heaven reducible to one's own final act of self-transcendence into God. Heaven is not attainable through human effort. There will certainly be the joy of fulfillment as our hearts find their final rest in the God for whom they have longed. But both the joy and the fulfillment presuppose the divine initiative, as we have been stressing. From the beginning to the end of human existence, all is from the grace of God. Only through such a divine gift can we aspire to and attain the fullness of life to which we are called. In this regard, in each of the blessed, the mystery of God comes into its own and finds a new dwelling and glory. In each of the blessed the Reign of God for which they prayed has finally come.

At the center of this "theological" heaven is Christ. It will mean being with him and sharing in his joy. St. Ambrose sums it up: "For life is to be with Christ; where he is, there is life; there is the kingdom."[10] Jesus does not cease to be the mediator between God and our humanity once his followers reach heaven. His role as "the way" (Jn 14:6a) is not terminated, so that he then drops into the background when the goal is reached. For heaven is the radiant unveiling of what has been true all along: "No one comes to the Father except through me" (Jn 14:6b). In the vision of God, the blessed see God precisely as the Father of our Lord Jesus Christ and share in the joy of his relationship with the Father: "If you know me, you will know my Father also" (Jn 14:7). In the end, those who have followed Christ as "the way" will find him revealed as "the truth and the life" (Jn 14:6a). God is seen as the divine mystery of self-giving that was incarnate in him in order to gather all into a God-dimensioned unity (Jn 17:22-23). Our "face-to-face" vision

---

10. Ambrose of Milan, "Vita est enim esse cum Christo; ideo ubi Christus, ibi vita, ibi regnum." (*In Luc. X* in *Patrologiae Cursus Completus: Series Latina*, 221 vols. [Paris: J. P. Migne, 1844-64], 15:1834.

of God is to see God in the face of Christ: "For it is the God who said, 'Let light shine out of darkness' who has shone in our hearts to give the light of the knowledge of the glory of God in the face of Christ" (2 Cor 4:6). Far from making Christ disappear into the shadows, the radiance of the divine light never loses its luminous Christ-centered intensity. The infinite divine mystery remains ever defined by what has been given in the beloved Son.

Looked at in this way, heaven is the space fashioned for us by Christ within the divine life. It is no extraterrestrial location, but the final dimension of creation.[11] It includes the spiritual and material universe. By making all this his own, Christ has introduced every dimension of existence into the divine realm. In assuming our humanity as the Word made flesh, in rising from the dead to a new realm of life, he takes with him our humanity, its world, and the whole universe into a final sphere of existence. In this perspective, heaven is experiencing what Paul proclaimed when he spoke of Christ in the following terms: "He is the image of the invisible God, the firstborn of all creation; for in him all things in heaven and on earth . . . all things have been created through him and for him. He is before all things and in him all things hold together" (Col 1:15-17).

THE HEAVEN OF MARTYRS

The divine self-gift is eminently achieved in the case of the martyrs. These, in their different ways, have died that the Reign of God might come. Heaven belongs in a special way to them. God will be revealed as their God, the vindicator and glory of those who have witnessed to divine truth and justice. However much it cost them, they have refused to live their lives dominated by the false gods behind the pride and violence of the world: "They have conquered [their accuser] by the blood of the Lamb and by the word of their testimony, for they did not cling to life even in the face of death" (Rev 12:11; cf. 15:5-7). These martyrs (literally, "witnesses") have contested the idols of a world that demand so much human sacrifice and imprison the world in hopeless subservience to God-less powers. In the courage and compassion of these followers of the Crucified, the Spirit reveals the true meaning of history. They have heard the divine Word. They have let the voice of God interrupt the self-glorifying tale of victory over the weak and the powerless. They have obeyed the summons to live in the world as the expanding field of life-in-the-making. For these martyrs, true life was to be lived in the service

---

11. Joseph Ratzinger, *Eschatology: Death and Eternal Life*, trans. M. Walstein (Washington, D.C.: Catholic University of America Press, 1988), 234.

of the Kingdom. They witnessed to eternal life already begun in the works of love and justice and mercy. By contemplating the heaven of the martyrs, hope rejects any vision of heaven as the dwelling place of a God indifferent to human suffering. The true God is the glory of those who have never tried to escape from the demands of justice, love, peace, and forgiveness.

Through their union with the Crucified, the martyrs have witnessed to the reality of "life to the full" (Jn 10:10). Their yes to human life and dignity receives its divine affirmation. The promise inherent in their decisions on behalf of love and justice is now eternally kept. The witness of the martyrs embodies a splendid defiant hope for the heaven of God. The highest values will not be forever vulnerable to the powers that work through the threat of death. Whenever hatred, violence, envy, and selfishness are accepted as the basic world-forming realities, then risking one's life and reputation in the service of truth or in care for the hopeless must appear to be a risk too great to bear. But if "charity and its works" remain (*Gaudium et Spes* #39), if authentic life will be vindicated in glory, if eternal life is already in the making through the decisions of our present history, these heroes of hope challenge all to ask, Why not live now? They have dared to love and hope even unto death. But when the dreaded reality of death comes up against the radiant witness of the martyrs, it is the meaning of death that changes. It becomes the door opening in welcome for all who have lived for God. The martyrs have stepped through the door of death into the eternity of God. They have entered the realm of ultimate life as the affirmation, the vindication, and the homecoming of true selfhood. To die in the Lord is to be glorified in what our Christ-conforming loves have made us.

HEAVEN AS THE FULLNESS OF LIFE

While the God of heaven must always be the God of martyrs, believers are called to the fullness of life through many vocations. The Spirit works through the witness of different lives and gives different graces in leading all to eternal life. Every calling costs a life in its own way. There is a dimension of martyrdom in every vocation. Here we will dwell on three features of eternal life that all vocations share, namely, love, vision, and resurrection.

Heaven as Love

The Spirit of love inspires love, and this love subsumes, transforms, and fulfills all the loves that make up our lives. However the worth and passion of life are expressed, the quality of any life is most surely revealed in its loves: "Where your treasure is, there is your heart also" (Mt 6:21). What is spontaneously called "real life" is essentially found in the loves and relationships that make up that life in its interpersonal, social, or global dimensions. Admittedly, the experience of love has its own ambiguities. The erotomania of contemporary Western culture immediately reduces all love to sexual relationships. Given, too, the fragility of marriage and family life, the experience of love is frequently associated with pain and the possibilities of self-destruction. Love, even if it is the most precious intimation of eternal life, has been often compromised by darker forebodings.

Still, there is something overwhelmingly positive. For anyone in love, not only the beloved other, but other persons, even formerly ordinary words, places, gestures, and the body itself are transformed. Everything is suffused with a new energy and enchantment. Isolated individuality is dissolved; one's whole being expands. There is a loss of self—as independent and isolated—but only for the sake of finding this self transformed in a transfigured world.[12] The Canticle of Canticles, literally, "the Greatest Song of All," remains the classic biblical affirmation of this fundamental ecstatic feature of human existence: "I am my beloved's, and his desire is for me" (Cant 7:10).[13] To the lover, the world is a new creation, even if hitherto unknown and unrecognized. As an astute psychologist remarked,

> It is a very common experience. Everyone who has truly fallen in love has had it, and sex, in the narrow sense, is not the important thing. It is the recognition of "our native country" through love of another. We glimpse his or her eternal destiny and so also our own—we know, in that moment, that we have the freedom of that country forever.[14]

The self-in-love with the beloved other experiences intimations of eternity and homecoming. That affective experience is the most evocative, and perhaps the most neglected, anticipation of the life of heaven. For all the loves of our heart are homing to a final fulfillment. Heaven, then, is where our God-ward hearts come home and find their peace. Eternal life is the ultimate state of being-in-love. It shares in the love life that God is.

---

12. P. Kreeft, *Heaven: The Heart's Deepest Longing* (San Francisco: Ignatius Press,1989), 100-108.

13. See Roland E. Murphy, "The Song of Songs," in *The New Jerome Biblical Commentary*, ed. Raymond E. Brown, Joseph A. Fitzmyer, and Roland E. Murphy (Englewood Cliffs, N.J.: Prentice-Hall, 1990), 462-65, for introduction and commentary.

14. Helen Luke in her commentary on Dante's *Divine Comedy*, as quoted in R. Haughton, *The Passionate God* (London: Darton, Longman & Todd, 1981), 50.

The eschatological experience of love in its fullness is the best context in which to ponder the sacramental meaning of marriage. The committed union of man and woman is a "visible sign of invisible grace." In this connection, the "invisible grace" of heaven is, indeed, ultimately a life of self-giving, ecstatic love. This is the deeper sense of the old saying: "marriages are made in heaven." Each marriage, whether in human judgment it succeeds or fails, is an act of hope, imagining the fullness of life in terms of the many-splendored experience of human love. Though, as Jesus teaches, in that final realm of love, procreation is no longer necessary (see above), it does not mean the cessation of love—as unreserved self-giving and delight in service of the other. It anticipates a transformed world that the present form of sexual union can only dimly foreshadow.

Not only the world's mystics and martyrs but also its lovers must be permitted a say in what "life to the full" (Jn 10:10) finally means. If "God is love . . . [and] those who love are born of God and know God" (1 Jn 4), there are consequences. Human loves sacramentally prefigure a final form of loving as a sharing in the ultimate being-in-love that is at the heart of trinitarian life. Though heaven will be immeasurably more than the fragility and incompleteness of earthly loves, it is not less.[15] The final transformation of love subsumes and fulfills everything that our present experience of love has found worthwhile. The passion, commitment, and generativity of our earthly loves remain the most vivid and the most familiar anticipation of what we shall be. None of this need be excluded from the great Pauline affirmation: "Love remains" (1 Cor 13:8). To adapt the Johannine expression, loving our neighbor, whom we can see, is the best preparation for meeting the God of love, whom we cannot see (see 1 Jn 4:21).

Dostoevsky pondered the limitations of earthly love. Loving another completely is always imperiled by the demands of the ego. Only Jesus himself represents the ultimate ideal of loving others as oneself. If we keep in mind that this expansion of our being into an ever fuller communion is a gift of the Spirit, we can appreciate more deeply what the great Russian novelist writes. For those who follow Christ,

It has become clear as daylight what the last and highest stage of the evolution of the personality must be. It is this: when our evolving is finished, at the very point where the end is reached, one will find

15. For wise remarks on heaven and sexual love, see Peter Kreeft, *Everything You Ever Wanted to Know about Heaven . . . But Never Dreamed of Asking* (San Francisco: Ignatius Press, 1990), 117-32.

out . . . with all the force of our nature that the highest use one can make of one's personality, of the full flowering of one's self, is to do away with it, to give it wholly to any and everybody, without division or reserve. And that is sovereign happiness. Thus, the law of "me" is fused with the law of humanity . . . This is exactly the paradise that Christ offers.[16]

Heaven as the Vision of God

Christian tradition has privileged the the "beatific vision" as the essential meaning of heaven. It is the "face-to-face" vision of God. St. Paul writes, "For now we see in a mirror, dimly, but then we shall see face to face. Now I know only in part; then I will know fully, even as I have been fully known" (1 Cor 13:12). As a church doctrine, the character of this vision of God was defined, from the early fourteenth century, as "intuitive or even face-to-face" knowledge of God. The divine essence is finally revealed "plainly, clearly, openly" to the mind strengthened with the *lumen gloriae*, "light of glory" (Council of Vienne, in 1312).[17]

The Thomistic tradition highlighted the beatific vision as the perfect act of human intelligence—even though it is necessarily accompanied by beatific love and joy. Through this God-given capacity to see God face to face, the human spirit is radically and finally divinized. It participates in the light of God's own knowledge of the divine essence, and, consequently, of everything in God. This eschatological mode of seeing and knowing God contrasts with the present human situation. Even in the holiest life there remains a basic limitation in our knowledge of God in this life. Through the gift of love we are united to the will of God, but the face of God is unseen. Our words, symbols, sacraments, and overall experience of the effects of God's saving action in the world offer only a clouded intimation of what God is like. The divine reality itself remains always in what the mystics refer to as the "the cloud of unknowing."[18]

But the limitation of our knowledge of God in this life is overcome in the beatific vision. The blessed "see" God in an immediate, face-to-face knowledge. In a final act of grace, the divine Word informs and actualizes human

---

16. Quoted by Yves Congar, *The Wide World My Parish* (London: Darton, Longman & Todd, 1961), 60-61.

17. See J. Neuner and J. Dupuis, *The Christian Faith in the Doctrinal Documents of the Catholic Church* (London: Collins, 1982), 684-88.

18. *The Cloud of Unknowing*, ed. William Johnston (Garden City, N.Y.: Doubleday, 1975).

intelligence to overcome its limitations and to expand its capacities so that it can receive the full evidence of the divine reality. In this way, the human mind catches up, as it were, with the reality of its love. For even in this life, love can pierce through the darkness in which God dwells and be united with God through surrender to the divine will. In a final vision, the mystery that love had lived is disclosed in its full clarity. What was loved in darkness is now known in light; and love is transformed into the joy and peace of possession.

It must be admitted that this account of the beatific vision has suffered from being too closely connected with a rather abstract notion of the soul with its different faculties of intellect and will. Theological traditions made different choices. The Thomistic tradition, as already mentioned, came down in favor of the intellect. In the beatific vision, love possesses its ultimate object through the intellect transformed in the divine light and sharing in God's own self-knowing. The Franciscan school was less intellectualist. It accented the role of the will as brought to its perfection in the fullness of love and union with God. It was a minor tragedy for theology that an abstract anthropology kept these two approaches apart. But it need not be so. The good points of both traditions can be brought together in a more concrete notion of human consciousness. Here we make a few remarks.

First, the knowledge concerned is too often understood in a very visual manner, based on an analogy with ocular vision. "Seeing" God is not the same as the eye's seeing colors and shapes. A full notion of knowing must go beyond gazing or having a good look. Knowing is more than simply "seeing." Take, for instance, the following experiences. When we have an insight, there is an experience of sudden release and delight. It is likely to be expressed in the exclamation, "Now I've got it!" Such occurrences are not unlike the "Eureka!" of the scientist, or the "Aha!" of the artist, or the pleasure of getting the point of a joke. More seriously, the moment of insight is experienced as a liberating breakthrough in the self-consciousness of the sufferer after successful therapy. In such instances, knowing something is more like an ecstatic expansion of what we are. We begin to exist more truly. We dwell more consciously in the real world. It results in a joyous self-expansion into the universe of what truly is the case. However modest any given instance might be, it occurs as a moment of homecoming for the questioning existence that we are.

The act of insight is even less like simply "seeing" when we consider it more deeply. In the experience of insight, the knowing self and the reality known come together as one. In that event, from one point of view, some aspect of the reality of the world comes to consciousness in the actively knowing self.

From another viewpoint, the self experiences an ecstatic expansion into the real world. Clearly, then, a simplistic notion of knowing as just "having a good look" tends to distort the far more mysterious experience of our knowing as an ecstatic form of self-realization within the mystery of things. From this perspective, if we understand the beatific vision as the deepest kind of knowing, any suggestion that the blessed simply look at God from the outside, as "out there" as it were, is precluded. Eternal life is rather the blessedness of being ecstatically immersed in the ocean of Light.

We can take this point a little further. A more philosophically attuned theology tended to think of our spiritual being in rather abstract terms. There is a spiritual soul, and that is equipped with the two separate faculties of intellect and will. The intellect intends truth, and the will reaches out to the good. It is more helpful, at least when we are considering the beatific vision, to give the primacy not to metaphysical psychology of different faculties but to our own conscious experience. Our human consciousness unfolds as an integrated movement and outreach. The truth we seek and the goodness we desire interpenetrate. The more we know, the more we love; and the more we love, the more intimate is our knowing.[19] Being-in-love is experienced as being-in-truth. Both the self and the other are disclosed in their fullest lived reality. Here we need ponder only the experience of significant relationships or, say, any great cause that has mightily drawn us out of ourselves. The more I study ecology, the more my love for nature increases. In that greater love, I find new energies to nourish the wonder and exploration of the natural world. Knowing and loving necessarily interfuse. The greater the love, the greater the capacity and the desire to know "the beloved other," be it an individual, a community, or a larger aspect of the world itself. A greater knowing nourishes a greater loving. The two activities work together to bring joy and delight. We are inspired to communicate the excellence, the beauty, the value of who or what has been so radiantly disclosed.

By reflecting on this kind of experience, we have a more satisfactory analogy of the beatific vision. God indwells the deepest center of our being as light and love. The final receptivity to the light and truth of God's Word can-

---

19. Bernard Lonergan writes,

> The transcendental notions, that is, our questions for intelligence, for reflection, for deliberation, constitute our capacity for self-transcendence. That capacity becomes an actuality when one falls in love. Then one's being becomes being-in-love . . . Once it has blossomed forth, and as long as it lasts, it takes over. It is the first principle. From it flow one's desires and fears, one's joys and sorrows, one's discernment of values, one's decisions and one's deeds. (*Method in Theology* [New York: Herder & Herder, 1972], 105).

not be separated from an ecstatic surrender to the love and unity of the Spirit. In that light and love, we see the face of the Father in its infinite beauty and mystery. In short, the beatific vision is more like an immersion in the fathomless depths of God, in which truth, goodness, and beauty are one in the trinitarian life. In that abyss of mystery, we are united with God and with all creation in God.

This is to say that the beatific vision must be understood—as with everything that can be said about heaven—in trinitarian terms. The vision of God is not simply beholding the Trinity "from the outside." God is not one object, however sublime, among many that the blessed now see. They do not so much see what God is like as become transformed into the divine likeness. To see God is to be "deified" or, if you will, "trinified." The essential meaning of the beatific vision lies in our future participation in God's own self-knowledge and joy. The blessed are enfolded into the communal life of the three divine persons. As the divine Spirit transforms our finite capacities, the human spirit becomes pure receptivity to the Word of God and lives in praise of the Father's glory (cf. Eph 1:3-14). As participants in this vitally trinitarian communion, the saints in heaven possess an "inside" knowledge of God. Transformed, they share in what God is—self-giving, infinite life. In this connection, theology, in its modest accounts of the beatific vision, has often had recourse to the words of the Psalmist,

> They feast on the abundance of your house,
> And you give them drink from the river of thy delights.
> For with you is the fountain of life;
> In your light we see light. (Ps 36:9)

Within the divine mystery, in communion with the divine persons, the blessed share in the divine life. A variety of sense analogies is applicable here. To be in heaven is to feast on the reality of God, to drink from the source of life. It is to taste the sweetness of the Spirit and inhale its fragrance. It is to plunge into the depths of divine mystery. We will hear the eternal music of the Word and touch and embrace what in life could never be grasped. We will move with the energies of divine life and see the beauty of perpetual light that shines upon us. Within God, the blessed not only meet God face to face but also see the universe, in every dimension of its being and becoming, as God's continuing and creative self-manifestation.

St. Thomas would say that the humble task of theology is, from the outset, deeply eschatological. Though theological wisdom draws its evidence from divine revelation, it finds its assurance in the clarity already enjoyed by the saints in heaven. Their present vision supports the faith, hope and love of our pilgrim state. Or, more technically, theology "proceeds from principles known in the light of a higher knowledge, which is that of God and the blessed" (*STh* 1, q. 1, a. 2). This is to say that the beatific vision is what can be described as a participative knowledge. It is not a matter of looking at God "from the outside" but a knowledge born of an immersion in the boundless ocean of trinitarian life. It is to live from, with, and in God: "After this life, God himself is where we will be" (*ipse [Deus] post istam vitam est locus noster*) (Augustine, *Ennar in Psal.* 30).[20]

There is a final point. Even though God is "seen" and "possessed" in the glory of heaven, God does not cease to be absolute and inexhaustible mystery. God is not an object bounded by the limits of finite vision. God is not possessed as something held and grasped. The immediacy of face-to-face vision does not mean that the mind now masters what was once too difficult or too obscure. No doubt many mysteries will be resolved in the light of God, but the abiding mystery of God is not one of them. For God can never be placed in some larger context. There are no other points or frames of reference or comparison. The infinite mystery essentially—and forever—surpasses all contexts, all reference points, and the universe itself.[21]

In other words, to see God face to face is finally to see that God is the limitless, all-surpassing, and all-giving mystery of true life. It will mean seeing God as the generative source of all creation, but always immeasurably more than creation or its limitless other possible forms. This all- and ever-surpassing transcendent excess of God is technically referred to as the divine "incomprehensibility." It does not, of course, mean that the beatific vision is somehow compromised or frustrated. The light of glory is the luminous space in which everyone and everything will appear to manifest the divine radiance. But that luminous mystery of God is revealed as limitlessly surpassing the created universe and all other possible universes, and the still-finite mind of the blessed, however enlarged its capacities. Caught up into such infinity, the human spirit finds its basic delight in the joyous experience of knowing that God—Father, Son, and Holy Spirit—is truly God, mystery unbounded. The depths of God are experienced as immeasurable by any created mind, yet as inexhaustibly attractive in its infinite expanse. Such a notion of the beatific vision inspires hope to imagine definitive union with God not only as the

---

20. *Patrologiae Cursus Completus: Series Latina*, 36:252.

21. Paul J. Griffiths ("Nirvana as the Last Thing: The Iconic End of the Narrative Imagination," *Modern Theology* 16 [2000]: 19-38) imaginatively suggests how the Buddhist notion of nirvana has similarities with the Christian tradition of the beatific vision.

peace of a final homecoming and eternal rest. It is also eternal *life*. It promises the joy of an ever-new beginning in a life of unending, adoring exploration.

The Resurrection of the Body

The full-bodied reality of Christian hope necessarily includes the resurrection of the body. Heaven is the home of the totally human. The risen Lord himself appeared not as a ghost but as the newly embodied source and form of an existence totally transformed in the Spirit. To share in his resurrection is to find that the joy of love and the light of vision overflow to transfigure our bodily being. As was previously remarked, human beings are never pure spirits. Without some form of embodiment, the human person can scarcely be said to exist. Because we are bodily beings, our existence is related to the totality of the world and its creative source. Hence, hope justifiably envisages the resurrection of the body as conformed to the body of the risen Lord: "He will transform the body of our humiliation that it may be conformed to the body of his glory, by the power that also enables him to make all things subject to himself" (Phil 3:21).

Because the power of Christ extends to "all things," the range of hope is cosmic in its scope. G. Martelet catches the point:

> We believe that Christ, *through his risen body* is the principle of a life so absolute that it embodies on the cosmic plane, the ultimate hope of a world that has been created for the resurrection.[22]

Hope for heaven can hardly claim to be "catholic" if either the universe is left out of consideration or our embodied existence within it. Part of the problem is the limitations in our way of imagining what our bodies are. We are inclined to think of the human body as a particular personal possession. It is regarded as an individualized self-contained unit in the universe. This singular parcel of matter is thought to exist as separate from the rest of the world. It marks a physical boundary over against other bodies. In contrast to this extreme material individualism is a more relational perspective—hence more personal, more cosmic and christological in its span. The body inserts the human person into the cosmic totality. It represents not so much a boundary as a focus of relationships. While the soul is "in some sense all things" in its

---

22. G. Martelet, *The Risen Christ and the Eucharistic World,* trans. René Hague (New York: Seabury Press, 1976), 82.

spiritual capacities, the body exists in a network of relationships extending to the whole physical universe. It is a particular focal point where each is grounded in the whole and the whole is embodied in and enriched by what each one is. The resurrection of the body is, therefore, of cosmic signifi-cance.[23]

Once more we allow Martelet to recall the christological focus:

> Christ's transfigured body is the archetype of the universe already introduced, in a hidden and mysterious manner, into the state of trans-figuration, and also of the human race permeated by the Spirit and eschatologically unified.[24]

In the full unfolding of the paschal mystery, Christ is revealed as the ultimate factor in the destiny and form of creation. All creation's energies and forces are made subject to him, reintegrated into a new wholeness (e.g., Eph 1:10; Col 1:15-20; Jn 1:1-5). In and through Christ, the reshaping of the universe has irreversibly begun. Christ himself is the transcendent space in which all the becoming of history and world takes place. In this regard, he is the absolute point by which all else is measured, the goal finalizing all genetic processes. Faith in the risen One affects our sense of reality: "From the metaphysical depths of the universe, new, divinised forces are already flowing into our exis-tential environment in the outer surface of things."[25] In other words, to be "in heaven" is to be "somebody" in a transformed universe. We are not disembod-ied spirits haunting the world to come, but totally human within it.

We must keep reminding ourselves that the resurrection of the body must not be thought of in the physical terms that are relevant to this pres-ent state of biological existence. Hope, in this regard, is not a covert way of clinging to this present, inherently mortal existence. On the other hand, current physics has a more relational understanding of matter and energy, with its models of particles and waves. The constitution of the human body in a cosmic field of dynamic relationships raises new questions. An analogi-cal understanding of what is to come must have some continuity with our present experience of the body in this temporal form of life. It is a biophysi-cal, ever-changing metabolic unit serving our incarnate existence at this stage. Through the body we enjoy a relational and self-expressive participa-

---

23. Ibid., 82-92.
24. Ibid., 157.
25. Ladislaus Boros, *The Moment of Truth: Mysterium Mortis*, trans. G. Bainbridge (London: Burns & Oates, 1962), 154.

tion in the world and its history. Yet there are discontinuities as well. Paul has already reminded us of this: "What is sown is perishable, what is raised is imperishable . . . it is sown a physical body, it is raised a spiritual body" (see 1 Cor 15:35-58).

The risen life of this "spiritual body" is not a continuation of this present life. Resurrection does not mean resuscitation, even if in a higher realm. The whole person is being raised to eternal life in a creation transformed in the Spirit in the pattern of Christ's resurrection. This looks to a different mode of existence compared to the biological pattern of our present earthly existence. Nonetheless, there is some kind of essential embodiment involved. The human self is inextricably linked to its history of earthly being and freedom. A too-physiological understanding of bodily resurrection, however, impedes the appreciation of the radical transformation that is promised. The seed of eternal life is germinating in our present earthly existence. It sprouts into a mode of being governed only by our relationship to God. It blooms by conforming us to the body of the risen Christ and bears fruit in relationship to all creation penetrated by the Spirit. To change the metaphor, this new embodiment inhales the free air of God's achieved creation, and that new creation is made to serve the communion of life and love that characterizes our final state.

Grace, the gift of eternal life in God, had been grafted onto our present biophysical existence, but there are limits. Even the greatest mystic will grow hungry and weary and be exposed to disease and suffering and death. There is a more general sense in Jesus' words, "The spirit is willing but the flesh is weak" (Mk 14:38). Our future spiritual embodiment, on the other hand, will breathe the life of God and unrestrictedly expand in a new communicative coexistence in the Spirit.

The relationship of the risen body to the present bodily form of our existence manifests both continuity and discontinuity. Embodied in this space-time world, the human spirit has been sustained and enabled to expand in a creativity proportioned to it. In this world we human beings have found beauty and have felt the breadth of our universal belonging. Within it, we have adored the creative mystery engendering everything that is and will be. In the evolutionary history of such a world, we have sought for and met the Christ. As the Advent antiphon sings, "Let the earth be opened and bud forth the savior" (*aperiatur terra et germinet salvatorem*). And into such a world, generation after generation of living things have been born and died, to make the earth fruitful and hallowed for the generations to come.

In the minds of our great thinkers, this world became a universe present to itself as an immeasurable wonder. To the inspiration of our artists, it offered its shapes and colors, its sounds and movements, to burst forth into ever-new forms. In our mystics, it is a world come home to itself as something holy, a vast sacrament bearing within itself the presence of all-creative mystery. In human science and craft, it yields itself to human use, no longer as a blind force threatening humankind but as the earth nurturing the emergence of a planetary humanity. The mystery of the cosmos has smiled on us in the wonder of a human face and has given birth to each of us from the womb of a woman.[26] It has given man and woman to each other in the life-giving intimacy and shared joy of sexual love. This material universe has become, as it were, the shared body of the human spirit. To hope for the resurrection of the body implies, then, a cosmic hope of being saved with, and in, our world.

The human spirit is embodied in a material world. This means that the world of matter has been taken up into new levels of being through the activity of the human mind and heart and hand. Indeed, in the incarnation of the Word, the material world has been occupied and possessed from within by the divine mystery itself. In the resurrection of Christ, it has become the beginning of a new creation. Neither for the New Adam, nor for us who believe in him, can heaven mean leaving this world behind. This world and ourselves within it are destined, through death and resurrection, for a final transformation. All the groaning of the cosmos will yield to the Alleluia of a creation finally at home with its Creator.

To believe in the incarnate Word is to be summoned to surrender to Christ's Spirit as it animates all creation, as a limitless field of self-transcending energy. This Spirit moves, connects, and, in the end, transforms all reality into the Cosmic Christ, the Lord of the universe of grace. St. Ambrose sums up the cosmic sweep of the mystery of Christ: "In Christ's resurrection the world arose. In Christ's resurrection, the heavens arose, in Christ's resurrection the earth itself arose" (*De excessu fratris sui*, bk. 1).[27]

It is here that the Catholic doctrine of Mary "assumed body and soul into heaven" has special significance. For the assumption of Mary is a concrete symbol of the creativity of our God-charged world. Early patristic theology thought of Mary as the New Eve, formed from the New Adam (Gen 2:21-23), as the "mother of all the living." Against such a background, the assumption is a unique Marian privilege. Yet, as now assumed into the glory of Christ, she is the anticipation of the heaven of a transfigured creation.[28] She

---

26. Kreeft, *Heaven*, 99-117.

27. *Patrologiae Cursus Completus: Series Latina*, 16:1354.

28. See Karl Rahner, "The Interpretation of the Dogma of the Assumption," in *Theological Investigations*, vol. 1, trans. C. Ernst (London: Darton, Longman & Todd, 1961), 215-27.

is the paradigm of creation open to, and collaborating with, the all-creative mystery of God. As the mother of Christ, she symbolizes the generativity of creation as it is penetrated by the Spirit. In her, the earth has been opened to bud forth the savior. Her assumption nourishes hope with an assurance that our nature and our history have already come to term in Christ. She embodies the reality of our world as having received into itself the mystery that is to transform the universe in its entirety. Through her assumption into glory, our world has already become heaven.

It is not as though a wondrous transformation of the material world is totally beyond our experience. Every time we sing or speak or dance, or make music or paint, the sounds and colors and movements of the natural world breathe with new life. The arts bring about a higher, more human embodiment in the world of cultural communication. The notes on a page plot the emergence of a symphony, as instruments made of animal tissue, metal, and wood work together with human skill and imagination to produce a great musical event. The energies of matter have been tapped to provide human intelligence with possibilities of communication as with the worldwide electronic Web. The creative human spirit is ever infusing matter with life and meaning and bringing about a new level of embodiment. When we speak of the resurrection of the body, the relevant question—if it can ever be positively answered—is this: How might the divine creator Spirit so penetrate and refashion the world of matter as to bring into being a risen body appropriate to life in Christ?

There were old answers; today they tend to raise a smile, and we may be well advised to follow Paul's advice to the Corinthians on this matter (1 Cor 15:35-58) and recognize the limits of our imagination. Still, medieval theologians, with an eye to the risen body of Jesus, spoke of the qualities of the glorified body in terms of its perfect atunement to the demands of the Spirit in the realm of eternal life.[29] Thus, it was gifted with "impassibility," or an inability to suffer. It would show a "subtlety" or material refinement. It would move with "agility" and be spatially unbound. It would shine with "clarity" or special radiance. The provocative feature of these seemingly curious suggestions is the readiness of past theology to think of the material constitution of body in another dimension, outside the space-time continuum of our present existence. Moreover, in the current science of matter, mass and energy are interrelated. Subatomic entities exhibit both particle and wavelike features. In the world of relativity, the "laws" of time and space as we experience them in the familiar sensory world are strangely indeterminate when

---

29. For example, Thomas Aquinas, *Supplementum*, qq. 82-85.

it comes to the innermost constitution of matter as quantum physics would describe it. The imaginative language of current physics already begins to sound like a description of the glorified body as the medievals thought of it. Clearly, theology, as it continues to work closely with quantum physics and the new cosmology, may well come up with a notion of the risen body that will take it beyond our present discretion and make for more eschatological excitement in this area.[30]

In the meantime, we continue to believe in the resurrection of the body and the life of the world to come. Bernard Prusak's evocative words can serve as a summary:

> All the notes which form "the melody" of an individual person's life, echoing through the movements of an unfinished symphony within history will, in the resurrection of the dead, become fully integrated within the once unfinished but now once and for all completed symphony of history and creation. In the final consummation, we will all together experience the entire symphony of our histories—after the final note has been written and played. All the *notes* of our individual melodies will have been composed within an embodied history, like molecules of ink on a material score, but in the completed cosmic symphony echoing in eternity in union with God, each individual, personal melody will resonate, together with all the others, the whole identity of our embodied history with a deeper reality than the molecules of the bodies in which the identity of our life was originally composed. In that dynamic finality, "matter and spirit will belong to each other in a definitive fashion."[31]

CONCLUSION

Heaven is, then, an irreplaceable symbol in the language of Christian hope for what is not yet and cannot be fully known. Reserve is in order, but also a quiet joy—perhaps even excitement, despite the "certain shyness" of which a great Christian writer, C. S. Lewis speaks:

---

30. The complexity of the issues is comprehensively brought out by R. J. Russell in his modestly entitled, "Eschatology and Physical Cosmology: A Preliminary Reflection," in *The Far-Future Universe: Eschatology from a Cosmic Perspective*, ed. George F. R. Ellis (London: Templeton Foundation, 2002), 316-54.

31. Bernard P. Prusak, "Bodily Resurrection in Catholic Perspectives," *Theological Studies* 61 (2000): 64-105, here 105.

In speaking of this desire for a far-off country, which we find in ourselves even now, I feel a certain shyness. I am almost committing an indecency. I am trying to rip open the inconsolable secret in each one of you—the secret which hurts so much that you take your revenge on it by calling it names like Nostalgia and Romanticism and Adolescence; the secret which also pierces with such sweetness that when, in very intimate conversation, the mention of it becomes imminent, we grow awkward and affect to laugh at ourselves; the secret we cannot hide and cannot tell, though we desire to do both. We cannot tell it because it is a desire for something which has never actually appeared in our experience. We cannot hide from it because our experience is constantly suggesting it, and we betray ourselves like lovers at the mention of a name.[32]

---

32. C. S. Lewis, *The Weight of Glory* (New York: Macmillan, 1949), 4.

9

Hope's Eucharistic Imagination

VATICAN II REFERS TO THE EUCHARIST AS "the summit and source of the life of the Church" (*Sacrosanctum Concilium* 10). Such a statement has an eschatological ring to it. As the summit, the eucharist is the height on which the church stands and looks toward its future. From that standpoint, the horizon of hope opens up in its manifold dimensions. It stretches out to what no eye has seen, nor ear heard, no human heart conceived, concerning all that God has prepared for those who love him (1 Cor 2:9). The eschatological sweep of the eucharistic vision takes in all the particular horizons of Christian life, practice, and organization. It anticipates the full realization of what is to come. The whole of history becomes a time of Advent as hope awaits the *parousia*, the final manifestation of him who is already giving himself in what the church is celebrating.[1]

The eucharist is also the source. Hope is ever renewed as the church proclaims the death of the Lord until he comes (1 Cor 11:26). The food and drink of the eucharist sustain the energies of hope. This sustenance provides the strength to act with world-transforming energies of "love, joy, peace, patience, kindness, generosity, faithfulness, gentleness, and self-control" (Gal 5:22-23a). These vital gifts are boundless in their scope: "There is no law against such things" (v. 23b). Possessed and inspired by the Spirit of Jesus himself, the hope of the church continually draws from this unfailing source.

St. Irenaeus of Lyons, eighteen hundred years ago, in his confrontation with Gnosticism, the heady "new age" spirituality of his day, expresses a basic rule: "Our way of thinking is attuned to the eucharist; and the eucharist in turn confirms our way of thinking" (*Adversus Haereses* 4.18.5).[2] This is especially the case for our way of thinking about the activity and object of Christian hope. In celebrating the eucharist, the hope of the church finds both its criterion and its most concrete expression.

---

1. For a valuable patristic approach, see G. Wainwright, *Eucharist and Eschatology* (London: Epworth, 1971).

2. *Patrologiae Cursus Completus: Series Graeca,* 161 vols. (Paris: J. P. Migne, 1857-66), 7/1:1028.

THE IMAGINATION OF JESUS

Attuning its way of thinking to the eucharist, the church looks forward from its summit and lives in contact with its unfailing source. There it obeys the command of Jesus, "Do this in memory of me" (1 Cor 11:24).[3] He has not left the church a theory but has commanded an action. Jesus, present in the power of the Holy Spirit, is a "commanding presence." He is not in the first instance a sacred reality contained in the bread and wine, but "the resurrection and the life" (Jn 11:25). His life-giving presence draws his disciples in every age into the self-giving existence represented in the eucharistic symbolism.

There is a point to make here. Even the best eucharistic theology tends to hurry on to theoretical considerations of the eucharist as a sacramental sign and symbol. It easily overlooks what is most obvious. The eucharist has its origins in the creative imagination of Jesus himself. His eucharistic gift means not only receiving his body and blood. It is also a matter of being imbued with his imagination. Paul had occasion to observe, "Let each of you look not to your own interests but to the interests of others. Let the same mind be in you that was in Christ Jesus" (Phil 2:4-5; cf. Gal 3:27). In the parables he told, in the meals shared with his followers and with the sinners and outcasts, Jesus was in effect inviting all these to share his subversive imagination. He imagined the world otherwise. The master symbol of his imagination was the Reign of God. This divine realm contrasted with the harsh, God-remote, segregated domains jealously defended by the religious and secular authorities of his day. That old world constantly reinforced the rules of exclusion. It expressed itself in a fierce etiquette of apartheid. The unworthy "nonperson" was no fitting companion to the worthy. He or she had no place at the table. Hospitality had definite limits.

As Jesus proclaimed the Reign of God, he was the focus of wondrous new hopes. He made room for all those whom the cultural idols of his day— and throughout time—had excluded and demeaned. In his imagination the murderous fantasies of the world are disarmed. To the poor in spirit belonged the great gift of the Kingdom of God. The meek, in their renunciation of violence and revenge, would be the decisive force in history; they would inherit the earth. The merciful would find themselves in a universe of mercy. The pure of heart, surrendered to God's will and God's Reign, would see

---

3. Cf. 1 Cor 10:16; Mt 26:26-29; Mk 14:22-25; Lk 22:15-20.

God—revealed in the love that Jesus embodied. Peacemakers would be called God's very own children. In the same way, all who accepted the struggle involved in doing what is right and in witnessing to what is truly good would find themselves anew in God's Kingdom. No matter how they might be vilified, they would have reason for rejoicing in what was coming into being (Mt 5:3-11).

The way Jesus imagined the world and the new age that had dawned is implicit in his eucharistic commandment. Past biblical scholarship surmised that he was mistaken in expecting the Reign of God to come about in his day. But it must be remembered that Jesus was not less than the prophets. He spoke for God, and for what God was doing and intending. Neither for him nor for any other prophet did this mean an empirical controlling knowledge of consequent historical events. He was speaking for what God was doing, in a final time of grace, beyond human possibilities or calculations. The only language that could express such consciousness of mercy, salvation, and judgment had to be symbolic and imaginative. The first age of Christian reflection had to begin unpacking this symbolic totality of Jesus' eschatological imagination. It could not be said all at once. The New Testament inevitably expresses the final age of grace in terms of a number of phases and events. Now was the acceptable time: Jesus had come, preached, healed, suffered, died, and risen from the tomb. But there was a "not yet." Hope was anchored in fact, but there were different interpretations of how near or how far in the future the consummation of God's plan would be. For that reason it seems oddly monodimensional to ask if Jesus was wrong about the timing of his Father's salvific plan. Because of his surrender to the will of the Father, he regarded the time frame of the coming of the Kingdom as neither his business nor that of anyone else—that is, neither his disciples nor "the angels of God" (cf. Mk 13:32). The closer we move to his God-centered imagination, the more we are drawn into the all-deciding character of his mission as it bore on the incalculable totality of God's design.[4]

In a final meal with those closest to him, he gave dramatic expression to his way of imagining his God-given mission to the world.[5] Paul wrote for the benefit of the Corinthian community, which was in danger of falling victim to other imaginations. He brought his readers back to what Jesus himself has done: "he took a loaf of bread, and when he had given thanks, he broke it

---

4. For a fuller discussion, see James D. G. Dunn, *Christianity in the Making*, volume 1, *Jesus Remembered* (Grand Rapids: Eerdmans, 2003), 790-824, 884-90.

5. See James Alison, *Raising Abel: The Recovery of Eschatological Imagination* (New York: Crossroad, 1996), especially chapter 3, "The Discovery of Jesus' Imagination" (pp. 57-76).

and said, 'This is my body that is for you. Do this in remembrance of me.' In
the same way he took the cup . . . 'This cup is the new covenant in my blood.
Do this . . . in remembrance of me'" (1 Cor 11:23-25). Jesus is here acting
in the most familiar of all human contexts, namely, the sharing of a meal
involving the most common of commodities, bread and wine. Yet he did this
in the most unpromising of situations. He was conscious of the arrival of a
final decisive hour. His disciples were full of foreboding. They feared for him
and for themselves. After all, one of them would betray him, and the rest
would abandon him. A conspiracy to do away with him had been gathering
momentum. His enemies were implacable in their determination to purge
their world of the imagination that he embodied. Yet, in the teeth of such
terminal opposition, he surrendered himself to the Father for the sake of all
who would follow him. In their turn, his followers would experience a world
inhospitable to everything his eucharistic gift represented. For Jesus, as for
them, there was no question of putting a nice construction in a violent world.
Yet his imagination was centered on the gracious power of God to give life
where death had reigned before. He imagined the world otherwise. For him,
something was happening that would change the world from top to bottom.

Whereas in the Synoptics and Paul, Jesus commands followers to remember
his self-gift through the symbols of the bread and wine, in John's Gospel this is
expressed in another form.[6] He washes the feet of his disciples: "For I have set
you an example, that you also should do as I have done to you" (Jn 13:15). He
imagined his self-giving love "unto the end" (Jn 13:1) in a way that included
his disciples. Conformed to him, they would become a community of loving
service. From one point of view, the eucharist proclaims the self-giving of Jesus
on the cross so as to nourish the life of his followers (1 Cor 11:26). But this
must be related to another aspect. The gift transforms those who receive it. The
love that gives itself calls into existence a community that must busy itself in
humble, mutual service: "If I, your Lord and Teacher, have washed your feet,
you also ought to wash one another's feet" (Jn 13:14).

This is to say that Christian hope draws its character from the creative
imagination of Jesus himself. The Spirit that possessed him will inspire the
young to see the visions and the old to dream as he himself did (cf. Acts 2:17).
His followers are invited to enter into his way of imagining God, themselves,
and the world. His imagination inspires the pilgrim life of each one. Clothed
with his imagination, nourished by his body and blood, breathing his Spirit,
hope goes on. It must allow for the patient recognition that "it has not yet

---

6. See Anthony J. Kelly and Francis J. Moloney, *Experiencing God in the Gospel of John* (New
York: Paulist Press, 2003), 141-68, 274-85.

appeared what we shall be" (1 Jn 3:2a). Yet it looks for his final manifestation: "What we do know is this: when he is revealed, we will be like him, for we will see him as he is" (1 Jn 3:2b).

In this eucharistic context, we have paused to emphasize the imagination of Jesus in which the church shares. Our purpose here is not to weaken any theology of Jesus' objective real presence, but to highlight its intimately personal character. Imagination is transformative. Any artist must be patiently imaginative, playing with many images before the luminous form emerges. Likewise, the scientist has to experiment with all kinds of formulas and symbolic equations before the moment of insight occurs. Most of all, the prisoner, the sufferer, the dying would be utterly overwhelmed without the seemingly impractical activity of imagining the world differently—in terms of release, healing, and life in another dimension. The ability to imagine is what makes and keeps us human. It gives our lives momentum, direction, and shape, molding our existence into something passionate, defiant, and creative. It is the ability to see the world "otherwise." Most of all, in grief and isolation, in those dark phases of human journey, imagination comes into its own as a creative energy. It works within the unfinished business of our lives and opens it to forgotten other dimensions. Into this world of hope, the imagination of Jesus has entered, to inspire hope for eternal life. In the time and space and opacity of our present existence, the eucharist draws us into the imagination of "Christ in you, the hope of glory" (Col 1:27).

OTHER IMAGINATIONS AND
THE EUCHARISTIC IMAGINATION

The imagination of hope disturbs our cultural fantasy worlds. Enacted in the eucharist, hope rejoices in the extremity of that love that impelled the Lord to give his body and blood as our food and drink. The gift that only God can give is a shock to the taboos of a culture wary of love, and which is incapable of understanding the divine passion. Yet the dimensions of God's gift cause our hearts "to burn within us" (Lk 24:32). The eucharist dissolves "the heart of stone" and replaces it with the "heart of flesh" that Ezekiel had promised (Ezek 36:24-28). Self-serving patterns of exclusion are deeply embedded in any culture. These are upset by the demands of a holy communion of selfless love, and all the subtle strategies of image making are torn open by the living imagination of him as the "real presence" of what is to come.[7]

---

7. William T. Cavanaugh, *Torture and the Eucharist: Theology, Politics, and the Body of Christ* (Oxford: Blackwell, 1998), is a powerful political statement of the meaning of the eucharist.

When hope is nourished by the imagination of Jesus and the imagination of the church, it finds in the eucharist a master symbol of what is present in its full promise. Without such a focus, imagination can degenerate into private fantasy, and any expression of hope becomes paper-thin. But in the concreteness of the eucharist, hope goes beyond fantasy and abstraction. The world is radically the field of trinitarian self-giving love. It is earthed in time and space. It comes to expression in a given community of unfinished human beings who, despite all weakness, can draw on an inexhaustible source of hope and courage.

The imagination that the eucharist nourishes sees the impersonal "objectivity" of science in a new way. Latent in the scientifically established world is the mystery of divine creation and incarnation. The universe is a field of divine communication. God has called everything into existence. The Father has sent his Son to dwell among us. The Holy Spirit makes us aware of the great mystery at work. The incarnate Word reveals the extent of divine giving in the passion of the cross. And his resurrection from the dead inspires in us even now the hope of a final universal transformation. The ultimate values of life, love, and communion are not confined to intrapsychic space. They enter into the texture of reality itself. "Hard science," taken to an extreme, is an illusion. The universe is not structured on impersonal universal laws. It cannot be adequately explored only through a science of inanimate objects. For even science knows that the universe owes its development to singular happenings. Under the influence of "strange attractors,"[8] it leaps into new levels of being. In this development, the ultimate "strange attractor" has been revealed as the risen Christ himself.

The eucharist, then, celebrates the universe as a great spiritual breathing space. The imagination, mind, and heart expand to apprehend the whole as a field of communion and multidimensional connectedness in Christ. In him "the whole fullness of the deity dwells bodily" (Col 2:9). In that God-filled space, hope must go beyond any self-enclosed individualistic viewpoint. The eucharist derives from Christ's own sense of reality; for him, it is a field of communion and mutual indwelling. In John's Gospel, Jesus prays "that they may all be one. As you, Father, are in me and I in you, may they also be one in us . . . I in them and you in me, that they may be completely one" (Jn 17:21-22). The implication is clear: our unity in God derives from the way

---

8. David Toolan in *At Home in the Cosmos* (Maryknoll, N.Y.: Orbis Books, 2001) explains this mathematical term as the mysterious influence that causes the developing system to branch in this way rather than at a point of bifurcation. It is "strange" because it leads to widely variant and unpredictable consequences (p. 171). For the christological analogy, see p. 200.

the Father and the Son are united in the one divine life. The divine persons are not independent entities somehow consenting to come together. The life of the Trinity consists in an eternal flow of each divine person into the others and of the others into each. In that realm of relationships life is expressed as mutual self-giving. Beatrice Bruteau nicely observes, "Instead of taking as the norm of Reality those things which are *outside* one another, he [Jesus] takes as a standard and paradigm those who are *in* one another."[9] Here we are challenged to imagine our interrelationships in terms of mutual indwelling modeled on the union existing between the Father and the Son. In such a life, each nourishes and sustains the being of the other. Human existence when it is most conformed to the divine manner of being means nothing less than the gift of ourselves. We are *within* one another for the life of each other. By being from the other, for the other, and *in* the other, our earthly human lives participate in God's own trinitarian love life. And this is exactly the character of the life that the eucharist already celebrates, even as it looks to its fulfillment.

THE EUCHARIST WITHIN COSMIC TRANSFORMATION

So far, we have considered the eschatological bearing of the eucharist in terms of imagination. Needless to say, the realism of the eucharist is in no way compromised. Admittedly, the Catholic doctrinal tradition usually spoke in philosophical and physical terms. It aimed to present some understanding of the change that occurs to bring about the "real presence." The hallowed term in this respect was "transubstantiation." It was introduced into theological discourse by Roland Bandinelli, later Pope Alexander III, in 1140. It then became a formal doctrinal term by entering into the definitions of the church at the Fourth Lateran Council (1215), and it remained part of Christian vocabulary thereafter. Thomas Aquinas elaborated and refined its meaning by employing technical Aristotelian categories such as substance, accidents and the manner in which change occurs. Nonetheless, it is not always remembered that he presented the eucharist first of all as a "sign" of God's gift.[10] Because the eucharist is the sign of Christ's self-gift to the church, he is present to us in a way that exceeds all worldly categories.[11] A new and

---

9. See Beatrice Bruteau, "Eucharistic Ecology and Ecological Spirituality," *Cross Currents* 40, no. 4 (Winter 1990-91): 499-514, here 502.

10. On the nature of the sacraments as signs, see *STh* 3, q. 60, a. 1.

11. The work of Louis-Marie Chauvet on eucharistic signification is of special importance as he exploits the possibilities of the postmodern context. See *Symbol and Sacrament: A Sacramental*

philosophically strange term was necessary to express the transforming power of the paschal Christ—hence, "transubstantiation" (*STh* 3, q. 75, a. 1). The self-giving love of God acts beyond the scope of any earthly form of change. The transforming power of Christ extends to all times and places (*STh* 3, q. 56, a. 1 ad 3). In the power of his Spirit, Jesus becomes a flesh-and-blood real presence through the eucharistic action. It is an answer to the prayer of the church to the Father, the Creator of all, as the current liturgical prayer has it:

> By the power of your Holy Spirit sanctify these gifts we have brought before you so that they may become the body and blood of your Son, our Lord Jesus Christ, at whose command we celebrate this eucharist. (Eucharistic Prayer III)

To appreciate the eschatological significance of this eucharistic transformation, we must place it in a larger frame of reference. There are two related perspectives. The first is the dynamic context of God's action in the universe at large. The second looks to the radical sacramentality of the church that is manifest in the eucharist.

The all-embracing significance of the mystery of Christ is expressed in the various Pauline and Johannine statements. It speaks of how "all things" are made through him, in him, for him (Jn 1:3; 1 Cor 8:6; Col 1:16). In this cosmic vision, Christ is both at the origin and at the end of what is coming to be. He is the one to whom all things are tending. He is the image in which all things are made. So utterly does he fill all dimensions of the universe that Paul declares that "all things hold together in him" (Col 1:17). As the coherence of all creation, he both unifies and reconciles. Christ embodies the Father's outreach toward a fragmented and alienated creation: "for in him all the fullness of God was pleased to dwell, and through him to reconcile all things . . . making peace by the blood of his cross" (Col 1:19-20). These metaphors of causing, containing, unifying and reconciling aim to express one thing: the cosmic and universal scope of what Christians hope for.

In relation to creation, Christ is "above," "before," and "beyond" all that is. He is the Word, the unique Son of the Father, and the Lord of all. The world neither utters the divine Word nor produces Christ nor contains him. Rather,

---

Reinterpretation of Christian Existence, trans. Patrick Madigan and Madeleine Beaumont (Collegeville, Minn.: Liturgical Press, 1995); idem, "The Broken Bread as Theological Figure of Eucharistic Presence," in *Sacramental Presence in a Postmodern Context*, ed. L. Boeve and L. Leijssen (Leuven: University Press, 2001), 236-62; idem, *The Sacraments: The Word of God at the Mercy of the Body* (Collegeville, Minn.: Liturgical Press, 2001).

he causes and contains everything that exists. Yet because he so precedes and exceeds all created reality, he is "within" the universe in a special manner. On the one hand, he is with God in the beginning and is identified with God (Jn 1:1-2). All creation came into being through him (Jn 1:3). On the other hand, this Word has become flesh, and dwelled among us (Jn 1:14). Lifted up on the cross, he draws all to himself (Jn 12:32). The cross, the marks of which continue into his risen life, reveals the extent of his self-gift and of the self-giving of the Father. To this degree, hope finds its center inscribed into the reality of history through the paschal mystery. A centrifugal expansion takes place from that point. The mystery of Christ unfolds into dimensions bounded only by the creative love of God.

The glory of the incarnate Word is disclosed only in his death and resurrection. To merely human eyes, he is "in the world." He is contained by it and is immersed in its cosmic processes. As a human being he is subject to the violence of its history. But to the horizon of hope, the universe is "in Christ." He embodies the ultimate life and transformation of all creation. Jesus exultantly cries out on the cross, "it is accomplished" (Jn 19:30). His mission is complete, and all creation is brought to its fulfillment. Creation, having originated in Christ, is condensed and fulfilled in him: "heaven is opened" (Jn 1:51). The God of love comes into the world through the Word and the Spirit; and that world opens into the infinite expanse of God. This universal context of God's self-giving is the setting for the sacramentality of the church, and the eucharist within it.

THE EUCHARIST WITHIN THE SACRAMENTALITY OF THE CHURCH

By celebrating the eucharist, the church celebrates the opening of heaven (Jn 1:51; 3:13; 5:26-27; 6:62; Mk 14:62). Hope moves through the course of history in the light of the divine communication that has occurred. As a gathering of believers, the church is a distinguishable presence in the world. Indeed, in its historical particularity, it is that part of the world that has awakened to the mystery that embraces all creation. Thus, the church becomes the visible witness to the invisible grace that is at work. In the totality of its life and mission, the church is the sacrament of the body of Christ being formed to its fullness as history unfolds and reaches toward its goal.

In this perspective, all the activity of the church is sacramental. It bears Christ within itself and witnesses to his presence through the ages. It is *Christopheric*, literally, "Christ-bearing." This fact is celebrated in the particularity of the sacraments as they are celebrated in the life of the body of

Christ. Yet these sacraments, and even the eucharist itself, would be an empty play of ritual signs if they were disconnected from the basic sacramentality of the church. Similarly, the sacramental reality of the church would be without substance if it were separated from the great cosmic sacramentality of creation in which the whole Christ is being born: "We know that the whole of creation has been groaning in labor pains until now" (Rom 8:22). God is at work through all time and space so that Christ "might be the firstborn within a large family" (Rom 8:29). Creation itself would be going nowhere unless, at its heart, there blazed the all-transforming mystery of Christ.

Still, we must go further. Unless the reality of Christ is understood as emanating from the self-giving love of God, it could be lost in a world of myths. It is important to distinguish between the icon and the idol, as Jean-Luc Marion has suggested.[12] In short, an idol is a human projection.[13] It is designed to reflect back to us what we are. In contrast, an icon lets another light into our world. Hence, Christ is not an idol, thereby reducing God to the limits of human vision. He is not a fabricated projection on the part of a religious system intent on bringing order into the chaos of experience. Rather, Christ is an icon, back-lit by a light not of this world. He embodies the offer of a gift unconditioned by any notion of mundane exchange or manipulation. In Christ, "the image of the invisible God" (Col 1:15), the divine light shines through. The Father holds the whole of creation in his loving gaze and summons it to hope and love. The light and the love coming from beyond the world disrupt the projections of any religious system. The disruptive excess of God's love finds its "trace" in the cross. Through the cross is disclosed the *kenōsis*, the self-emptying of Jesus, as the revelation of the unconditional love that gives itself for the world's salvation. For this reason, through the eucharist, the church proclaims "the death of the Lord until he comes" (1 Cor 11:26). It presumes a presence, and indeed, "the real presence" in traditional language. But the Lord is with us under the appearance of folly and abasement. The wounds of the cross that marked Jesus' death still indelibly mark his risen body as it is given in the eucharist. It is true to say that the eucharistic experience of the church contains within it both an assurance of Christ's "real presence" and a sense of what we might call his "real absence." For this presence can be acknowledged only in patience and hope, and this

---

12. Jean-Luc Marion, *God without Being*, trans. Thomas A. Carlson (Chicago: University of Chicago Press, 1991), 7-24.

13. How subtly these projections or counterfeits can work is powerfully described by William Desmond in his *Hegel's God: A Counterfeit Double?* (Burlington, Vt.: Ashgate, 2003): "An idol is no less an idol for being wrought from thought and concepts as from stone or gold or mud" (p. ix).

absence can be overcome only when he who is already with us in word and sacrament comes forth in his full eschatological disclosure. It is the experience of "now, but not yet." The oldest liturgical formula prays, "Come, Lord Jesus!" (Rev 22:20; cf. 1 Cor 16:21)—or, in the current eucharistic proclamation, "Christ has died, Christ is risen, Christ will come again!"

The shock of the cross grounds eucharistic hope in the reality of history. To attempt to bypass it would lead merely to an ideology of cosmic optimism. The stark shape of the cross pricks the inflated balloon of all human projections. It brings hope down to earth. In his crucifixion Jesus is transfixed by the reality of our violent history. Yet there is the trace of another reality that is not contained by any worldly power. Inscribed into the self-enclosed history of violent systems structuring the evils of the world, is the gift of God. It discloses a level of self-giving that owes nothing to a world where a pure gift is unintelligible. In the horizon of hope, however, the self-giving of Jesus on the cross reveals the self-giving love of the Trinity reaching out to all creation: "God is love, and those who abide in love, abide in God and God abides in them" (1 Jn 4:16). The Father expresses his love by giving what is most intimate to himself, his only Son (Jn 3:16). Further, he gives everything into the hands of the Son (Jn 13:3). The Son responds in love. He clings to nothing of his own. He surrenders all to the Father (Jn 4:34). The Holy Spirit witnesses to this love by drawing all into the self-giving relationship that exists between the Father and the Son (cf. 1 Jn 4:13; 5:6-7). For their part, the Father and Son now refuse any presence in the world other than through their Spirit of truth and love.

Yet the gift of God is made to the real world that has crucified the Son: "God so loves the world" (Jn 3:16). Here the bread and wine are offered as "the fruit of the earth and the work of human hands." These elements distil the meaning of nature, history, society, and culture. Through the transformation of these offerings, eucharistic hope is all-inclusive in its expectation. It envisions a universe already moving toward its ultimate transformation in Christ. The very modesty of these symbols of bread and wine makes a point. They prevent those celebrating the eucharist from pretending that they are already participating in the fullness of the eschatological banquet. The end is not yet. Hope, if it is to be realistic, must show a proper patience. It moves on in the midst of historical horrors and the deadly weight of the world's evils. There is no possibility of resorting to the eucharist as a spiritual solution impervious to the harshness and violence of history.

Still, these modest symbols of bread and wine, of common food and drink, do earth and anchor hope in the real world of nature and history. Hope begins *here*. It deals with what is. It longs for the transformation of this present reality. For into this here-and-now, the Word has become flesh and dwelled among us. In this history he has died; and in this history his tomb lies empty. In this history, witnesses to his resurrection have lived and died. And it is within this history that the church in its visibility as a community of faith and hope exists. In this world and in no other, hope must make its patient way in the vitality of Christ's Spirit. It cannot exult in the perfect possession of what is yet to be given. Yet it exalts, in praise and thanksgiving, the One from whom the end will come, who will be "all in all" (1 Cor 15:28).

Understood in this way, the eucharist is an antidote for fundamentalist fantasies about the future. It keeps open the play of the "now" and the "not yet." It lives in the in-between of Christ present and yet to come. It communicates in the common symbols of bread and wine yet acknowledges the inexpressible otherness of the gift never to be contained in worldly forms or categories. It lives in this the actual community of imperfect human beings and yet defers to the future that "God has in store for those who love him" (1 Cor 2:9). The eucharistic community is inescapably aware of limitation and imperfection of itself and its world. Nonetheless, it envisions a future that is more than the individualistic salvation of pure spirits. For such a community is not made up of shades haunting the world. It is the gathering of those who eat and drink the bread and wine of the world. In doing so, it is sustained by what only God can give, "for the bread of God is that which comes down from heaven and gives life to the world" (Jn 6:33).

TRANSUBSTANTIATION REVISITED

The transformation of the bread and wine into the body and blood of Christ begs to be related to the larger scope of divine transformation. This is instanced in the incarnation, as the Word was made flesh, and in the resurrection of the Crucified. In other words, the eucharist is primarily a sign of the total mystery of God's redeeming love at work. The transformation of the eucharistic bread and wine is not a strange, even arbitrary, miracle. It cannot be isolated from God's love for all creation. If it is considered outside this larger context, then the bread and wine are simply "the matter of the sacrament," the raw material, as it were. Transubstantiation would be simply a divine replacement of one substance with another—even though, as the scholastics would say, "the accidents" remain.

The eschatologically unnerving aspect of such accounts of transubstantiation is that the real presence of Christ is understood as ousting the reality or substance of the created earthly realities. The heavenly Christ is crudely imagined as coming from the outside, from beyond, our world. The risen Jesus is imagined to replace the "inside" of the realities we know and use. If transubstantiation is thought of in this way, the remaining appearances of the bread and wine seem like a kind of shell, providing temporary camouflage for Christ hidden within them. The implication is that the Lord's presence demands a price: the abolition of some part of created reality. The eucharist contains the heavenly Christ in a mysterious fashion, but the earthly realities of bread and wine are emptied of their substance, that is, their deepest reality. It would be hard to avoid the impression of the human reality of the fruit of the earth and the work of human hands as reduced to mere "accidents" that have no place in the final revelation of Christ. But that position can hardly square with the teaching of Vatican II's *Gaudium et Spes*:

> When we have spread on earth the fruits of our nature and our enter-prise—human dignity, fraternal communion and freedom—accord-ing to the command of the Lord and his Spirit, we shall find them again, this time cleansed from the stain of sin, illuminated and trans-figured, when Christ presents to his Father an eternal and universal kingdom . . .

The council envisages a purifying transformation of "our nature and its enterprise." In bringing about the Kingdom, God does not appear to be engaged in any destructive activity or any radical replacement of the human realities concerned. While appreciating the intense realistic thrust of the tra-ditional accounts of transubstantiation, we must ask whether it does justice to the eschatological character of Christ's presence in the eucharist.

F. X. Durrwell points us in another direction—or "elsewhere," as he puts it:

> The principle of intelligibility of the Christian mystery is in itself. Neither the bread, nor the wine, nor the meal, nor the gathering, whether grasped according to a philosophy of intention or of nature, can verify the Eucharistic presence. The key of the mystery is else-where.[14]

In a larger perspective, we must not imagine Christ "contained" in the eucharistic elements in some way. It is more a matter of the bread and wine being themselves "contained" in Christ in an eschatological and transforma-tive manner. From this point of view, the reality of Christ does not supplant or replace the innermost reality of the bread and wine. Christ's action frees

---

14. F. X. Durrwell, *The Eucharist: Presence of Christ*, trans. S. Attanasio (Denville, N.J.: Dimen-sion Books, 1974), 9.

and lifts up these elements of nature and culture to attain their fullest reality in him. By being transformed into his body and blood, they are not less than what they were previously. They attain the full and final reality of what they were meant to be: "for my flesh is true food, and my blood true drink" (Jn 6:55).[15] Familiar elements of our earthly life are constituted in their ultimate significance—food and drink of eternal life. The eucharistic food is not "the food which perishes, but . . . the food which endures to eternal life" (Jn 6:27). It is the "true bread from heaven" (6:32), "the bread of God which . . . gives life to the world" (6:33). This "bread of life" (6:35) nourishes those who receive it with the life-giving reality of Christ—"my flesh for the life of the world" (6:51). Through the transforming action of the Spirit, the eucharistic elements are no longer mere nutrients of biological life—"not such as the fathers ate and died" (6:58). They are transformed into the food and drink of eternal life in God.

By eating and drinking what Christ gives us, we have a foretaste of life in a transformed universe. This comprehensive vision sees the transformation of the fruit of the earth and work of human hands into the body and blood of Christ as an anticipation of the universal transformation that God intends. The transformed bread and wine anticipate the radical transformation of all creation in Christ. It is already in progress.[16] What is offered as bread and wine are products of nature and human culture. Yet they are given back to us as bearing their final "christened" form. In the eating and drinking of this "true food" and "true drink," Christian hope expands to cosmic proportions. The eucharistic "holy communion" embraces the whole of creation. Hope is hope for the transformation of all that is.

To appreciate this point, we must keep clearly in mind the relationship of Christ to the whole universe, as mentioned above. For in Christ "all things hold together," just as he "sums up" all creation (Eph 1:10). He is "the firstborn" of all creation and its final homecoming. He draws into himself creation in all its forms. In this extended sense, all of creation is on its way to being "transubstantiated." Transformed in Christ, it will achieve its final reality. There is a critical issue here. Christ's relationship to creation is not tyrannical. For the grace of the Holy Spirit "heals, perfects, and uplifts" all created nature. The Spirit invoked over the humble earthly offerings of the church, gives a completion and perfection beyond anything imaginable in terms of philosophical or physical categories.[17]

---

15. See especially F. X. Durrwell, *L'eucharistie: Sacrament Pascal* (Paris: Cerf, 1981), 89-113.

16. See also G. Martelet, *The Risen Christ and the Eucharistic World*, trans. René Hague (New York: Seabury Press, 1976), 160-97.

17. Hans Urs von Balthasar, *The Glory of the Lord: A Theological Aesthetics*, vol. 1, *Seeing the Form*, trans. Erasmo Leiva-Merikakis (New York: Crossroad, 1982), 679-80.

By locating the doctrine of transubstantiation in this eschatological setting, nothing is lost of its realism, and a great deal is gained. The eucharist is understood more fully as the sacrament of historical and cosmic hope. We will try to tease this out more fully in what now follows.

HOPE FOR NATURE AND CULTURE

The eucharistic symbolism brings nature and culture into a hope-filled milieu.[18] With the threat of ecological disintegration, the artificiality of a technological culture uprooted from nature is increasingly apparent. Human consciousness is not regarded as a dimension or *a part* of nature. It has been set violently *apart* from nature. In this ambivalent situation, the eucharist is an ever-renewable resource for reconciliation and hope.[19]

The great emancipations of the modern age from former oppressive structures have been achieved at some cost. The liberated individual became uprooted from nature understood as limiting or threatening personal freedom. As the sense of a sacred nurturing universe diminished and the autonomous modern person became the measure of reality,[20] a deep sense of alienation resulted. The natural world appeared to be no more than a limitless resource to be channeled and exploited for human purposes. Where an exploitative freedom reigns, there is room neither for God nor for nature.

Still, there remain ever-renewable resources of Christian hope and its accompanying eucharistic imagination. The eucharist brings together what the modern world keeps completely apart. Here eucharistic hope finds its focus in another perspective. God is so much *God*, so infinite and creative in goodness, that the divine presence reaches into the innermost depths of matter. The physical world plays a part in communicating the most divine of gifts.[21] Conversely, the material world is fully God's creation. Physical reality is so intimately possessed and held in being by the Creator that it is the medium through which the divine mystery communicates itself to human beings.[22] The Word becomes flesh, and the body and blood of Christ become the food and drink of eternal life.

---

18. For a more thorough treatment of the ecological significance of Christian faith, see my *An Expanding Theology: Faith in a World of Connections* (Sydney: E. J. Dwyer, 1993); and revised, 2003: http://dlibrary.acu.edu.au/staffhome/ankelly/. See also Peter C. Phan, "Eschatology and Ecology: The Environment in the End-Time," *Irish Theological Quarterly* 62 (1996): 3-16.

19. For a discussion of the modern situation and the value of the eucharist, see Simon Oliver, "The Eucharist before Nature and Culture," *Modern Theology* 15, no. 3 (July 1999): 331-53.

20. Mircea Eliade, *The Sacred and the Profane: The Nature of Religion*, trans. Willard R. Trask (New York: Harcourt, Brace & World, 1959), 179.

21. See Toolan, *At Home in the Cosmos*, 210-19.

22. Ibid.

This sacramental reality of the real presence is brought about by the transformation of the shared fruit of the earth and the work of human hands. The bread that is offered becomes for us "the bread of life." The wine we bring becomes "our spiritual drink." In this way, the eucharist anticipates the transformation of all creation, in which matter, spirit, nature, and culture are connected in the one God-created universe. The fruits of nature and the work of human creativity are integrated in the cosmic scope of God's self-communication in Christ. Nature and the history of human creativity interpenetrate. The produce of the earth is instanced in the wheat and grapes. Human creativity is effective in changing the grain and grapes into bread and wine. The reality of human culture is disclosed in that such food and drink are used in the convivial communication of our meals and festive celebrations. This cultural component enters into the eucharist to constitute the sign of Christ's self-giving on the cross. In its turn, Christ's self-gift incarnates the self-giving love of the Father and the grace of the Holy Spirit.

The eucharist brings together all these gifts and all these forms of giving. It locates our hope in a universe of grace and giving. From nature's generosity we have the grain and the grapes. Through the manifold collaboration of human work and skill, we have the gifts of bread and wine. From the hospitality of family and friends flow the gifts of good meals and festive celebrations. Jesus' self-giving at the Last Supper is actualized in the gift of his body and blood as the food and drink of eternal life. Working in and through all these gifts and modes of giving is the gift of the Spirit sent by the Father who so loved the world. When the church celebrates the eucharist, all these gifts come together to nourish Christian hope with "the gift of God." We are bound together in a giving universe, at the heart of which is the self-giving love of God. We are living and dying into an ever-larger selfhood: "Unless a grain of wheat falls into the earth and dies, it is just a single grain; but if it dies, it bears much fruit" (Jn 12:24). Our true identity expands in a network of relationships pervading the whole of the universe, and the deepest dimension of our relational selves reaches into the trinitarian relationships that constitute the very being of God. In the eucharist, Paul's prayer begins to be answered:

> I pray that you may have the power to comprehend, with all the saints, what is the breadth and length and height and depth, and to know the love of Christ which surpasses knowledge, so that you may be filled with all the fullness of God. (Eph 3:18-19)

FORETASTE OF ETERNAL LIFE

To sum up, in the sacrament of the eucharist are interwoven the many strands that make up the texture of Christian hope. This sacrament discloses the interconnection of many mysteries: Trinity and creation, the incarnation, the death and resurrection of Jesus, the gift of the Spirit, and the sacramental reality of the church itself. Yet the eucharist earths all such mysteries in the familiar natural and cultural realities of "the fruit of the earth and work of human hands." What is most familiar is charged with immense new significance. As a result, the eucharist figures as an intensely compact symbol of what Christian hope is about.[23]

The eucharist celebrates what is as the presence of what is not yet. It anticipates what is still to be fully realized. In the time of hope and waiting, the eucharistic community eats, drinks, tastes, breathes, and touches the future as it is already coming in Christ. Hope expresses itself in terms of the familiar, yet is beholden to the inexpressible otherness of what is in our midst. The now but not yet, the present and the absent, what is and what is to come, can be expressed in a number of complementary ways.

First there is the maternal realism of hope. Here I refer to the ancient symbolism of "Mother Church," historically represented in Mary, the mother of Christ. Through the eucharist, the Marian and maternal church conceives Christ and his members within her. This pregnancy is both a presence and a concealment. The true face of Christ, head and members, will only appear when the child of hope is born. In the meantime, the eucharist is the womb of the church. It is pregnant with the Christ who is truly and really present, but it must await the moment of birth. On that day, Christ will be born as the embodiment of the "one new humanity" (Eph 2:15; 4:12-14)). The hitherto divided human family will in this birth find the joy of its final peace and reconciliation (see Eph 2:15-22).

Second, as the Christian community acts in obedience to the Lord's command to "do this in memory of me," a healing of memories occurs. The recollection of sin, failure, hurt, and conflict, with all the horror and evil involved, has worked powerfully to form the historical identity of each individual and

---

23. Note Vatican II on this point: "Christ left to his followers a pledge of this hope and food for the journey in the sacrament of faith, in which natural elements, the fruits of man's cultivation, are changed into his glorified Body and Blood, as a supper of brotherly fellowship and a foretaste of the heavenly banquet" (*Gaudium et Spes* #38).

group. But all this is now brought into contact with that other way of remembering the past.[24] The past is reclaimed in the love and forgiveness that the crucified and risen Christ embodies. The eucharist enables the community to remember the past by assimilating and imbibing the self-giving love that alone determines the future. Each eucharist is a celebration of the mercy that can heal the memories of the evils that have been suffered or caused. The power of evil to infect history is radically undone. Time is not reduced to a history of conflict. It is more than a catalogue of violence and evil. It contains the memory of the gift of love that is greater than all human destructiveness. In the celebration of the ongoing gift of this love in the present, the past, even in its failures, can be peacefully reclaimed as the history of redemptive love at work. It continues in the present as the seedbed of hope once the destructive power of the past is broken. By looking forward from the eucharistic summit of hope, the community is freed to retrieve in its past the traces and evidences of an ultimate love and mercy.

The healing of memories flowing from the Lord's command "to do this in memory of me" is not only looking back into history, but looking forward to the ultimate reconciliation of all in Christ (2 Cor 5:17). The eucharistic tone of "Give us this day our daily bread" leads on to the next petition, "Forgive us our trespasses as we forgive those who trespass against us." The eucharist cannot be separated from this desire for reconciliation (Mt 18:35; Mk 11:25). For each eucharistic celebration is one in the number of the "seventy times seven" acts of unending forgiveness throughout history that Jesus demands (Mt 18:22). Through the eucharist, the church is formed as a historical agent of the healing of memories and ultimate reconciliation, as it intercedes for all (1 Tim 2:4). A historic outcome of this eucharistic grace is the unprecedented request of Pope John Paul II for forgiveness from all who have suffered at the hands of the church, its agencies or its people.[25]

Third, the eucharistic experience consists in various ways of "sensing" the Gift of God. As a sacred meal, it offers hope a taste of eternal life. It gives hope new eyes to envision the future in what is already present, and a new hearing to catch the ultimate promise of the Word that is spoken. In its eucharistic setting, hope can inhale the Spirit as the atmosphere of the new creation. It touches and handles the tokens of a transfigured creation. And so, as hope eats, drinks, hears, touches, and tastes its "real food and real

---

24. On this point, see Alison, *Raising Abel*, 114-16.

25. See International Theological Commission, "Memory and Reconciliation: The Church and the Faults of the Past," December 1999, http://www.vatican.va/roman . . . /rc_con_cfaith_doc_20000307.

drink" (Jn 6:55), it anticipates the festivity of the heavenly banquet.[26] Here is found the inspiration that brings forth the various liturgical arts as eschatological anticipations of the new creation. Don Saliers writes at the conclusion of an article on this theme,

> Poet, painter, music-maker; mystic, dancer, bread-baker; dreamer, potter, tent-maker; story-teller, vessel-bearer, feast-partaker. This is the eschatological art of the faithful liturgy. This is the hope of the Word made flesh. This is our embodied proclamation and our cry, "The Lord has come—Come Lord Jesus!"[27]

Human experience and imagination can never adequately depict the full extent of what God has promised. Yet hope has "tasted the heavenly gift" (Heb 6:4) in the familiarity of the flesh-and-blood reality of this present life. The eucharist gives hope an immediate contact with the divine gift. Its communal celebration locates this gift in concrete experience of time and space. Without this eucharistic immediacy and concreteness, eschatological thinking could drift toward an abstract theory or a private fantasy. In contrast, the eucharist offers a taste of the future, already present and nourishing hope into its fullest dimensions. The eucharistic community has "tasted the goodness of the Word of God, and the powers of the age to come" (Heb 6:4). Eschatology must take the psalmist's exhortation seriously, to "taste and see that the Lord is good" (Ps 33[34]:8). In the sacramental realism of eating and drinking the body and the blood of Christ, the senses of hope are heightened and intensified. St. Thomas Aquinas remarks on the appropriateness of the metaphor of tasting related to God's presence:

> One experiences a thing by means of sense, but the experience of a thing present differs from the experience of something absent. One experiences a distant reality by sight, smell, and hearing. Whereas one experiences a present reality by touch and taste. Still, while touch attains this present reality in an extrinsic way, taste attains what is present in an interior way. Now God is neither distant from us nor

---

26. "The Eucharist opens up the vision of the divine rule, which has been promised as the final renewal of creation, and is a foretaste of it . . . the Eucharist is the feast at which the Church joyfully celebrates and anticipates the coming of the Kingdom in Christ (1 Cor 11: 26; Mt 26:29)." *Baptism, Eucharist and Ministry*. Faith and Order Paper, no. 111 (Geneva: World Council of Churches, 1982), 15.
27. Don Saliers, "Worship as Christian Eschatological Art: Word and Grace Come to Life," *Uniting Church Studies* 9, no. 1 (March 2003): 9-21.

outside us . . . and so the experience of the divine goodness is called tasting. (*Postilla super Psalmos* 33, 8 [my translation])

Pope John Paul II develops this metaphor further:

The Eucharist is a straining towards the goal, a foretaste of the fullness of joy promised by Christ (cf. Jn 15:11); it is in some way the anticipation of heaven, the "pledge of future glory." . . . Those who feed on Christ in the eucharist need not wait until the hereafter to receive eternal life: they already possess it on earth, as the firstfruits of a future fullness which will embrace the human in its wholeness. For in the eucharist we also receive the pledge of our bodily resurrection at the end of the world: "He who eats my flesh and drinks my blood has eternal life, and I will raise him up at the last day" (Jn 6:54). This pledge of the future resurrection comes from the fact that the flesh of the Son of Man, given as food, is his body in its glorious state after the resurrection. With the eucharist we digest, as it were, the "secret" of the resurrection.[28]

CONCLUSION

We have presented the eucharist as the summit and source of Christian hope. Hope finds its fundamental expression in the imagination of Jesus himself as he invites his followers through the ages to share in his sense of God, human community, and the future of the world. Hope anticipates the future by celebrating the gift that is already present and nourishing itself on the true food and true drink that Jesus is. Theological words will always fail. But in this sacrament we "digest the 'secret' of the resurrection" and live by the promise that will be kept—the transformation of the universe itself.

28. John Paul II, encyclical *Ecclesia de Eucharistia: On the Eucharist in Its Relationship to the Church* (Strathfield, NSW: St Pauls Publications, 2003), par. 18, pp. 19-20.

10

Living Hope

THIS FINAL CHAPTER SERVES IN SOME WAYS as a summary of what has been treated so far. Its main focus, however, is practical—hence, "living hope," that is, hope as animating every aspect of the conduct of Christian life. It will always be in the form of a practical involvement in the paschal mystery of Christ. In union with him, people of hope are confronted with evil—in themselves and in their world. They must suffer their exposure to the power of evil by not contributing to it. Only a love that "hopes all things, [and] endures all things" (1 Cor 13:7) can find a way beyond the violence and hatred of a desperate situation.

ESCHATOLOGY AND HOPE

In its patience and endurance, hope is always reaching beyond what theology alone can deliver. As the gift of the Spirit, hope is from God, in God, and for God. As a theological virtue, it is defined only by infinities of divine wisdom and mercy. Still, an eschatologically focused theology serves to refine and inspire the energies of hope. It can do this in two ways.

First, eschatology makes clear what Christian hope is not. It is not an optimistic feeling. The gift of hope is expressed in the "character" of the patient endurance of suffering through the whole fate of human history and creation itself (Rom 5:1-5). The more hope expands in the light of the paschal mystery, the more vividly it recognizes the hopelessness of the death-bound world. The more, too, it is set in opposition to the desperate violence of that world that, by attempting to hurry history to its end, succeeds only in leaving behind a trail of victims.

In contrast to all forms of impatient apocalyptic prediction—religious or secular—hope offers no detailed knowledge of the future. It may resort, in urgent situations, to the exuberant biblical symbolism of the Book of Revelation. There is no other way to depict the power of evil. Even though the forces of evil have been cast down to earth in the heavenly war (Rev 12:7-9), the world still remains a battleground. The great dragon seeks to devour the offspring of the woman (Rev 12:3-6, 13-17), and the beast rises from the abyss, drawing the world to worship it and to make war on the elect (cf. Rev 13:1-10). These and other luridly imaginative representations of the power of evil are born out of crisis. They are inspired by the terminal experiences of struggle, persecution, and judgment. The world—or better, perhaps, a world—is ending, at least a world that has proved implacably hostile to Christian existence. Yet even here the englobing image is that of Jesus, the Alpha and the Omega, the source of eternal life (Rev 1:17-18; 22:12-17). In him all the forces of the creation are concentrated (Rev 1:12-16). He is the Lord of history, but as the Lamb who was slain (Rev 5:6-12). The terrible travail that is described throughout the subsequent appalling visions culminates in a new heaven, a new earth, and a new Jerusalem (Rev 21:1-5)—the luminous dwelling place of God and the Lamb (Rev 21:22-22:5). In its "patient endurance" (e.g., Rev 1:9; 2:2-3; 2:19; 3:10), the prayer of the church is condensed into the cry of confident longing, "Come, Lord Jesus" (Rev 22:20).

This apocalyptic style of imagination and expression must be related to the more general "negative eschatology" of the New Testament, as was mentioned previously. Hope looks beyond any clear and definite description of the last things to yield "to him who by the power at work within us is able to accomplish abundantly far more than all we can ask or imagine" (Eph 3:20-21). Hope is assured that we are already the children of God, but recognizes that "what we will all be has not yet been revealed" (1 Jn 3:2).

Second, a truly theological eschatology underlines what hope positively is. For hope moves through time in an energy flowing from the heart of Christ, crucified and risen. Its forward movement is powered and sustained by the Spirit of Jesus (Rom 5:5). Yet its path is traced and earthed in the eucharist. The sacraments of the church anticipate a universe transformed and brought to its fulfillment. Hope imagines the end out of its present experience of what is already being given. The stream of eternal life has already begun to flow. It springs up in care for one's neighbor, reconciliation with one's enemies, and in all liberating activities that refuse to leave the world at the mercy of death and violence.

THE ESCHATOLOGY OF HUMAN CONSCIOUSNESS

Clearly the gift of hope is not a surreal, unearthly addition to human life. Indeed, we can argue that our conscious existence is, in a radical and dynamic sense, natively eschatological. The self-transcending movement of our living, conscious being anticipates some ultimate completion. Aquinas would say that we have a natural desire to see God. This "natural desire" for the ultimate Good can never be in vain (*STh* 1, q. 12, a. 1). Human existence cannot be a living contradiction.[1]

The Dynamism of Existence

Bernard Lonergan's *Method in Theology* speaks of this natural desire for God in a more contemporary, psychologically attuned idiom.[2] The self-transcending drive toward limitless truth and goodness constitutes the basic dynamism of our conscious living. Lonergan is not talking about a theory. He is appealing to a set of experiences intimately accessible to everyone. We are present to ourselves in our questioning of what and why and how. The open-ended dynamic evident in our questioning attains solidity in our honest judgments about what is the case. It becomes responsible in the decisions we make for the truly good. We are in this way registering the attraction of meaning, truth, and goodness. The dynamism driving our conscious existence is ever taking us beyond all limited attainments. The meaning of all meaning is the goal. The ultimate worth of all we have found to be good is the promise. It would seem, then, that hope is inscribed into the dynamism of our being. Yet there is a question. Lonergan asks,

> But is the universe on our side, or are we just gamblers and, if we are gamblers, are we not perhaps fools, individually struggling for authenticity and collectively endeavouring to snatch progress from the ever mounting welter of decline?[3]

A hopeful answer to such questions, however it is expressed, has a profound effect on attitudes and resoluteness. Lonergan gives point to the questions implicit in our living:

> Does there or does there not necessarily exist a transcendent, intelligent ground of the universe? Is that ground or are we the primary instance of moral consciousness? Are cosmogenesis, biological evolu-

---

1. A many-sided and profound reflection on this point is found in Fergus Kerr, *Immortal Longings: Versions of Transcending Humanity* (Notre Dame, Ind.: University of Notre Dame Press, 1997).

2. Bernard Lonergan, *Method in Theology* (London: Darton, Longman & Todd, 1972).

3. Ibid., 102.

tion, historical progress basically cognate to us as moral beings or are they indifferent and so alien to us?[4]

The mind and heart cannot rest content with a little bit of meaning, truth, or goodness. We look to the full disclosure of the reality that is already sustaining our existence. We cannot be content with "partly living." The ultimate exerts a gravitational pull on our intelligence and freedom. Our present participation in being and goodness impels mind and heart to anticipate a fulfillment and completion. An anticipation of a final homecoming is built into conscious existence. Hope stirs in our every waking moment. Lonergan refers to the open dynamism at the heart of our being as our "transcendental subjectivity." It is what we consciously experience as the deepest orientation and longing of our being. It resists any form of self-enclosure, for it unfolds in the limitless horizon in which our search for meaning, truth, and goodness must move forward. In this sense, the dynamism of our conscious existence borders on "a region for the divine, a shrine of ultimate holiness."[5]

Such an account of human experience can, of course, be dismissed by various systematic manifestations of despair and cultural depression. For instance, the atheist will say that there is nothing there, that this radical openness and longing of our being are an illusion; that it means nothing, and is going nowhere. An agnostic can hesitate over the direction of this radical hopeful thrust of life and assert that it lacks any real proof. A humanist concern to improve the world might consider that any hope for a transcendent, eschatological fulfillment is a distraction from the real challenges that face society. But however the question of hope is asked or answered, the deeper question of life keeps recurring. Is our search for meaning, our concern for truth, our struggle against evils and celebration of the good nothing but a journey to nowhere and an eternally frustrated hankering for the unattainable? Is there no "last thing," no eschatological reality, in which the heart comes home and toward which the universe is tending? Hope gives a positive answer.

The Gift from Above

Yet the fullness of Christian hope is not reducible to an upward movement from the core of our being. However precious the intimations of our deepest

---

4. Ibid., 103.
5. Ibid.

thinking, our most passionate loves and creative actions, we never simply think or will ourselves into this ultimate realm. This upward and forward journey leads to an impenetrable darkness and silence. Our failures can seem too great. The sheer weight of the world's ills and evils tempt us to lose heart. The "one thing necessary" is something so "other," so far outside the "system," at once so unattainable and all-demanding, that courage can fail. If hope is to be a world-shaping energy, it is desperately in need of a gift that will make all the difference. But such a gift from above is exactly the source and foundation of Christian hope. The Word has become flesh and dwelled among us, to take on himself what we most fear. His tomb is empty; and his Spirit is the fresh air our souls now breathe. The gift of God has been given, and a fountain of living water is springing up to eternal life. Hope is not disappointed. St. Paul understands it as continually sustained by the love that is poured forth in our hearts by the Holy Spirit (Rom 5:5). In this sense, hope is born of a gift; and that gift is precisely the energies of God-given love. The fulfillment of this gift of "grace" or "being in love" is eloquently described by Lonergan:

> As the question of God is implicit in all our questioning, so being in love with God is the basic fulfillment of our conscious intentionality. That fulfillment brings a deep-set joy that can remain despite humiliation, failure, privation, pain, betrayal, desertion. That fulfillment brings a radical peace, the peace the world cannot give. That fulfillment bears fruit in a love of one's neighbour that strives mightily to bring about the Kingdom of God on this earth.[6]

This gift makes all the difference. Without it, life would be dissipated and directionless. The power of evil would be too great, and the most noble lives of self-sacrificing love would be futile gestures in a meaningless universe.[7]

Deep peace and joy resulting from self-surrender to God and love of others are the stuff out of which a life of hope is made. The gift of love makes all the difference. It inspires a passionate hope for the fulfillment of what God's love has promised. The love of God necessarily includes being loved by God and the capacity to love God in return and to be one with the divine will as

---

6. Ibid., 105.
7. Ibid.: "On the other hand, the absence of that fulfillment opens the way to the trivialisation of human life in the pursuit of fun, to the harshness of human life arising from the ruthless exercise of power, to despair about human welfare springing from the conviction that the universe is absurd."

it creates and guides the whole created universe. To live in hope is to live in a universe in which the really "last thing" is God's self-giving love. The eschaton of the love of God has predestined the universe to be transfigured in the glory of the risen Christ, "to the praise of his glorious grace which he freely bestowed on us in the Beloved" (Eph 1:5-6). It directs everything and everyone to that final state in which "God may be all in all" (1 Cor 15:28).

This final gift of God is already enacted in history through the incarnation, death, and resurrection of Jesus Christ: "For God so loved the world that he gave his only Son" (Jn 3:16). He is the yes to all God's promises and the Amen to all our prayers (2 Cor 1:20). He is the first and last letter of the alphabet of God's creative Word—"the Alpha and Omega, the First and the Last, the Beginning and the End" (Rev 22:13). All hope has its focus and foundation in him who "is before all things, in [whom] all things hold together" (Col 1:17).

The Word of God, irrevocably incarnate though it is, does not kill the ongoing conversation of human history. It comes to its fullest human hearing only in the kind of hope that welcomes the creativity of dialogue among all peoples and their deepest hopes. The Word becomes flesh, and the flesh is the story of a conversation unfolding throughout the whole human story. Because the Word was made flesh, this whole human story is fundamentally the autobiography of God. It includes the life stories of individuals and communities, of societies and cultures, and the great cosmic story of the universe itself. Everything we are in this corporeal, earthed, communal, and individual historical existence is now part of the story of the incarnate Word. The gospel story is told and retold in all the variety of contexts that make up our human condition. The good news is offered to all the longings and fears and hopes that animate human history. It provides no catalogue of information about the future, but illuminates the direction of life at whatever point hope stirs and despair threatens.

While the center is always Christ, the human telling point can be anywhere in a vast and expanding circumference. The expression of Christian hope will vary. It will speak with differing accents on the lips of, say, the young or the old or the dying. For the condemned and the guilty, it will be expressed as a plea for mercy and forgiveness. Those suffering physically or mentally will see it in terms of release and healing. It will stir in a language of liberation and justice in those oppressed by hopeless poverty or menaced with political violence. It will promise a refreshed sense of creation to those who have wakened to ecological wonder and responsibility. Those who have dedicated their lives to making peace among nations will state their hopes in terms of a final reconciliation and a new beginning. For those who have borne the brunt of some dreadful natural disaster—say in fires, earthquakes, floods, or in the recent catastrophic tsunami that affected so many on the coasts of the Indian Ocean, hope looks beyond death and grief to life beyond this world. Hope speaks in different accents and uses the whole scale of human experience for its music and song. The ever-changing human condition does not permit a monotone expression. Because any expression of Christian hope can come across as an absurd or fantastic answer to an unasked question, Christian hope demands a new imagining in every age and in every shifting context in which people are confronted with despair, meaninglessness, and loss.

The gospel of hope is, then, addressed to the inconclusive and fragmented reality of human history. It offers, however, a first and last word on what is coming to be. It does not lose its definitive character. For creation as a whole, and human history within it, has been claimed and welcomed by God. Karl Rahner makes the point:

> For since we are living in the eschaton of Jesus Christ, the God-Man who was crucified for us and who has risen for us and who remains forever, we know in our Christian faith and in our unshakeable hope that, in spite of the drama and ambiguity of the freedom of the individual persons, the history of salvation as a whole will reach a positive conclusion for the human race through God's own powerful grace.[8]

This "all-powerful grace" is nothing other than the gift of the Spirit, the God-given energy moving everything and everyone to its ultimate form in Christ: "If the Spirit of him who raised Jesus from the dead dwells in you, he who raised Jesus from the dead will give life to your mortal bodies also through his Spirit who dwells in you" (Rom 8:11). The groaning of all creation in its cosmic activity of giving birth, along with the groaning of those who hope for their full redemption (Rom 8:22-23), is supported by the "unutterable groanings" of the Holy Spirit praying in the hopeful prayers of all Christians. The abiding witness of the Spirit opens hope to expand, beyond its hesitations and often self-imposed limits, to its fullest dimensions (Rom 8:26).[9]

Hope, then, lives at the intersection of two vectors, the gift of God from above and our spiritual searching from below. The downward vector of grace

---

8. Karl Rahner, *Foundations of Christian Faith*, trans. William V. Dych (New York: Seabury, 1975), 435.

9. For commentary, see Brendan Byrne, *Romans*, Sacra Pagina 6 (Collegeville, Minn.: Liturgical Press, 1996).

meets, intensifies, and transforms the upward vector of our anticipations from below. Or, as the venerable theological axiom states, "grace heals, perfects, and elevates nature." This is not to suggest that there is a perfect symmetry. The gift of God never fits neatly into a human system of anticipation and expectation. The shock of the cross and the surprise of the resurrection are always too much for human wisdom or human capability (1 Cor 1:25). Against the temptation to homogenize "what God has prepared for those who love him" (1 Cor 2:9) as a mere extrapolation of human experience, hope needs to live in another sense of proportion. Only God can give the final moment of the end. Yet the self-giving and transforming love of God is already at work in the freedom and fabric of creation. It will reach its completion in God's time and on God's terms. Grace, the gift from above, will heal, perfect, and fulfill the "upward" longing and expectation of nature and its history. The creative Spirit will form the fragmented vocabulary of our present existence into the great poem of the new creation. In its divine dimensions, it is beyond our understanding and control. Here a singularly evocative passage from Vatican II's *Gaudium et Spes* points theology in the right direction:

> We know neither the moment of the consummation of the earth or of the human, nor the way the universe will be transformed. The form of this world, distorted by sin, is passing away; and we are taught that God is preparing a new dwelling and a new earth in which righteousness dwells, whose happiness will fill and surpass all the desires for peace arising in the hearts of men. Then with death conquered, the sons of God will be raised in Christ, and what is sown in weakness and dishonor will put on the imperishable: charity and its works will remain, and all creation which God made for human beings will be set free from its bondage to decay. (39)

It may be that little more can be said about the time and character of the end. But in the present, the life-giving Spirit inspires in those who hope the restlessness of a love and compassion beyond human calculation. Not to enter that field of self-giving love through care for the other, forgiveness of enemies, and solidarity with the hopeless is to be left out of what is the force of the future. In short, hope places us actively in the world understood as God's reign. It keeps on posing the question: If eternal life is actualized only in the self-dispossession of love, why not start living now? One way or another, hope demands a love unto death. The life of hope peaks in self-surrender to God and the divine purpose for all creation. Its eschatological openness immunizes against the attractions of the false gods, which demand so many victims to feed the needs of pride, greed, and the lust for power. Such idols seek to deprive the present of hope. In its turn, genuine hope adores the God to whom the future really belongs. The oppressive power of every idol is called into question.

HOPE AS CONVERSION

The conduct of hope expresses itself in a life of radical hopefulness. No one is once and for all hopeful (see Rom 5:5). A continuing process of conversion must take place. It affects mind, heart, and imagination in the effort to understand what we are hoping for and on whom we rely. Through participation in the mystery of Christ, we are given new capacities to understand, new values to express, a new relational self to discover, and a new perspective on the world and its history. Let us briefly dwell on these various dimensions of the hopeful self.

Religious Conversion: The Reign of God

In terms of horizon, the conversion of hope leads to the unconditional adoration of the God of hope. It means moving from the idols of culture to entrust oneself to the living God. Through God-given and God-directed hope, the Holy Spirit draws us out of ourselves, into a self-surrender that goes beyond the limited perspectives of optimism or pessimism. Through the Spirit we move beyond all worldly supports and systems to yield unreservedly to the Reign of God. In the self-surrender of adoration, hope rejects the idolatrous self-projections inherent in any life, culture, or society. It takes to heart the last words of John's letter, "Little children, keep yourselves from idols" (1 Jn 5:21). Positively, the horizon of hope is limitless, bounded only by the infinity of God's freedom and saving intention to be "all in all" (1 Cor 15:28). The consciousness of hope shares in the divine consciousness itself, as the three divine persons embrace in communion the universe of created persons. Hope adores the Father as the infinite source and goal of all creation. It breathes the divine Spirit, the infinite wave of freedom moving all into a future that only God can give. In the light of the Word, it finds the world already claimed by God and on the way to transformation.

The more trinitarian the eschatology, the more it permeates every aspect of theology.[10] The Greek theological tradition speaks of *theiōsis*, the deification of our finite being as we are transformed in the very life of God. This implies the "trinification" of human existence as it is drawn into the love life of the divine persons, as members of Christ, temples of the Spirit, and children of the Father. Similarly, there is a trinitarian implication in the doctrine of the incarnation. The Word alone is incarnate; but the Spirit is poured forth to dwell in all hearts, and the Father is the horizon in which all creation comes home. In such a perspective, the end point of creation is the "enworlding" of the Trinity. As the ancient philosophical tradition had it, the good consists in its capacity to share what it essentially is (*bonum est diffusivum sui*). Theologically speaking, God is essentially self-giving. Or, as Pannenberg would say, "God's being *is* God's rule."[11] This is not to say that God depends on creation to be God. It does mean, however, that the holy Trinity has freely and eternally chosen to create the universe in order that it might be saved, healed, and fulfilled by participating in God's own life.

Christic Conversion: The Parousia

The historical focus of this religious conversion always remains Christ. As hope is more fully converted to Christ, it is not looking backward, but forward. It becomes a longing for the return of the Lord. Through sacramental and mystical union with Christ, hope participates in his mind and heart and imagination. The key to every phase of Christ's being, in life, in death and in his risen existence, is always the Reign of God, his Father. To pray for the coming of the Kingdom and the final coming of Christ is to pray for the same thing. He sums up the whole of history as "the Alpha and the Omega, the first and the last, the beginning and the end" (Rev 22:13). He comes as the incarnate meaning of all history. For that meaning is not decided by victors dictating their memoirs of triumph over lesser mortals. It will be decided by him who has made himself one with the lost and the victimized who, however anonymously, have suffered in the name of the Crucified.

Jesus is risen precisely in the cruciform character of his whole existence. His risen and glorified body still bears the wounds of the cross. The self-giving love that marked his death on the cross is the very form of his risen

---

10. We note here the deep trinitarian structure of Pannenberg's eschatology. See Christiaan Mostert, *God and the Future: Wolfhart Pannenberg's Eschatological Doctrine of God* (Edinburgh/New York: T&T Clark, 2002), 183–225.

11. For citation and comment, see ibid., p. 137.

existence. Already from his heart flows the stream of eternal life, even though
it bear the marks of its collision with the lethal powers that still seek to dom-
inate our life in the world. Even though we are not of the world, we are still
in it (Jn 17:11), and being in it leaves its mark. Yet hope longs for the coming
of the "Other" who has, in his life, death, and resurrection, drawn near to
the closed, defensive house of our being, "Listen! I am standing at the door,
knocking; if you hear my voice and open the door, I will come in to you and
eat with you, and you with me" (Rev 3:20).

Ecclesial Conversion: The Community of Hope

The religious and Christic dimensions of hope provoke a conversion that is
corporate, communal, ecclesial. Hope is not an individualistic spirituality
but a communal life. The God of hope is the focus of the shared hope of the
pilgrim people of God.[12] For the church is the milieu that nourishes and
supports the praxis of hope. In that communal life, the gospel is proclaimed,
the eucharist is celebrated, and the witness of its members is manifested in
the abundance of the Spirit's gifts: "to each is given the manifestation of the
Spirit for the common good" (1 Cor 12:7). Yet no individual Christian is
offered a free ride in the communal hope of the church. Hope cannot pas-
sively live *off* the community of hope, but *for* it and *within* it, as it contests
the depression and despair of every age. Yet without this communal, historically realized dimension, hope would be a flimsy individualistic posture. In
its corporate form, however, hope expands in the quickening field of the
church's experience of the Spirit. The divine witness calls to mind the "dangerous memory" of Jesus' involvement with the sinners, outcasts, and poor of
the world and impels hope to its cosmic proportions (Rom 8:18-27).

The ecclesial community, breathing an atmosphere of trinitarian communion (Jn 17), must cultivate a culture of hope to counter and cure the
social culture of despair and violence. Hope takes on its historical form in the
flesh-and-blood reality of the church, as it reaches forward to full arrival of
the Reign of God over all creation. Particular issues in eschatology arise not
as the disconnected themes in an abstract or inconclusive hope, but as extrap-
olations within the flow of the trinitarian life already pulsing within the life
of the church. It represents the totality of the creation already enfolded into
the realm of trinitarian life: "this life was revealed, and we have seen it and
testify to it" (1 Jn 1:2).

---

12. See *Lumen Gentium,* chap. 8, "The Pilgrim Church," ##48-51.

Moral Conversion: Solidarity with the Hopeless

Hope inspires a moral conversion. It is expressed in a conduct or praxis that turns from spiritless conformism to moral creativity and collaboration. The moral dimension of hope challenges the politics of its time, national and international, to look beyond their natural alliances with power and wealth. It embraces the tasks of making peace and forming a more just social order. Only hope can cause economics to envision a global situation in which the world's goods can be decently shared. It would be a form of despair to allow anyone to be degraded to a subhuman existence through greed, neglect, or exploitation. Though often unnoticed in its effects, hope underpins the relationships of marriage and family. For it fosters both a sense of the family of humankind and the irreplaceable uniqueness and transcendent worth of each human life. Further, the impulse of moral conversion raises questions for the mass media. Can it function as an instrument of more hopeful communication of the human reality? Need the news of the day be a catalogue of misfortune, scandal, and failure? Must the virtue ennobling the great and small lives that make up existence on this planet go unreported and be deemed unworthy of comment? Most of all, hope allies itself with the hopeless, the exhausted, the forgotten, whom official history has relegated to the margins of worthlessness.

The "self-transcendence" of which the philosophers speak is realized on a new spiritual level, as it appreciates more effectively the claims of the other. This outgoing movement leaves behind despair and all forms of limited hope. It looks for an inclusive and compassionate practical involvement with "the hopeless"—at the point where there is no earthly hope. In anticipation of an ultimate community of life, hope works to achieve appropriate social, economic, political, and cultural expressions in order to bring about an all-inclusive common good. Admittedly, these concerns make their own martyrs. But without their witness, hope would be a worthless posturing.

The history of mutual victimization is challenged by the community of hope. The church is called to be the agent of another history. Its gifts and its goals are reconciliation and the peace of God's Kingdom. The moral impetus of hope is sustained by the conviction that the world in which it acts has already been changed. For the human world is no longer terminally defined by the threat of death. Human beings no longer need to cling to the present form of life in a defensiveness intent on mere survival against all odds. The world is defined by the reality of the resurrection. It is not a graveyard, but a garden. A gracious Spirit is at work. True life is realized in love. Others are not a threat but a responsibility and a blessing, even if they are presently perceived as enemies and persecutors.

When hope works for a God-defined future, it contests the economy of competition and greed. The psychotic mind-set that goes under the name of "economic rationalism" is confronted with another possibility, the divine economy of gift and giving. Life, from its beginning to its fulfillment, is never something earned or hoarded. It is an unimaginable and particular gift, to each for the sake of all, and to all for the sake of each one. While no created being can give life and existence, hope inspires the freedom to serve the purposes of the "Lord and giver of life" in a spirit of giving and care for the other. This generosity of giving, beyond the limits of strict justice or self-serving calculation, anticipates the community of eternal life. In that final form of communion, the divine gift, the divine giver, together with the gifted, the forgiven, and the graced, are united in one life of endless giving.

Intellectual Conversion: Hopeful Intelligence

Hope manifests itself as an intellectual conversion as well. It brings forth its own kind of intelligence and expresses itself in habits of mind and creative imagination. It is "hope seeking understanding" in all that can be learned about God, our own selves and our world. Hope can, of course, be dismissed as irrational attitude, divorced from the "real world" of calculation, planning, and control. Managerial planning may feel little need of something as ethereal as hope. Its Christian version is peculiarly impractical. Why should it so curiously linger around the cross of an executed criminal and then go on to speak of a resurrection in a world where the dead do not rise. In contrast to a hope that is seeking for further intelligence, this flatly managerial attitude comes dangerously close to despair seeking its own confirmation, and to cultural depression seeking its own justification. In that desperate perspective, the rule of law means a bigger police force, larger prisons, and the unsleeping, technological surveillance of every life in its every transaction. The recognition of human rights collapses into a welter of litigiousness, with the resultant huge hemorrhaging of social resources. A huge carapace of political and economic bureaucracy, unable to envisage any good other than maintaining itself, exercises ever tighter controls. It sees freedom only as its enemy. The transcendent values of human dignity, honesty, justice, loyalty, and moral conscience are of little value for the good order of society. The inevitable tendency is presumptively to criminalize every citizen and to turn even the most peaceful society into a kind of prison farm. The tensions inherent in any human culture feed a mindless adversarialism. The "other" is automatically demonized and scapegoated. The resultant absurdity is magnified by image-obsessed media exchanges in which no one ever learns, no mind ever changes, and no one can admit to being wrong.

When a culture loses its hope, it loses a good deal of its intelligence as well. The depressed mind confronting any difficult situation is already closed to the grace of a larger humanity and a more imaginative intelligence. The virtues of humility, forgiveness, compassion, and religious faith are unrecognized and unseen. The hopeless intelligence loses much of its cognitive power. A sense of proportion vanishes. Only problems remain. The depressed intelligence works with a sense of history reduced to a catalogue of defeats and dangers. In that dismal perspective, the only way forward is more oppressive control. Intelligence settles into a kind of psychic and social permafrost that no appeal to community or compassion can melt.

In contrast to this bleak, oppressive outlook, the intellectual dimension of hope inspires a larger conversation. Hope must never recover from its initial surprise when the Lord rose from the tomb. As the Spirit breathes, there is always room for more surprises; the great human conversation is never over. Hope must gently insist that no one be left out of the unending human search for our common good. Each individual brings his or her own hopes, sufferings, and even guilt to the table of life. Each is to be welcomed in the open space, beyond any human imagining, of God's saving will for the salvation of all.

Despair underwrites a culture of oppressive conformity. Nothing new can happen. The good and the bad are clearly identified as the received adversarialism becomes the thinking machine of any given society. But hope looks beyond frozen alternatives to refresh the human condition with a culture of the alternative. People and systems can change, because something that makes all the difference has occurred. Here hope shows its long-term patience. It accepts the reality of dialogue with different faiths, philosophies, scientific explorations, and the arts. A hopeful intelligence opens into a horizon shaped by the conviction that "God our Savior . . . desires everyone to be saved and to come to the knowledge of the truth" (1 Tim 2:4). To hope, therefore, is not to fear genuine intelligence but to be confident in its abilities to search for, and find, the truth. In the horizon of hope, the universe is radically intelligible, no matter what the evils and the experience of absurdity which tempt to despair.

Though the Kingdom of God is yet to be fully realized, it expands from the irreversible fact of the resurrection of the crucified Jesus. The glory of the cross communicates a subversive irony into all domains of the worldly glory. The rewards and recognition deriving from the idolization of power, riches, and celebrity are called into question (Jn 5:39-47). Another form of cultural and social intelligence is at work.

Psychological Conversion: The Self Renewed

There is another side to the conversion of hope that we can call "psychological." It is turning from the violence and isolation of the desperate—and depressive—ego to the hopeful self. Our social identity has been deeply formed through the imitation of examples of violence and prejudice embodied in the society into which we were born.[13] To this degree, our identity has been formed precisely at the expense of others. We are who we are by being against *them*. We are defined by threat and envy in a dynamic of mutual victimization. The gods of the culture promise an exclusive heaven reserved for "people like us," and consign the different, and the "other" in general, to outer darkness.

It is precisely this dynamic of violence that is subverted by the cross. The Son of God himself takes the place of the defenseless victim. He refuses all complicity in the web of violence (see Lk 6:27-36). He prays for the forgiveness of those who have condemned and crucified him (Lk 23:34). His cross unmasks the violence of human culture ruled over by death and despair (see Is 53; Jn 17; Lk 6:27-39; 23:34). His resurrection is the divine vindication of the self-giving love he has shown. Love keeps on being love, leaving no room for vengefulness, human or divine. The risen One breathes the Spirit of forgiveness and peace into the hearts of his frail disciples (Jn 20:23). They would find themselves anew as loved by the God revealed in Jesus, and so begin to inhabit the world as agents of peace and universal reconciliation. For them, the world is no longer governed by "licentiousness, idolatry, sorcery, enmities, strife, jealously, anger, quarrels, dissensions, factions, envy . . ." (Gal 5:19-21). To hope is to inhabit another place in a life of "love, joy, peace, patience, kindness, generosity, faithfulness, gentleness, and self-control" (Gal 5:22-23). Hope, then, lives in the buoyancy of an identity conformed to

---

13. This process has been impressively described by James Alison in his two books *Raising Abel: The Recovery of Eschatological Imagination* (New York: Crossroad, 1996) and *The Joy of Being Wrong: Original Sin through Easter Eyes* (New York: Crossroad, 1998), through his insightful recourse to the cultural anthropology of René Girard.

Christ and imaging God. It is a manifestation of the vitality of the "new self, created according to the likeness of God" (Eph 4:24; Col 3:10).

In the universe of grace, this new self lives in a redeemed coexistence.[14] It is related to others in an open circle of communion. We belong inextricably to one another. Our common receptivity to the divine gift was conditioned by no merit on our part. For all allow themselves to be forgiven—where guilt and failure had before been paralyzing forces. Hope celebrates a release from defensive isolation into an active life of relationships. In that exchange, the people of hope forgive as they have been forgiven, and give from the gift that they have received, sharing in the bounty of what has been given to all. Hope further manifests itself in intercession. We pray for one another. Neither we ourselves nor others are "finished," until our community in God is finally established. In this way, hope, relying on God's unstinted giving, lives in a generous interdependent universe of giving and receiving. It witnesses to the world the great communion of life and love that is in the making (Jn 17:2-24).

Bodily Conversion: The Materiality of Hope

At first glance, to speak of hope in terms of a "conversion to the body" must seem a strange way of putting it. It is not so strange, however, once we realize that Christian hope in fact rejects any disembodied, dematerialized sense of the future. Our risen existence will still be embodied. It is difficult to say more on the transformed materiality of the risen body without trivializing this unique aspect of Christian hope. The full-bodied expectations of hope are necessarily focused on the risen Jesus. They are further sustained by the food and drink of the eucharist. The sacrament of Christ's body and blood uniquely concentrates the physicality of hope and expresses dimensions of bodily and cosmic hope that are otherwise beyond words.

We have commented extensively on the resurrection of the body in the chapter on heaven. There we stressed that the continuity of personal identity beyond death cannot depend on the physical-chemical composition of the body we "possess" in this life. The physical atomic and molecular substrate of our existence is always in a metabolic state.[15] Nothing in our genes was

---

14. This is the deep point of the theology of women's liberation. For the feminist turn in eschatological thinking, see Peter C. Phan, "Woman and the Last Things: A Feminist Eschatology," in *In the Embrace of God: Feminist Approaches to Theological Anthropology*, ed. Anne O'Hare Graff (Maryknoll, N.Y.: Orbis Books, 1995), 206-28.

15. David Toolan, *At Home in the Cosmos* (Maryknoll, N.Y.: Orbis Books, 2001), 188-89.

present a year ago. The skin is renewed monthly and the liver regenerated every six weeks. Each time we breathe we take in billions of atoms breathed by others on this earth. Blood transfusions and organ transplants point to a larger, less individualistic physicality. Our individual bodies cannot be the single identifying factor in what or who we are. But hope for the resurrection of the body is not looking for the resuscitation of this little bit of recyclable matter.

It is not as though our bodies were ever our exclusive possession of a part of the physical universe. It is more that they are contingent distillations of the whole, individually patterned condensations of the cosmic energy pervading the space-time universe.[16] In short, not only is our spiritual being "to some degree all things" (Aristotle and Aquinas), but our bodily being as well is a microcosm formed by and interacting with the whole physical cosmos, a *somebody* existing by the grace of everybody. The universe, though always radically God's creation, embraces us and bears us on in its cosmic unfolding. Hope envisages no escape from the material world, but welcomes the prospect of sharing in its transfiguration. Neither the world nor our humanity is sacrificed in God's gracious design. Still, this *self*, this "somebody" that each of us is, when we are conformed to the death and resurrection of Christ, looks to its final embodied form within a transformed universe.

Hope in its most intense form is not looking to some kind of "out of body" experience. In the name of the risen Christ it claims for the future the whole corporate character of our existence. It looks to the final affirmation of our incarnate being. In the light of the divine incarnation of the Word, what we are and the way we are enter into the future that God will give. Hope is bound, then, to attempt to express itself in an appropriate body language. Sense, imagination, voice, and movement come together in the arts. Music, architecture, song, dance, poetry, painting, and sculpture are hopeful anticipations of the body transformed. Don Saliers describes the liturgy, in its every movement, as a "dance of transformation," including all dimensions of the body and its language.[17] As an eschatological art, the eucharistic liturgy brings all senses into play and into relation to one another:

Authentic, vital and faithful liturgy invites a synaesthetic participation—seeing with the ears (poetry, music, rhetorical power of preaching). Hearing with the eyes—color, form, texture, hue—"sounds" the

---

16. For the big picture, see ibid., especially chapter 10, "The Voice of the Hurricane" (pp. 178-91).
17. Don Saliers, "Worship as Christian Eschatological Art: Word and Grace Come to Life," *Uniting Church Studies* 9, no. 1 (March 2003): 9-21, here 19.

souls as well. Seeing with taste: "O taste and see the goodness of the Lord." The cross-over of the senses is involved.[18]

The arts inspire an experience of refreshment and release in regard to our sensuous and embodied selves. If hope drifts too far from the arts, it is hard pressed to suggest anything credible on the resurrection of the body. If, however, hope contains within itself a "conversion," it can be endlessly productive of anticipations of how our earthly being can be transformed by the power of the divine imagination.[19] In contrast to the finitudes of our present fate, when aging, disease, and accidents occur as limits to the self-expressive capacities of the body, a hope searching for its true art anticipates that eschatological freedom when the body will be the perfect expression of love for God, neighbor and neighborhood, in its corporate and cosmic dimensions.

THE WITNESS OF HOPEFUL VOCATIONS

We must be always working toward a more adequately formulated eschatology. Hope goads intelligence to do the best it can. It takes time. But hope, while it might profit from theology, cannot wait for the fullest and best exposition. It is caught up immediately in the drama of life. This includes all the particularities of time and place, the context of a particular community, the experience of specific sufferings, and the grace of a given vocation. Theology must recognize that the hope of each of us is expressed in a particular eschatological or even "apocalyptic" form.[20] The movement of one's life witnesses to the hopeful conviction that something is actually happening in the here and now. Whether we live in Nairobi or Beijing, Mumbai or Rio de Janeiro, Sydney or Washington, Manila or Berlin, we are each involved in something decisive for the future of the world.

---

18. Ibid., 19-20.

19. For a reflection on J. R. R. Tolkien in this respect, see Anthony J. Kelly, "Faith Seeking Fantasy: Tolkien on Fairy Stories," in Anthony J. Kelly, "Faith Seeking Fantasy: Tolkien on Fairy-Stories," *Pacifica* 15 (2002): 190-222.

20. "Apocalyptic" is a notoriously slippery word in modern biblical and theological thought. In general, it stands for a tendency to imagine the future out of an intense dissatisfaction with the present, in the conviction that the judgment of God will be revealed in a precise historical form, as justifying the suffering elect and as bringing destruction on their persecutors. This, of course, can lead to all kinds of destructive fantasies. But the basic usefulness of this word today, it seems to me, lies in indicating the power of eschatological hope to inspire a new imagining of one's way of being in the world, critical of the prevailing culture. The person of hope thus becomes conscious of his or her life as a unique vocation, the dramatic expression of hopeful solidarity with the suffering and "hopeless" other. See Mostert, *God and the Future*, 32-38.

By stepping out of the securities of the present, people of hope give expression to what is hopeful within them.[21] They are staking all, not without cost, on what is coming to be. Hope finds its voice as it utters a clear, strong word in the daily conversation that makes up our lives. It means not being defeated by those apparent dead ends and failures that always tend to enclose one's world in despair. But hope shows its endurance especially by occupying the most hopeless point in our particular worlds. It moves in solidarity with all those who are furthest from hope—those in one's world who are unloved, who are judged as worthless, who no longer count, who have been left behind as failures. Its special companions are the casualties in the dominant success story of any given culture. Regardless of the judgments of society, hope can exclude no one from the future.

Living hope is defiant. It longs for God's judgment and prays for the truth of Christ to be revealed. Its passion is not always respectable. The resurrection of the crucified Jesus makes suspect any alliance with the banal, self-congratulatory scenarios fabricated by "the rulers of this world." Clothed with the imagination of Jesus and inspired by his Spirit, hope begins to imagine the world "otherwise." We could give the impression that the countercultural witness of hope is reserved only for heroic individuals. It has in fact been claimed as the basic vision of the church itself. Vatican II's Pastoral Constitution on the Church in the Modern World opens with these words:

> The joy and the hope, the griefs and the anguish of the people of our time, especially those who are poor or afflicted in any way, are the joy and the hope, the grief and the anguish of the followers of Christ as well. Nothing that is genuinely human fails to find an echo in their hearts. For theirs is a community composed of human beings, who, united in Christ and guided by the Holy Spirit, press onward to the Kingdom of the Father, and are bearers of a message of salvation intended for all. (*Gaudium et Spes* 1)

Such a passage signals the entry of a new kind of hopeful imagination into the life of the church. The people of God have to live in a world in which the image counts more than the reality. But radical hope is intent on a face-to-face vision of God. In anticipation of future union with God, hope is impelled to establish eye-to-eye contact with the suffering other in the world

---

21. Part 3 of Alan E. Lewis's *Between Cross and Resurrection: A Theology of Holy Saturday* (Grand Rapids: Eerdmans, 2001) is especially valuable here, as he considers what is involved in living the paschal story in world history, contemporary society, and personal life (pp. 261-460).

of the present. It reaches beyond the image and the mask, to recognize the face of Christ and his summons to service. The First Letter of John asks, "How does God's love abide in anyone who has the world's goods and sees a brother or sister in need and yet refuses to help?" (1 Jn 3:17). This deeply love-centered and theological letter gives a warning that pierces to the heart of theology: "Those who say, 'I love God' and hate their brothers and sisters, are liars; for those who do not love a brother or sister whom they have seen, cannot love God whom they have not seen" (1 Jn 4:20).

Classically, this eschatological imagination is expressed through the three vows of religious profession. In that developing and variegated tradition, Christian communities embark on a life of radical self-offering "for the sake of the Kingdom of God" (see *Lumen Gentium* 44). In a way that goes beyond the normal patterns of human fulfillment in career, possession of property, and family, religious life is a form of exposure to the ultimacy of what is to come. That witness continues and is being continually renewed. But today it is not difficult to discern this "exposed" character of hope in many other styles of life. Given the drastic erosion of personal value in technocratic culture, the measure of fidelity and generosity demanded in marriage and parenthood is often (always?) felt to be excessive. To resist the bias of the culture toward impermanent relationships by giving oneself in unconditional, exclusive love to one's spouse is a powerful witness to the mystery of the other. This other person is worth the love of a lifetime. Likewise, to opt for the future by having a family and accepting the radical demands of nurturing and supporting one's children, is a powerful testimony—usually unnoticed—to a uniquely subversive hope. The human and Christian values involved demand a continual and intimate self-sacrifice—in the face of the fragility of human relationships in the present cultural context. More conspicuously, the same quality of subversive hope can be discerned in those who care for the suffering, the incurable, and the dying. Then there are those who are patiently accepting great suffering throughout a lifetime. To others, they might appear to be victims of an unkind fate. But that is not their sense of themselves. Theirs are other gifts, above all that of giving themselves over to the divine will for its purposes. There are endless other examples, instanced in those who are involved in the risks of peacemaking and disarmament—with its vulnerability to failure and vilification from all sides. Some commit the social folly of renouncing class, position, and privilege in the interests of solidarity with the oppressed and the suffering. Noteworthy, too, are those exploring new lifestyles in order to respond to the current ecological crisis brought about by the addictive consumerism of our day.

It is precisely when and where a culture tends to make its peace with hopelessness that Christian hope must exhibit what has been imaginatively called "an apocalyptic sting."[22] This is the point at which hope demands a defiant creativity. If hope stands against dehumanizing forces and structures, it also stands with any movement of liberation that works for a more human future. In the name of the God "who will be who he will be" (Ex 3:14), hope must remain resolutely open to "what has not yet appeared" (1 Jn 3:2) in terms of the fullness of our humanity.

The above-mentioned evangelical instances of losing one's life in order to save it all manifest the "apocalyptic sting" inherent in Christian hope. Each is an experience of the grief of a world ending—even if the world in question is limited to the particular world of one's own comfort, security, and autonomous disposition of one's life.[23] Christian believers have no choice but to face what is unfinished in themselves and undecided in their world. But that is where hope comes into its own. It is the expression of the energy and imagination intent on the world's transformation in God. Solidarity with the hopeless, the suffering, and the oppressed suggests the form of the coming Kingdom of God by way of negation and absence, the "not yet." Still, at the same point, there is that "now." The Spirit of Christ inspires the conduct of defiant hope in this time, in this place, in this cultural context, in the society of these people in all the particularity of character, commitment, and attitude. Hope is lived out in this time of the Spirit. Note the words of Jesus to his disciples on the eve of his death:

I still have many things to say to you, but you cannot bear them now. When the Spirit of truth comes, he will guide you into all truth; for he will not speak on his own, but will speak whatever he hears, and will declare to you the things that are to come. He will glorify me, because he will take what is mine and declare it to you. All that the Father has is mine. For this reason I said he will take what is mine and declare it to you. (Jn 16:12-15)

The Spirit has come. There were "many things" that could not be borne by the disciples before the resurrection of Jesus.[24] But now that has happened, and

22. Johann Baptist Metz, *Faith in History and Society: Toward a Practical Fundamental Theology*, trans. D. Smith (London: Burns & Oates, 1980), 74, 169-77. For analysis and critical appreciation, see James Matthew Ashley, *Interruptions: Mysticism, Politics and Theology in the Work of Johann Baptist Metz* (Notre Dame, Ind.: Notre Dame University Press, 1998), 169-204.

23. Christopher Dawson, *The Historic Reality of Christian Culture* (New York: Harper & Row, 1960), 23-24.

24. Anthony J. Kelly and Francis J. Moloney, *Experiencing God in the Gospel of John* (New York: Paulist Press, 2003), 317-24.

two millennia later the Spirit is still guiding the followers of Christ into "all truth." The Spirit leads further, by declaring "the things that are to come." The Holy Spirit thus glorifies Jesus in what most intimately characterizes him. This is always to be found in the self-giving love that has its origins in the Father's love for the world: "For God so loved the world [*kosmos* in Greek], that he gave his only Son, so that everyone who believes in him may not perish but may have eternal life. Indeed, God did not send his Son into the world to condemn the world but in order that the world might be saved through him" (Jn 3:16-17). In this horizon of the *cosmic* love of God, the conduct of hope becomes the practice of love:

> Beloved, let us love one another, because love is from God; everyone who loves is born of God and knows God . . . for God is love. . . . Beloved, since God loved us so much, we also ought to love one another. No one has ever seen God; if we love one another, God lives in us, and his love is perfected in us. (1 Jn 4:7-12)

God is the unseen source of our deepest life and the source and goal of all our loving. Hope moves in the current of this life and grows in the generosity of this love to long for the final vision of what still lies hidden in the future.

Selected Bibliography

Alison, James. *The Joy of Being Wrong: Original Sin through Easter Eyes*. New York: Crossroad, 1998.

———. *Raising Abel: The Recovery of the Eschatological Imagination*. New York: Crossroad, 1996.

Ashley, James M. *Interruptions: Mysticism, Politics and Theology in the Work of Johann-Bapist Metz*. Notre Dame, Ind.: Notre Dame University Press, 1998.

Averill, James R., G. Catlin, and K. K. Chon. *Rules of Hope*. New York: Springer-Verlag, 1990.

Barbour, Ian G. *When Science Meets Religion: Enemies, Strangers or Partners?* New York: HarperSanFrancisco, 2000.

Becker, Ernest. *The Denial of Death*. New York: Free Press, 1973.

Benz, Arnold. *The Future of the Universe: Chance, Chaos, God*. New York: Continuum, 2000.

Bevans, Stephen B., and Roger P. Schroeder. *Constants in Context: A Theology of Mission for Today*. Maryknoll, N.Y.: Orbis Books, 2004.

Bloch, E. *The Principle of Hope*. Translated by Neville Plaice, Stephen Plaice, and Paul Knight. 3 vols. Cambridge, Mass.: MIT Press, 1996.

Boros, Ladislaus. *The Moment of Truth: Mysterium Mortis*. Translated by G. Bainbridge. London: Burns & Oates, 1962.

Braine, D. *The Human Person: Animal and Spirit*. Notre Dame, Ind.: University of Notre Dame Press, 1992.

Bregman, Lucy. *Death, Dying, Spirituality and Religions: A Study of the Death Awareness Movement*. New York: Peter Lang, 2003.

Brown, Warren S., Nancey Murphy, and H. Newton Maloney, eds. *Whatever Happened to the Soul? Scientific and Theological Portraits of Human Nature*. Minneapolis: Fortress Press, 1998.

Byrne, Brendan. *Romans*. Sacra Pagina 6. Collegeville, Minn.: Liturgical Press, 1996.

Cavanaugh, William T. *Torture and the Eucharist: Theology, Politics, and the Body of Christ*. Oxford: Blackwell, 1998.

Chauvet, Louis-Marie. "The Broken Bread as Theological Figure of Eucharistic Presence." In *Sacramental Presence in a Postmodern Context*, edited by L. Boeve and L. Leijssen, 236-62. Leuven: University Press, 2001.

———. *The Sacraments: The Word of God at the Mercy of the Body*. Collegeville, Minn.: Liturgical Press, 2001.

———. *Symbol and Sacrament: A Sacramental Reinterpretation of Christian Existence*. Translated by Patrick Madigan and Madeleine Beaumont. Collegeville, Minn.: Liturgical Press, 1995.

Connell, Martin F. "*Descensus Christi ad Inferos*: Christ's Descent to the Dead." *Theological Studies* 62 (2001): 262-82.

Couture, A. "Réincarnation ou résurrection? Revue d'un débat et amorce d'une recherche." *Science et Esprit* 36, no. 3 (1984): 351-74; 37, no. 3 (1985): 75-96.

Daley, Brian E. *The Hope of the Early Church: A Handbook of Patristic Eschatology.* Cambridge: Cambridge University Press, 1991.

Deane-Drummond, Celia E. *Creation through Wisdom: Theology and the New Biology.* Edinburgh: T&T Clark, 2000.

Denzinger, Henricus, and Adolfus Schönmetzer, eds. *Enchiridion Symbolorum Definitionum de Rebus Fidei et Morum.* Freiburg: Herder, 1965.

Desmond, William. *Hegel's God: A Counterfeit Double?* Burlington, Vt.: Ashgate, 2003.

Dupuis, Jacques. *Toward a Christian Theology of Religious Pluralism.* Maryknoll, N.Y.: Orbis Books, 2001.

Dunn, James D. G. *Christianity in the Making.* Volume 1, *Jesus Remembered.* Grand Rapids: Eerdmans, 2003.

Durrwell, F. X. *The Eucharist: Presence of Christ.* Translated by S. Attanasio. Denville, N.J.: Dimension Books, 1974.

———. *L'eucharistie: Sacrament Pascal.* Paris: Cerf, 1980.

———. *The Resurrection: A Biblical Study.* Translated by Rosemary Sheed. London/ New York: Sheed & Ward, 1960.

Edwards, Denis. *Breath of Life. A Theology of the Creator Spirit.* Maryknoll, N.Y.: Orbis Books, 2004.

———. *Jesus and the Cosmos.* Homebush, N.S.W.: St Paul Publications, 1991.

———. *Jesus the Wisdom of God: An Ecological Theology.* Homebush, N.S.W.: St Paul Publications, 1995.

Ellis, George F. R., ed. *The Far-Future Universe: Eschatology from a Cosmic Perspective.* London: Templeton Foundation, 2002.

Fingarette, Herbert. *The Self in Transformation: Psychoanalysis, Philosophy and the Life of the Spirit.* New York: Harper Torchbooks, 1963.

Flannery, Austin, OP, ed. *Vatican Council II: The Conciliar and Post Conciliar Documents.* Revised edition. Dublin: Dominican Publications, 1988.

Ganoczy, A. "Cerveau et conscience en anthropologie théologique." *Recherches de Science Religieuse* 92, no. 3 (2004): 349-81.

Greer, Rowan A. *Christian Hope and Christian Life: Raids on the Inarticulate.* New York: Crossroad, 2001.

Gutiérrez, Gustavo. *A Theology of Liberation: History, Politics and Salvation.* Translated and edited by C. Inda and J. Eagleson. Maryknoll, N.Y.: Orbis Books, 1973; rev. ed. 1988.

———. *The Truth Shall Make You Free: Confrontations.* Maryknoll, N.Y.: Orbis Books, 1990.

Hayes, Zachary. *Visions of a Future. A Study of Christian Eschatology.* Wilmington, Del.: Michael Glazier, 1989.

Hunt, Anne. *Trinity: Nexus of the Mysteries of Christian Faith.* Maryknoll, N.Y.: Orbis Books, 2005.

————. *The Trinity and the Paschal Mystery: A Development in Recent Catholic Theology.* Collegeville, Minn.: Liturgical Press, 1997.

Hurtado, Larry W. *Lord Jesus Christ: Devotion to Jesus in Earliest Christianity.* Grand Rapids: Eerdmans, 2003.

International Theological Commission. "Questions in Eschatology." *Irish Theological Quarterly* 58 (1992): 209-43.

Johnson, Elizabeth. *Friends of God and Prophets: A Feminist Theological Reading of the Communion of Saints.* New York: Continuum, 1998.

Kehl, Medard, and Werner Löser, eds. *The von Balthasar Reader.* Translated by R. J. Daly and F. Lawrence. Edinburgh: T&T Clark, 1985.

Kelly, Anthony J. *The Bread of God: Nurturing a Eucharistic Imagination.* Liguori, Mo.: Liguori Publications, 2001.

————. *The Creed by Heart. Relearning the Nicene Creed.* Melbourne: Harper Collins, 1996.

————. *An Expanding Theology: Faith in a World of Connections.* Sydney: E. J. Dwyer, 1993; revised edition (2003) available on Anthony J. Kelly, CSsR, home page, http://dlibrary.acu.edu.au/staffhome/ankelly/.

————. "The Gift of Death." *Compass Theological Review* 31, no. 1 (Autumn 1997): 37-42.

————. *The Trinity of Love: A Theology of the Christian God.* Wilmington, Del.: Michael Glazier, 1989.

Kelly, Anthony J., and Francis J. Moloney. *Experiencing God in the Gospel of John.* New York: Paulist Press, 2003.

Kerr, Fergus. *Immortal Longings: Versions of Transcending Humanity.* Notre Dame, Ind.: University of Notre Dame Press, 1997.

Körtner, U. *The End of the World: A Theological Interpretation.* Translated by Douglas Scott. Louisville: Westminster John Knox Press, 1995.

Kreeft, P. *Everything You Ever Wanted to Know about Heaven . . . But Never Dreamed of Asking.* San Francisco: Ignatius Press, 1990.

————. *Heaven: The Heart's Deepest Longing.* San Francisco: Ignatius Press, 1989.

Küng, Hans. *Eternal Life? Life after Death as a Medical, Philosophical and Theological Problem.* Translated by E. Quinn. New York: Doubleday, 1984.

Lafont, Ghislain. *Peut-on connaître Dieu en Jésus-Christ?* Paris: Cerf, 1969.

Lane, Dermot. *Keeping Hope Alive. Stirrings in Christian Theology.* Dublin: Gill & Macmillan, 1996.

Lash, Nicholas. *A Matter of Hope. A Theologian's Reflections on the Thought of Karl Marx.* London: Darton, Longman & Todd, 1981.

Le Goff, Jacques. *The Birth of Purgatory.* Translated by A. Goldhammer. Chicago: University of Chicago Press, 1984.

Lewis, Alan E. *Between Cross and Resurrection: A Theology of Holy Saturday.* Grand Rapids: Eerdmans, 2001.

Lynch, William F. *Images of Hope: Imagination as Healer of the Hopeless.* Notre Dame, Ind.: University of Notre Dame Press, 1965.

Manson, Neil A., ed. *God and Design. The Teleological Argument and Modern Science.* London: Routledge, 2003.

Marcel, Gabriel. *Homo Viator: Introduction to a Metaphysic of Hope.* Translated by E. Craufurd. New York: Harper & Row, 1966.

Martelet, G. *L'au-delà retrouvé. Christologie des fins dernières.* Paris: Desclée, 1975.

———. *The Risen Christ and the Eucharistic World.* Translated by René Hague. New York: Seabury Press, 1976.

McDannell, C., and B. Lang. *Heaven. A History.* New Haven: Yale University Press, 1988.

McGinn, Bernard. *Antichrist: Two Thousand Years of Human Fascination with Evil.* San Francisco: HarperSanFrancisco, 1994.

———. *Visions of the End: Apocalyptic Traditions in the Middle Ages.* New York: Columbia University Press, 1998.

McGrath, Alister E. *A Brief History of Heaven.* Oxford: Blackwell, 2003.

———. *Dawkin's God: Genes, Memes and the Meaning of Life.* Oxford: Blackwell, 2005.

Metz, J. B. *Faith, History and Society: Toward a Practical Fundamental Theology.* Translated by D. Smith. London: Burns & Oates, 1980.

———. *A Passion for God: The Mystical-Political Dimension of Christianity.* Translated by J. Matthew Ashley. New York: Paulist Press, 1998.

Moltmann, Jürgen. *The Coming of God—Christian Eschatology.* Translated by Margaret Kohl. Minneapolis: Fortress Press, 1996.

———. *In the End—The Beginning: The Life of Hope.* Minneapolis: Fortress Press, 2004.

———. *Theology of Hope.* Translated by James W. Leitch. London: SCM Press, 1967.

Mostert, Christiaan. *God and the Future: Wolfhart Pannenberg's Eschatological Doctrine of God.* Edinburgh/New York: T&T Clark, 2002.

Neusner, Jacob, Bruce Chilton, and William Graham. *Three Faiths, One God: The Formative Faith and Practice of Judaism, Christianity, and Islam.* Boston: Brill, 2002.

Novello, Henry. "Death as Privilege." *Gregorianum* 84, no. 4 (2003): 779-827.

Pannenberg, Wolfhart. *Systematic Theology*, volume 3. Translated by G. W. Bromiley. Grand Rapids: Eerdmans, 1998.

Peters, Ted. *God—The World's Future: Systematic Theology for a Post-modern Era.* Minneapolis: Fortress Press, 1992.

Phan, Peter C. "Current Theology: Contemporary Context and Issues in Eschatology." *Theological Studies* 55, no. 3 (1994): 507-36.

———. "Eschatology." In *The Cambridge Companion to Karl Rahner*, edited by Declan Marmion and Mary E. Himes, 174-92. Cambridge: Cambridge University Press, 2006.

———. "Eschatology and Ecology: The Environment in the End-Time." *Irish Theological Quarterly* 62 (1996): 3-16.

———. *Eternity in Time: A Study of Karl Rahner's Eschatology.* Selinsgrove, Pa.: Susquehanna University Press, 1988.

————. *In Our Own Tongues: Perspectives from Asia on Mission and Inculturation.* Maryknoll, N.Y.: Orbis Books, 2003.

————. "Woman and the Last Things: A Feminist Eschatology." In *In the Embrace of God: Feminist Approaches to Theological Anthropology,* edited by Anne O'Hare Graff, 206-28. Maryknoll, N.Y.: Orbis Books, 1995.

Pieper, Joseph. *Hope and History.* Translated by Richard Winston and Clara Winston. London: Burns & Oates, 1969.

Pieris, Aloysius, SJ. *An Asian Theology of Liberation.* Maryknoll, N.Y.: Orbis Books, 1990.

Plantinga Pauw, Amy. "'Where Angels Fear to Tread.'" *Modern Theology* 16, no. 1 (January 2000): 39-59.

Polkinghorne, John. *The God of Hope and the End of the World.* London: Yale University Press, 2002.

Polkinghorne, J. C., and M. Welker, eds. *The End of the World and the Ends of God.* Harrisburg, Pa.: Trinity Press International, 2000.

Prusak, Bernard P. "Bodily Resurrection in Catholic Perspectives." *Theological Studies* 61 (2000): 64-105.

Rahner, Karl. *Foundations of Christian Faith.* Translated by William V. Dych, New York: Seabury Press, 1978.

————. "The Hermeneutics of Eschatological Assertions." *Theological Investigations,* 4:323-46. Translated by Kevin Smyth. Baltimore: Helicon Press, 1966.

————. *On the Theology of Death.* Translated by C. H. Henkey. New York: Herder & Herder, 1962.

————. "The Question of the Future." In *Theological Investigations,* 12:181-201. New York: Crossroad, 1974.

Ratzinger, Joseph. *Eschatology: Death and Eternal Life.* Translated by M. Walstein. Washington, D.C.: Catholic University of America Press, 1988.

Sachs, J. R. "Apocatastasis in Patristic Theology." *Theological Studies* 54 (1993): 617-40.

————. "Current Eschatology: Universal Salvation and the Problem of Hell." *Theological Studies* 52 (1991): 227-54.

Saliers, Don E. *Worship as Theology: Foretaste of Glory Divine.* Nashville: Abingdon Press, 1994.

Sauter, Gerhard. *Eschatological Rationality. Theological Issues in Focus.* Grand Rapids: Baker Books, 1996.

————. *What Dare We Hope? Reconsidering Eschatology.* Harrisburg, Pa.: Trinity Press International, 1996.

Schmidt-Leukel, Perry, ed. *Die Idee der Reinkarnation in Ost und West.* Munich: Eugen Diederichs Verlag, 1996.

Schönborn, C. *From Death to Life: The Christian Journey.* Translated by B. McNeil. San Francisco: Ignatius, 1995.

Schwager, Raymund. *Jesus in the Drama of Salvation: Toward a Biblical Doctrine of Redemption.* Translated by James G. Williams and Paul Haddon. New York: Crossroad, 1999.

Schwarz, Hans. *Eschatology*. Grand Rapids: Eerdmans, 2000.

Schwöbel, Christoph. "Last Things First?" In *The Future as God's Gift: Explorations in Christian Eschatology*, edited by David Fergusson and Marcel Sarot, 219-41. Edinburgh: T&T Clark, 2000.

Sesboüé, Bernard. "L'enfer est-il éternel?" *Recherches de Science Religieuse* 87, no. 2 (1999): 189-206.

Smart, N., and S. Konstantine. *Christian Systematic Theology in a World Context*. London: Marshall Pickering, 1991.

Song, Choan-Seng. *Third-Eye Theology: Theology in Formation in Asian Settings*. Maryknoll, N.Y.: Orbis Books, 1979.

Teilhard de Chardin, Pierre. *The Divine Milieu*. New York: Harper & Row, 1960.

Tugwell, Simon. *Human Immortality and the Redemption of Death*. London: Darton, Longman & Todd, 1990.

Uzuku, Elochukwu E. "African Inculturation Theology: Path of Liberation." http://www.theo.kuleuven.ac.be/dt/pub_uzukwu_text_1.htm

Valliere, Paul. *Modern Russian Theology: Bukharev, Soloviev, Bulkakov; Orthodox Theology in a New Key*. Grand Rapids: Eerdmans, 2000.

Volf, Miroslav. "The Final Reconciliation: Reflections on a Social Dimension of the Eschatological Transition." *Modern Theology* 16, no. 1 (January 2000): 91-113.

von Balthasar, Hans Urs. *Dare We Hope 'That All Men Be Saved'?* Translated by D. Kipp and L. Krauth. San Francisco: Ignatius Press, 1988.

———. *The Glory of the Lord: A Theological Aesthetics*. Volume 1, *Seeing the Form*. Translated by E. Leiva-Merikakis. New York: Crossroad, 1982.

———. *Mysterium Paschale: The Mystery of Easter*. Translated by A. Nichols. Edinburgh: T&T Clark, 1990.

Wainwright, G. *Eucharist and Eschatology*. London: Epworth, 1971.

Wink, Walter. *Engaging the Powers. Discernment and Resistance in a World of Domination*. Philadelphia: Fortress Press, 1992.

———. *Naming the Powers*. Philadelphia: Fortress Press, 1984.

———. *Unmasking the Powers. The Invisible Forces That Determine Human Existence*. Philadelphia: Fortress Press, 1986.

Wright, N. T. *The Resurrection of the Son of God*. Minneapolis: Fortress Press, 2003.

Index of Biblical References

Index of Subjects

abortion, 97

Abrahamic faiths: eschatology and, 26-27

Acts of the Martyrdom of St. Perpetua: and purgatory, 116-17

Africa: inculturation and liberation in, 35-36

agility: as quality of glorified body, 178

aging population, 1

agony in the garden, 86-87

Alexander III (pope): and term "transubstantiation," 187

alienation of humans from nature, 195-96

Alison, James, 37

Ambrose

    on cosmic dimension of resurrection of Christ, 177

    on life in Christ, 164

analogy

    and afterlife, 121, 163

    and beatific vision, 171-72

    and purgatory, 131-32

    and resurrection of body, 175-76

    and theology of hell, 153

    and truths of faith, 67-69

Angela of Foligno, 156

Anselm, St.: theology described by, 53-54

Anthropic Principle, 38-39

Antichrist

    conflict with Christ, 150

    as symbol, 146, 150

    vanquished in hell, 146

apocalyptic: meaning of word, 218n. 20

Aquino, María Pilar: and oppression of women, 36

Arendt, Hannah: on fear of hell, 139

art: and transformation of material world, 178

Asia: oppression in, 36

assumption. *See* Mary: assumption of

Augustine, St.

    on fate of human beings, 153

    prayer of, at death of Monica, 117

    and purgatory, 114-15

    on suffering of love, 127

Auschwitz, 34

Bailie, Gil, 37

Bandinelli, Roland. *See* Alexander III (pope)

Barth, Karl

    and divine self-revelation, 70

    transcendental approach to eschatology of, 30

beatific vision

    analogy of, 171-72

    as meaning of heaven, 169-74

    as perfect act of human intelligence, 169

    Trinity and, 172-74

Becker, Ernest, 109, 132

    on denial of death, 98-102

Big Bang

    and creation, 37

    and time, 49

Bloch, Ernst, 28-29, 32

    analogy and, 69

    on Christianity, 14

    creative approach to hope of, 4-5

body

    glorified: qualities of, 178-79

    resurrection of, 39, 40-41, 174-79; analogy and, 175-76

    and soul, 39-48; dualism of, 39-40; terminology relating to, 40-48

    spiritual, 175-76

Boff, Clodovis, 32

Boff, Leonardo, 32

Bonaventure, St., 24

Boros, Ladislaus, 98, 109

    on death, 102-5

    on encounter with Christ, 125

brain, human, 46-47

and death, 105-8
  original, 106-7
Sölle, Dorothea, 33
Song, Choan-Seng: on barbarism of
  power, 34-35
Soskice, Janet Martin: on nihilism, 106
soul
  and body, 39-48; dualism of, 39-40;
    terminology relating to, 40-48
  creation of, by God, 43
  death and, 40-41
  faculties of: intellect and will, 171
  as form of human body, 40, 43
  God-relatedness of, 44-45
  materialistic reductionism and, 45-46
spirit
  human: embodied in created universe,
    42, 177
  and matter, 39-48
Spiritual Franciscans, 24
spirituality: hope as dimension of, 6
sterility, 1
Stoeger, William R.: on catastrophes in
  universe, 96
subtlety: as quality of glorified body, 178
suffering: of purgatory, 121-23
suicide, 97
Synod of Constantinople, 142n. 13, 157n.
  38
Synoptic Gospels
  negations in, 57-58
  view of heaven in, 159-61
  See also New Testament

Taoism, 26
technology: and communications, 3
theology
  of church as community of hope, 12
  and eschatology, 30-37, 53-72
  eucharistic, 182
  liberation (*see* liberation theology)
  and particularity and universality, 15-
    16
Theodore of Mopsuestia, 157
Theory of Everything (TOE), 43
Thérèse of Lisieux, St., 156
Thomas Aquinas
  analogical thinking of, 69

on beings of pure spirit, 48; freedom of,
    150-51
  on duration of creation, 49
  eschatological vision of, 24-25
  on God's creative love, 43
  on hope, 17
  on human spirit, 41
  on invisible and visible missions of per-
    sons of Trinity, 51
  on Jesus' dead body, 84
  on Jesus' risen body, 83
  on metaphor of tasting, 199-200
  on natural desire to see God, 203
  on sufferings of damned, 153
  on task of theology, 172-73
  on transubstantiation, 187-88
  on unity of human person, 40
Thomistic tradition: and beatific vision,
    169-70
Tillich, Paul: on purification by suffering,
    121
time
  end of, 51-52
  eschatological value of, 50
  hope and, 7, 14-15
  paschal sense of, 73-75
  relationship of, to eternity, 48-52
transmigration of souls. *See* reincarnation
transubstantiation. *See under* eucharist
Trinity
  and beatific vision, 172-74
  and eucharistic imagination, 186
  mutual self-giving of, 187
  and time, 51-52

universality: and particularity, 15-16
universe
  actions of God in, 188
  changing: and time, 49
  as field of divine communication, 186
  relationship of Christ to, 194
  spiritual dimension of, 46
  transformation of, 200

Vatican II. *See* Second Vatican Council
vocations, hopeful: witness of, 218-22
Volf, Miroslav: on purgatory as leading to
  final reconciliation, 128

von Balthasar, Hans Urs
  emphasizing contemplative and imagi-
    native dimensions of hope, 31
  on Holy Saturday, 89
  and paschal mystery, 70, 155-56
  spiritual eschatology of, 31

Weiss, Joachim, 30
will
  as faculty of soul, 171
  See also intellect
witness: of Christian hope, 11-14
women: oppression of, 36